TAR HEEL
North Carolina Football

TAR HEEL
North Carolina Football

By
Ken Rappoport

THE STRODE PUBLISHERS, INC.
HUNTSVILLE, ALABAMA 35802

To the fairy tale castle
on
Owens Road
and its inhabitants
who live happily ever after

All photographs courtesy of North Carolina Athletic Department

Contents

Foreword

Football Saturdays are very special days in a college town. That is especially true in Chapel Hill, home of the University of North Carolina. That special feeling that the town, the University, and Carolina fans have for football was one of the main reasons I took the head coaching job here.

Carolina has a rich football tradition. The University has produced such great players as Charlie Justice, Chris Hanburger, Ken Willard, Don McCauley, Ron Rusnak, and Ken Huff. Throughout its football history Carolina has fielded outstanding teams—from the undefeated team of 1898 to the glory years of the late 1940s to the 11-1 team of 1972.

The story of Carolina football is an exciting one. It is a story not only of games and teams but also of the individual young men and coaches who have represented a great university.

Bill Dooley
Head Football Coach
University of North Carolina

The Little Train That Could

"At the football game he does all the stunts. He runs, he passes, fakes, and punts.
"Between the halves he leads the band; then sells peanuts in the stands...
"All the way Choo, Choo, all the way!
"A chug, chug, chugga with a hip hooray.
"Bing, bat, boot that ball around;
"Open that throttle and cover ground."—From "All The Way Choo Choo" by Orville Campbell and Hank Beebe.

Charlie Justice braced against the biting early morning wind. He tucked his hands into his overcoat and lunged across the rolling green carpet of the North Carolina campus, side-stepping cherry trees and blazing wisteria with the dexterity of a tailback. His destination was the Monogram Club.

"Hi y'all," he greeted teammates in that familiar, affable manner, then sat down for the pregame meal.

Thoughts of the impending football war clouded his mind, and the usually gregarious Justice ate his breakfast in comparative quiet while digesting the game plan. He was the first one to leave the dining room and the first on the scene at Kenan Stadium, that gleaming showpiece nestled in majestic southern pines.

"How ya doin', Mr. Justice?" equipment manager Morris Mason greeted the Carolina "Choo Choo."

Welcome to Tar Heel Country.

"Fine, Morris, just fine," Justice said.

The football demigod dressed in silence, then sauntered to a seat under the field house stairway to contemplate the day's forthcoming battle. His body exploded with energy, and it took a long time to bring himself to that supreme moment of readiness. Finally, he had won the war with his nerves.

Back in the locker room, his teammates were dressing in their gorgeous powder blue uniforms, stuffing their heads into brilliant white helmets. Justice then made his motivational pitch.

"We're gonna lose!" he shrieked in his near-falsetto voice. "We're gonna lose if y'all don't start thinkin' about football. 'Bout playing a game of football for Carolina."

Heads bobbed in unison, the superb group of giants acknowledging their leader.

"We'll get 'em," snarled Art Weiner.

"We're ready," shouted Irv Holdash, who dressed next to Justice.

The players lined up in the tunnel leading to the field and tingled as the school band struck up the Carolina song. Many shivered with anticipation, tugging at their white pants.

Justice, his head held high and body taut, led his team on the field for the supreme moment. A passionate crowd choked Kenan Stadium and rocked when Number 22 appeared on the field in front of the blue Tar Heel legions.

"Choo Choo, Choo Choo! All the way, Choo Choo!" the berserk audience of more than 43,000 chanted. Justice grinned. He loved the adoration. Triumphantly he led his team to the North Carolina bench.

This was Fat City for Chapel Hill. The game had been a sellout. In fact all the games had been sellouts, the monster crowds magnetized by the golden lure of Justice. Scalpers had retreated, for there were literally no tickets to scalp. There had been the story of the rich woman who had flown into Chapel Hill on the day of the game. Unable to beg, borrow, or steal a ticket, she was shut out and forced to listen to the game on radio.

The game began....

Charlie Justice answered the phone.

12

"Charlie Choo Choo Justice speaking."

"Do you have time to talk?"

"Well, I have a client with me...hold on."

Some conspiratorial whispers followed.

"Yes, I can talk now...go ahead. Ask me whatever you want, and I'll try to answer it as best I can."

He had not lost his graciousness after all these years. Some people mellow as they get older. Charlie Justice started out mellow. Friends said he had never changed, and that was amazing for all his conquests. He had been the ultraviolet ray at North Carolina in his time, a folk hero of Paul Bunyan dimensions.

Charlie Justice runs—and leaves an enemy football player in his dust.

Now he was a working man among fellow North Carolinians. The body had thickened, and the hair had grown thin. The "Choo Choo" Justice of old was just a phantom now.

"Everybody else can grow old," Charlie said, a smile in his voice. "Everybody else can get bald and fat, but we're not supposed to. We're not supposed to lose our hair and put on weight. We're supposed to look the same, to be little boys all our lives."

Justice sells insurance now in Greensboro. Back in the 1940s, directly after the Second World War, he was selling football to the masses. And they were eating it up in big gulps.

"I never played before an empty seat in Kenan Stadium," he remembers with nostalgia. "We went to three bowls when I was there. When our teams left Chapel Hill after 1949, they had $500,000 in the black."

Justice paused to reflect a moment.

"I just loved it all. I loved Carolina, the people here, and I loved football....What I was was a football player, and that's all I ever wanted to be. I didn't even mind practice. Heck, I would have stayed out there all night if they'd let me."

Unflagging modesty prevents Justice from estimating his total impact on football in his time. It is wholly insufficient to say just that North Carolina's dazzling All-American player ran and passed for 5,176 yards, averaged 42.5 yards on punts and 16.2 on punt returns, scored 39 touchdowns, and threw for 26 more in four years from 1946 through 1949. There were some who could pass better, others who could run faster, and a few who could kick farther, but there was no one who could do all these three things as well in one man. Far from the classic runner, Justice nevertheless would leave infuriated tacklers in the dust with his gorgeous feints, a wriggle of the hip here, and a twist of the head there.

"He wasn't very fast," says veteran North Carolina newspaperman Dick Herbert, "I mean not real fast. And he ran a little spraddle-legged. But when he got hold of the ball, well, everybody got excited. In fact, his one run against Duke is regarded as one of the greatest of all time. I think it was for 43 yards, and I think everybody on the Duke team had at least one shot at him. There was that old story about how one of the Duke players missed him at the line of scrimmage, and somebody said, 'Why don't you get up?' And he said, 'I'm staying here because he's going to come back this way again.'"

He ran like a choo-choo train on a snaking, uneven track. That was how he got his nickname. He was a brilliant star in a constellation of stars.

Ernie Williamson remembers.

"Charlie to me was one of the greatest runners I ever saw," says Williamson, who used to block for Justice on the Carolina line. "He and Glenn Davis, the great Army back, were the two best running backs of their day, in my opinion. I'll tell you what, there may be others, but they're the only two I can recall seeing newspaper shots during a ball game, that when they passed the last man, the last defender's back was completely to them. In other words, they had faked him so completely, that when they faked outside, and this guy of course was coming outside, and they turned back in, when they actually went by him, he was completely turned around. They had faked him out that badly!

"One of the interesting things about his ability was the way he could cut on a football field. When the other team kicked off to Charlie, they would put five men on him. They'd kick that ball off to Charlie, but not one would lay a hand on him, because he could stop right in his tracks, and then he'd go in another direction. He was just as fast on that first step as he was at full speed. And he was easy to block for. You really didn't have to block anybody. All you did was have to screen, because he'd use you to break one way or another, and you really didn't have to block anybody, he was so great at the cutback. I remember once Charlie went 93 yards with a pitchout, and nobody laid a hand on him, and I told some people after that he could run faster sideways than I could run forward."

Art Weiner remembers.

"I'm very prejudiced on Charlie, but I think he was the greatest player who ever lived," says Weiner, the All-American end of the Justice era. "His contribution to the team was quite significant. He did everything. He ran, kicked, threw, and was quite an inspiration because every time he would enter the game, he was a marked man. Everybody was keying on him, and he had a big load to carry. He carried the ball or handled it about 75 percent of the time. He was an all-around threat. You

15

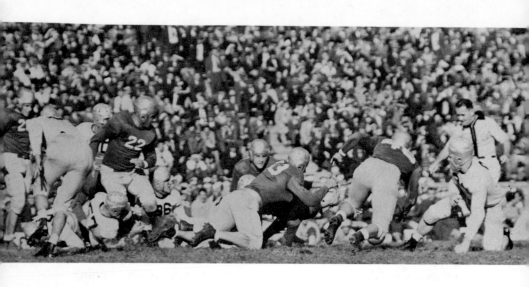

Great excitement in the line before "choo-choo" trains came to Carolina.

couldn't play him for a pass because he would run on you. If you did try to stack the defenses too much on the run, he'd pass. It would be hard to measure the contribution that he made to the team. So much depended on him."

Ken Powell remembers.

"Charlie Justice was one of these football players who comes along once about every 10 years," reflects Powell, another of Carolina's All-American ends of that period. "I believe to this day I've never seen a better football player than Charlie...really. Charlie was a tremendous competitor."

In a highly flattering article in 1949, *Life* magazine applauded Justice for his theatrical performance.

"He brings a sense of drama to the game," the magazine said. "When Justice goes back to receive a punt, he somehow looks like a man who is going to run 60 or 70 yards for a touchdown. He often does. In 1948 Justice averaged 5.2 yards by rushing, completed 50 percent of his passes, and led the nation in punting with an average of 44 yards. Although he is not phenomenally fast, he is extremely adept at sidestepping would-be tacklers. He has been described as the greatest southerner since Robert E. Lee."

Justice tensed in the backfield, his body in the familiar stance espoused by Coach Carl Snavely. His forearms rested on his thighs, and his hands were open to receive the snap from center Joe Neikirk.

The play called was a power sweep to the right. The Duke players had stacked their defense against it, but it was too late to change signals now. On the sidelines, Snavely choked down apprehensions of a broken play. He almost called time out, then snarled his displeasure.

Justice sailed toward right end, but found no running room. He cut back and skittered along the line of scrimmage, jabbing for daylight. Still nothing. He reversed his field once more and this time was tripped up by a Duke tackler. He nearly fell, but saved himself with one hand. Now he was bolt upright again, dancing a tightrope.

He darted through a sliver of space, and hurried through a crowded secondary. Now he was all right, wiggling and shaking off defenders. The open field beckoned. Justice sliced to his left, fooled the last Duke player with a head fake, and soon he was free. Chan Highsmith, the rugged Carolina lineman, was the only player near Charlie. "Glad it's you," Justice said as he crossed the goal line after a brilliant 43-yard run that broke the ice in the third quarter.

The crowd noise was nearly unbearable. An excited fan in the end zone fell out of his seat onto the field. Snavely, usually coldly impassive, was slapping Justice on the back and hugging him. "Great! Great! Great!" he said. Then the chants began rolling down from the stands, "Choo Choo! Choo Choo! Choo Choo!"

Ballad Of A
Running Back

They had waited for his arrival. Time wore heavily on Sarah Justice. She had gone to the window often, keeping an impatient vigil. Finally the car pulled into their driveway, and two men got out.

"He's here!" Sarah called to her husband. "Coach Snavely's here!"

Carl Snavely, the impassive "Gray Fox" of North Carolina football, assessed his newest recruiting target, Charlie Justice, then said:

"Let Mr. Erickson sit in the back of the car with your wife. You can sit up front with me, so we can talk."

Chuck Erickson, the assistant athletic director of North Carolina, squeezed in back with Sarah Justice, while her husband slid in next to Snavely in the front seat. The Tar Heel coach put the car into gear, pulled out of the driveway, and then picked up speed. Some time passed before Snavely turned to Justice.

"How much do you weigh?" he asked.

"One hundred and fifty-five pounds, Mr. Snavely," Justice answered.

Justice laughs about that episode today.

"He didn't say another word to me the whole trip, and it was a 55-mile drive from High Point, North Carolina, to Chapel Hill," Charlie says, somewhat amused. "He didn't open his mouth once. I thought that he really wanted to talk to me when

19

he asked me to sit up front with him. But all he asked me was how much did I weigh, and I told him 155, and he just shut up after that."

The occasion of Justice's first meeting with Snavely found no overtures from the frosty North Carolina football coach. In fact, the notorious "King Carl" had seemed downright insouciant on this recruiting mission.

"It was the first time I ever met the coach," Justice recalls. "We had just visited Duke, and he wanted me to come straight over from Duke to Chapel Hill, and I told him I wouldn't do it. I told him I'd meet him in High Point, where my sister lives. So he came over to pick me up, and he had Erickson with him."

After that gravely quiet car ride to Chapel Hill, Justice was not so sure that Snavely wanted him to come to North Carolina. And he was further convinced of it when the coach failed to visit him the next morning.

"He didn't even bother to come by and see us, or anything," says Justice. "He just left town and said he had to go to Pennsylvania to recruit. So I figured that he didn't even want to talk to me anymore. So we left and went back home and didn't have any intention of going back. If it hadn't been for my brother, I wouldn't have gone back."

Justice thought for a moment.

"I had almost decided to go to the University of South Carolina. In fact, I had already told Rex Enright there that I was coming. But I had an older brother, Jack, who had gone out of the state of North Carolina to play ball. And one day he called me into the kitchen and said, 'I've always helped you and always been a kind of advisor to you.' He said, 'I want to tell you this: You belong in the state of North Carolina. If you're going to live in this state and make your living here, this is where you belong and this is where you ought to go to school.' So he said, 'If you don't go to North Carolina, I'm going to disown you. I don't want to have anything else to do with you.' So I said, 'If you feel that hard about it, maybe I am making a mistake.' So I went back to Chapel Hill and visited with them and decided while I was there that I'd go. And it turned out it was right. And Rex Enright told me later before he died that he thought I was right, too, that they had better material at Chapel Hill, and that South Carolina wouldn't have been able to give

Coach Tom Young, right, greets Charlie Justice and his wife Sarah upon their arrival in Chapel Hill.

me the support that they did at Chapel Hill."

A little boy dreams. He runs through the streets of Asheville, and he is the best breakaway runner in North Carolina. It is the holiday season, and the streets are flooded with shoppers. Charlie Justice sees only enemy tacklers and dodges through artfully until he hits paydirt. The curb comes up to meet him and he skitters in the snow and ice, scattering the shoppers.

"Many a lady with a bag packed with toys and groceries shut her eyes and awaited impact with the wild-looking kid charging in her direction," Bob Quincy and Julian Scheer relate in their book, *Choo Choo, The Charlie Justice Story.* "Little did she know she was a practice dummy helping to develop one of the most elusive runners in the history of football."

"It got so bad," Justice revealed in the book, "the police began to watch for me. All of them knew me as 'that crazy kid who's always running the blocks.'"

They harnessed all that wild energy and put it to more significant use by the time Justice was in his teens. His star clearly began to rise along with his accomplishments at Asheville's Lee Edwards High School. The swashbuckling Justice was awash in admiration and acclamation as the bulwark of one of the finest high school teams ever produced in North Carolina. "If Asheville isn't acclaimed national champions, there ain't no justice-except Asheville's own great Charlie Justice," wrote Scoop Latimer in the *Greenville* (S.C.) *News.*

The Navy brought Justice down to earth.
"What do you want?" snapped the coach at Bainbridge Naval Station.
"I'm a halfback," Justice said.
The coach sized up this shockingly young, comparatively smallish applicant and dismissed him with the suggestion that he "catch punts at the far end of the field." Justice did, but he also kicked some himself. This brought him instant attention.
"You kick like that all the time?" the coach asked.
"Yes sir," said Justice.

"I went out for football primarily for one reason," Justice says. "To get out of KP. I knew just enough to know that if you played football you were automatically jerked from KP duty. Joe Maniaci, the Chicago Bears' back, was our coach. I'd heard about him but frankly didn't know other pro names were on deck until I reported for practice."

The team was a virtual array of pro football all-stars: Washington's Bill de Correvont, Philadelphia's Phil Ragazzo, Carl Tomasello of the New York Giants, Green Bay's Carl Mulleneaux and Chicago's Len Aiken. There were some golden college players in camp, too: William and Mary's Harvey Johnson and Buster Ramsey, Georgia's Jim Gatewood, Oregon State's Don Durban, and Auburn's Lloyd Cheatham. Justice was lost in this forest of talent.

"For the first three or four days I didn't even rate shoes, just ran around in sweat socks," he says. "But I was happy to be off KP at least until I was cut from the squad."

If the war had not broken out, Justice would have most certainly gone to college immediately. His gaudy high school credentials had earned him high football marks from the universities, and he had his choice of more than a dozen good schools. Instead he enlisted in the Navy and after passing indoctrination tests for aerial gunnery, he was shipped off to Bainbridge, Maryland. Before he could shoot a gun, Justice was blasting through lines of football players.

"I wound up at left halfback in our T-formation," recalls Justice. "I spent the rest of the war, including a few games in Hawaii, in that berth. We were a hell of a good team. They tell us we contributed to morale. I hope so. I'm no hero. I'm lucky. Most of the guys I started with for gunnery school were lost in the Pacific."

It was at Bainbridge that Justice earned his well-known sobriquet. "Say, that Justice kid runs just like a choo-choo train," a naval officer was supposed to have remarked in the stands during one game. It was a doubly appropriate line, since Justice's father was a railroad man. Later, when Justice starred at North Carolina, he would get mail addressed to "Choo, Choo, N.C."

Justice led Bainbridge to the top of the class among the nation's service teams during his two years there. Later he was transferred to the Pearl Harbor Navy All-Stars and kept fast company with another group of brilliant players. It was literally

23

a school of hard knocks for Justice, and he learned his lessons well. When he headed home after the war, he was armed with the experience of a professional football player and the exuberance of a college freshman.

Choo Choo Justice opens the throttle and covers ground.

Blue Heaven

In the euphoria of the winner's locker room, Charlie Justice was besieged by triumphant alumni.

"Shake, Charlie," one of them said.

"Just shake Holdash's hand," Justice said. "I don't need that."

The visitor reached over and extended his greetings to Irv Holdash, who dressed next to Justice's locker.

"Good grief," he said, finding a $20 bill in his hand. "I need a new pair of shoes and a haircut. Is there more of this around?"

"Stick with me," Justice said, "and I'll help you out."

The story of the Justice magnanimity triggers other golden memories for Irv Holdash.

"Charlie was a generous person," says Holdash, a center on the Justice teams. "In addition to trying to take all his fame lightly, he was very generous. It was something. There was one time when he was presented with a big floor-model radio-stereo unit for making an All-American team, and he said that he was going to raffle it off because he wanted one of the team members to have it. Art Weiner, who was getting married, I think that month, was the winner. I cite this as an example of his generosity, his concern for others. It was a beautiful thing."

There had also been the time after a game with Louisiana State in Baton Rouge.

"It was a night game, and some of the players decided to

go across the Mississippi to a gambling house," Holdash recalls. "We were supposed to be back at one o'clock, but nobody quite made it. And the coach was waiting for us in the lobby of our hotel. Most of the players walked in and gave themselves up, but I and three other guys decided to sneak around the back end. And there was Charlie at one of the windows. He had been hurt in the game and had not gone with us. So Charlie got the freight elevator and ran it down for us so we could get in without the coach seeing us. Charlie was just concerned about all the guys."

Justice's nobility is further enhanced in this reflection from teammate Ken Powell:

"One day in my freshman year I stopped by to talk to Jake Wade, our publicity director. I wasn't planning on eavesdropping, but I happened to be sitting outside his office when Charlie was in there. Charlie said, 'Now, Jake, we've got some good football players here...guys like Chan Highsmith, Walt Pupa, and these people. I think we ought to get these guys more publicity.' And Jake said, 'Well, Charlie, when sportswriters come here, they all want to talk to you.' Charlie said, 'Yeah, Jake, but if you tell them how good these guys are, then they'll want to talk to them, too...that will make us a better team.' That's the type of guy he was...a super individual. I mean if I had been in his shoes, I'd have been in there crying for more publicity...."

As it was, Justice was as famous as any movie star in his day. Hundreds of babies were named for him. A store in Greensboro once sold 900 "Choo Choo Justice" T-shirts in an hour. Mail to him was addressed simply, "Number 22, Chapel Hill." A song about him, "All The Way Choo Choo," sold 50,000 records nationally. When a small-town high school class in North Carolina was asked to name the greatest American, five named Franklin D. Roosevelt, four Dwight Eisenhower, two Robert E. Lee, and the other 58 named Choo Choo Justice. After Justice was graduated in 1949, a school spokesman reported: "Everyone was in a state of mourning."

Justice was flooded with presents and showered with affection. They held a Charlie Justice Day once in Asheville, and the player received enough building material to construct a house. "People were always pressing money on him," relates a teammate. "He always had a new car, and we'd heard through the grapevine that he never had to buy any gas."

Aside from his obvious talents as a football player, his enormous popularity was explainable. Justice thrived in a heavy romantic period of American life, points out Orville Campbell, a close friend: "He came along at a time when every little kid wanted to grow up to be somebody else, a football hero or even president...nobody captured the imagination of the American public the way he captured the imagination of the people of North Carolina."

Billy Carmichael, another close friend, reflects: "Charlie was every mother's dream—clean-cut, modest, generous, didn't smoke or drink, small, boyish."

Justice was the classic campus hero to Irwin Smallwood, a North Carolina newspaperman. "Wherever he went, there was an entourage. It was the times, I guess. Now we're fed up to here with superstars. We see them on television every day and twice on Sundays. Down here then, Charlie was THE superstar."

The Justice phenomenon was mind-boggling, Holdash remembers.

"Women, young and old, all sorts and varieties, just fawned over him and wanted to touch him," Holdash notes with amusement. "It was something to see. We had gone to Columbia, South Carolina, and good grief, you know, the women would come out just to touch him. These weren't silly people...."

"Charlie did not have any private life at all," says Ernie Williamson, a lineman from Carolina's salad days. "He could not get out of the stadium, he could not walk uptown without being completely mobbed. It was a real rat race for him to get home after a ball game. He'd go out of the stadium one way, and there were just crowds of people waiting. He did everything he could, he just wanted to get home, to get away from the crowds, he was so tired after a game, you know. But the same thing happened uptown...more crowds."

None of this turned his head. Despite his majestic stature as the Number One man on campus, Justice was just a friendly country boy who preferred the role of football player to celebrity. His feet were always on the ground—literally and

Charlie Justice, flanked by his wife and by Coach Tom Young, takes a gulp at the Well, a Carolina campus landmark.

figuratively.

"When they recruited him to play here, after his great football career in the Navy, it was a little like getting Clark Gable to appear in a local little-theater production," says Kay Kyser, the onetime North Carolina cheerleader who became a famous band leader. "He was a star even before he got here. But he was just the opposite of a prima donna. It never got to him. Let me tell you a little story. I took Charlie to a big Hollywood party once. The Hollywood people were dying to meet him. Charlie was flabbergasted. His face must have fallen a foot when he walked into that place. He didn't act like a football hero at all. He acted like the smallest of small-town hicks. He was the one impressed with them. All those movie stars. He'd never seen anything like it. I remember he came over to me and said, in that high voice of his, 'Man, this is tall cotton.' He just kept saying, 'Taaa-lll cotton.'"

Justice actively pursued his love affair with life and people. "Heck," he says today, "I'd just walk along the campus, messin' around and sayin' 'Hi' to everybody I saw. You do that now, and they'd think you were plumb crazy."

There was uncommon rapport between Justice and the university citizenry. The player went so far as to show football movies in his spare time to the avid student body, providing appropriate narration.

"For the students who couldn't get to the away games, Charlie and I used to run movies in the campus auditorium," recalls teammate Art Weiner. "They filled the place to see these movies without sound or anything else, just commentary from Charlie. We enjoyed doing it. It gave everyone a chance to see it, and the students were very interested and really turned out."

Justice's rapport with his teammates was no less magical. This story from Campbell, publisher of *The Chapel Hill Newspaper*, confirms that:

"Charlie got with Coach Carl Snavely right at the beginning of practice, and he took about 25 questionnaires home each night about the players. For about eight or ten days he and his wife Sarah went over those players. They say at the end of two weeks, Charlie knew the names and the backgrounds and more about the players on the field than any of the coaches did. Then he'd go up to a kid and say, 'Chuck, I hear you were the greatest when you were in Charlotte. We're going to have a great football team here....' Charlie Justice was the leader from the day he walked on the Carolina campus. He was an exception, having spent those years in the service, but he was still the leader, and the seniors on that football squad looked up to Charlie as much as the freshmen did. He had that innate ability that God had given him to extend the confidence in his ability to the other players...."

Holdash enhances that aspect of the Justice portrait: "Charlie recognized his position. He showed some authority, but in reflection it impressed me that he was cognizant of all the publicity. He was very friendly and outgoing and tried to push the publicity down and not let it bother anyone. So as a result, the relationship with all the players was just excellent. They all responded to him. He had a very shrill voice, and he was a kind of cheerleader type of fellow, talkative...always talking and moving around and cheering people up."

A crowd of some 1,000 had come to embrace North Carolina's newest royalty. Charlie Justice stood on the sidelines, his hands stuffed deep into his blue parka to combat the February cold. This was 1946, and Coach Carl Snavely was winding up his winter practice with a scrimmage against Guilford College.

"Justice," Snavely called.

The player looked at his coach with an air of expectancy, his stomach twisting.

"Try tailback for a while."

The ball was on the North Carolina 35 yard line when Justice entered the game. Guilford's defenders tensed at the appearance of the most sought-after prospect in Southern football history. They determined not to give ground. But Justice got the ball on the first snap, found a glimmer of daylight between tackle and end, and faked out several defenders en route to a 65-yard touchdown run.

Snavely met Justice at the sidelines, clutched his shoulders, and shouted gleefully: "That's enough, that's enough! Good boy, good boy!"

Before Charlie Justice came to North Carolina, the Tar Heels had never been asked to attend a bowl game. When he was there they went to three and rejected an invitation to a fourth.

"North Carolina may be the only team in history that was outscored for the season and played in a major bowl game," says a newspaperman, referring to the 1949 team that went to the Cotton Bowl. "Justice was such a big attraction that the Cotton Bowl took Carolina on that year. It was strictly the name of Justice that got them there, nothing else."

The irony of it all was that Charlie Justice almost did not go to North Carolina. And when he did, it seemed that he was at first considerably unappreciated by Snavely. There was Snavely's classic understatement when informed that Justice

30

Charlie Justice tries on a helmet for size while Coach Carl Snavely looks on. Choo Choo's head never got too big for his headgear.

would come to Chapel Hill.

"Yes, I hear he's here," the coach said coldly. "I hope he comes out for football."

Deep In The Heart
Of Texas

The game was hopelessly lost for the Texas Longhorns.

"It's going to be a long ride back to Texas," needled North Carolina's Bill Wardle.

"Why, you...." Ed Kelly snorted, his Texas-size temper flaring.

The big Longhorn tackle leaped through players and belted Wardle in the jaw. The Tar Heel guard abruptly crashed to the Kenan Stadium turf.

"Okay, you guys," the referee snapped, "that's enough!"

Kelly was led off the field, a chorus of boos ringing in his ears. The game rocked on, none too gently....

One rich Texan offered the lease on his oil well for two tickets, they said. There were reports of huge bribes being passed to ticket takers. Anything to get into Kenan Stadium.

"I believe it was the only game I've been to where you couldn't buy a ticket," remembers North Carolina newspaperman Dick Herbert. "I mean, you couldn't even get them from scalpers. They were giving gatekeepers $10 and $20 just to let them in."

All this tumultuous activity took place when North Carolina played Texas in 1948. It was obvious why tickets were so scarce. The Longhorns were ranked No. 1 in the country and the Tar Heels not far behind.

"The engagement was billed as the intersectional classic of the year, and the Texans didn't want to miss it," Bob Quincy

32

and Julian Scheer wrote in their book, *Choo Choo, The Charlie Justice Story*. "Chapel Hill's little airport bulged with small aircraft carrying big Longhorns."

Texans with 10-gallon hats and even bigger bankrolls were eager to put their "smart" money on the Longhorns. They got plenty of action from North Carolina's followers, who hoped to avenge the previous year's 34-0 disgrace by Texas. It was a perfect setting for a game and a perfect place for an upset....

Texas won the toss and decided to receive. A happy choice, decided Carl Snavely.

"I was amazed but delighted when Texas, after winning the toss, elected to receive," the North Carolina coach said. "Usually it wants to kick off.

"We had checked Texas for several games, and we discovered that every time Texas kicked off to a team they stopped the return somewhere between the goal line and the 15-yard line. If we received and they stopped us, we would be in a hole right at the start. So we decided that the best thing to do was to kick off to them and try to stop them near their own goal line and force them to punt out of a hole."

The Tar Heels at once established their defensive superiority. Then it did not take them long to establish their offensive superiority.

Texas received the ball but was unable to budge the Tar Heels. The Longhorns punted, and Charlie Justice ran the ball back 37 yards to the Texas 42. The Tar Heels moved the ball at will against the Longhorns, scoring in three plays. Justice hit Art Weiner with a 20-yard touchdown pass.

A minute and a half later, North Carolina scored again after Johnny Clements recovered a Texas fumble on the Longhorns' five yard line. Justice drove it in from the four over left tackle.

Three and a half minutes before the end of the first quarter, North Carolina shocked Texas with another score. The Tar Heels marched from their 43 on three running plays and three passing plays. The last pass, covering four yards, went from Justice to Bob Cox.

"That's the most excitement I've experienced in my life,"

recalls Ken Powell about the 1948 game, which ended in a sweet-revenge 34-7 victory over mighty Texas. "That's the year they broke the fences down to get into the game. The fans at the North Carolina State–Duke game just a few miles away had heard the score of our game, how we were beating Texas so badly, and left that game to come over and watch ours. There were no seats left, just standing room, so they broke the fences down to get in. We must have ended up with 60,000 people."

It was not quite that size, but it was one of the most animated and raucous crowds in Carolina history. Reported the *Daily Tar Heel*: "Kenan Stadium rocked from stem to stern with victory chants, yells from semi-conscious drunks and occasional brawls. A few drunks threw money wildly about the stands on foolish wagers and others threw hats on the field in fits of joy. At the same time, still others rose gallantly, though somewhat clumsily, to their feet and threw fists at one another."

Ken Powell: He had to fight his way through 50 ends.

Only the year before, North Carolina followers were lamenting the loss in Texas. Although the players would not give excuses then, there had been a rough plane ride where almost everyone got sick and unbearable heat in the Longhorns' Stadium that thoroughly wilted the Tar Heels.

"We flew in on a Friday afternoon," recalls Powell, "and when we hit the lower altitude, the guys got airsick and started throwing up. Well, we ended up with about 90 percent of our guys throwing up. And they either had nausea or diarrhea or all of this crap. And it was one of those damn hot days...."

Art Weiner, in retrospect, dismisses the sickness and the heat as factors.

"You hear a lot about the heat and the plane trip in 1947," Weiner remembers. "There was a great deal of sickness. But that wasn't the reason we got beat in Texas. We got beat by a better team down there."

In 1948 North Carolina clearly was the better team. And Justice clearly was the game's busiest player, scoring two touchdowns, passing for two, and kicking with surgical skill.

"The outcome amazed me," Justice said while stripping off his uniform. "Last night I didn't think we had it in us. I was worried. Before the game, our boys had little to say. You couldn't figure it. But from the first tackle by Bobby Weant, I sensed something extra. We were sharp. Our moves were right. Texas players noticed it, too. It was that perfect game you're always hoping for but seldom get."

Weiner gives a lion's share of the credit to Snavely for his astute preparation.

"Snavely did a marvelous job of getting the team up," Weiner points out. "The night before the game we had a team meeting, and he told the fellows what he thought the outcome was going to be—and convinced everybody that was what was going to happen. And it did. He just pointed out again how humiliating the defeat the year before had been in Austin and how, in so many words, the team had gone down there and had not given a good account of itself, had let the state down, and let all of our people and the alumni down. He told us that we'd had a year to think about it, and here they were, No. 1 again, and they had come a long way to Chapel Hill, and we could give them the same long ride home that we had the year before. He

Happy Tar Heels after the magnificent victory over Texas in 1948.

Carl Snavely has a handful here, flanked by Art Weiner (left) and Eddie Knox.

then predicted that we could beat them as bad as they had beat us, and it was almost an identical score."

One sportswriter was unable to decide which he enjoyed watching more—North Carolina's offense or defense. "It is like choosing between a Cadillac and a Lincoln Continental," said Billy Carmichael III of the *Daily Tar Heel*. "They both run rather smoothly."

Newspaperman Ray Howe preferred the defense, however: "Len Szafaryn, Haywood Fowle, Bob Mitten, Larry Klosterman, Chan Highsmith and Mike Rubish were bulls among Long-horns, as they drew much of the sting out of Texas' famed passing attack by rushing Paul Campbell before the T quarter-back could make his windup and delivery."

Outside Asheboro, a Ford jalopy with garish orange mark-ings had wound up in a ditch. The lettering hailed the Longhorn might and boasted that it was going from Texas to North Caro-lina "...or bust."

The symbolism was clear.

"It busted, and so did Texas," a newspaper story said.

In the years following the Second World War, the student population at North Carolina was about 6,500, many of them returning servicemen attending college on the GI Bill. Service expressions such as "Roger" and "Snafu" spiced up the campus language. Students dressed well at Chapel Hill. Sport coats and fraternity sweaters were the vogue. A good evening's entertain-ment could be found at the Rathskeller, Amber Alley, or Jeff's. Almost everybody eagerly waited for the weekend, though, for North Carolina football was at its height.

"God, that stadium used to rock," recalls Irv Holdash. "But in a very pleasant manner. No violence as such. They just were so delighted to be there to watch the team and cheer for them. There was no booing. I just don't ever recall any booing. And our best supporters were the blacks. As we came out of the dressing room onto the field, there was a small section there in the end zone filled with blacks, and that thing was always filled and jammed and jumping and popping. They knew every player by name...these guys."

The Tar Heels gave them something to cheer for. It is academic, of course, but still quite possible that this was the best array of talent ever seen at Chapel Hill.

"I think college football in my time, as far as actual mate-rial and actual talent went, was probably as good as it'll ever be," Charlie Justice reflects.

There is plenty of evidence to support Justice's statement. The postwar boom in America produced what is generally recognized as the golden era in college football. Teams over-flowed as returning servicemen hit the beachheads of univer-sities in waves, providing the richest assortment of talent in the

Irv Holdash: "That stadium used to rock."

sport's history.

"We had a lot of people that had been in military service, and several of them had been around, had played with different schools in the naval preflight programs and ROTC programs," Justice recalls. "Most of us were quite a bit older than your average college student today. And we had a couple of more years experience. You take myself. Even though I was a freshman in 1946, I had been in service and played three years of what you might say was pro football because I played with nothing but professionals and All-Americans. Most of us were just older and mature. And we knew what we wanted out of life. We knew you had to pay the price to be successful...and we were willing to pay the price."

Justice's exquisite talents were complemented by extraordinary blocking backs such as Joe Wright, Don Hartig, Eddie Knox, Phil Rizzo, and Bobby Weant and two fullbacks who could pass as well as run, Hosea Rodgers and Walt Pupa. The line included an array of what Justice would call "tall cotton"—ends Art Weiner, Joe Romano, Ken Powell, George Sparger, Dan Logue, John Tandy, Bob Cox, and Mike Rubish, tackles Ted Hazlewood, Stan Marczyk, Len Szafaryn, Haywood Fowle, and Ernie Williamson, guards Larry Klosterman, Sid Varney, Ralph Strahorn, Bob Mitten, and Emmett Cheek, and centers Chan Highsmith and Irv Holdash.

"We had a backup of six or seven classes," remembers Powell, "and I'll tell you how deep we were: On the first day of fall practice in 1946, when the ends started lining up to catch passes, we had 50 ends going out for the team. You know, Carl Snavely had so many people at North Carolina that Coach Peahead Walker of Wake Forest would come over to the campus every night after supper and would park his car near the cafeteria and wait for the players to come out. He'd talk to anybody who wasn't happy at Chapel Hill. That's how he got his players."

Powell recalls that one player who made the all-Southern team in 1945 dropped to fifth string in 1946 when all the veterans returned to Chapel Hill. There was also the story about the four third-string players who had quit the Tar Heels in 1946 and become immediate stars with the Charlotte Clippers, a professional team. A fullback from Mississippi was cut and sent home, and he eventually became an All-American at Ole Miss. ("They simply didn't have a chance to look at him, they were so overloaded with players," points out Holdash.) Bill Maceyko, one of the nation's top rushers at Cornell, was brought to North Carolina by Snavely and wound up being a defensive back because of Justice.

"Bill was a very fine ballplayer," Holdash recalls, "but there just wasn't room for two people at tailback. When we'd get ahead in a game, they'd put Bill Maceyko in, and he'd run and everybody would cheer like mad. They felt sorry for Bill Maceyko. But nobody had any animosity toward Charlie, he was so good."

With heavyweights like Williamson, Marczyk, Hazlewood, and Highsmith on the scene, North Carolina could start an offensive line that averaged about 275 pounds.

"They talk about athletes being bigger and faster today, and obviously people are jumping higher and running faster," Powell interjects. "But I feel honestly that the talent then, with the depth across the board, was better than the talent is today. Because of the backup of classes, the coaches had about six or seven times as much talent to work with in that particular era. And don't forget the athletes were older in college then, too. I think the average age on our team was about 24 or 25."

Holdash, an Ohio product, remembers that he had to work his way up through 11 centers before he became an All-American.

"I had to fight my way up through all those people," Holdash recalls, "and a good number of them were North Carolina boys. You had to get identified there very quickly, and I took on Ted Hazlewood in a scrimmage. I told myself if I didn't get noticed, I was going to be washed out of Chapel Hill. But I never realized that I took on the best tackle they had. He was about 245 pounds and fast! I was one of the dummies they put in there to serve as cannon fodder for the Sugar Bowl team. We'd run a play, and I'd go crazy, knocking down Hazlewood like it was a war. This went on for two days. And he was beating the hell out of me, and he'd just fall on me and grab me and shake me and say: 'This is a dummy scrimmage, frosh.' And he'd throw me down again.

"On the third day an assistant coach came over and said:

42

Three linemen on the first day of fall practice at North Carolina in 1945 huddle around Carl Snavely. From left are Del Leatherman, Ed Twohey, Snavely, and Arthur Collins.

'Holdash, we gotta get some practice going. And with you and Hazlewood, this isn't working. So consider yourself a permanent fixture. Send home, get the rest of your clothes. Tell your folks you're set here.' From that day forth, I knew I had found a home in Chapel Hill. This I will always remember."

Battle Of The Charlies

"The University of North Carolina has won some ball games, has lost some, and a few have ended in ties, but yesterday was the first time the Tar Heels have been robbed of a victory. To coin a phrase used by many of the spectators 'the officiating was lousy—the worst seen in any game a native Carolina team has played.' It was the opinion of the coaches and players alike that two illegal plays the officials failed to see 'robbed' the team of victory."—Carlton Byrd, Winston-Salem Sentinel.

Before the 1947 Sugar Bowl game was staged in gay old New Orleans, everybody talked about the two Charlies—Charlie Justice of North Carolina and Charlie Trippi of Georgia. After it was over, the talk was more about Gabe, George, Wiley, and Alvin. Those were the names of the officials in one of the most controversial bowl games ever played.

Gabe Hill, George Gardner, Wiley Sholar, and Alvin Bell were obviously not as famous as Justice and Trippi, but they got as much press as the football stars at the completion of the 20-10 Georgia victory in Tulane Stadium. It was the considered opinion of many that the officiating cost North Carolina the game, and these men were held up to clinical inspection and ridicule for some time afterward.

"Carl Snavely will always be satisfied to know that he won the 1947 Sugar Bowl," a sportswriter noted with rancor. "The score will go down in the books as favoring Georgia, 20-10, but

44

the Tar Heels figured lax officiating cost them the game. From supporters of both North Carolina and Georgia the opinion was that the Bulldogs scored their first touchdown on an illegal forward lateral pass, and their second touchdown came on a pass play in which a Georgia linesman was across the line of scrimmage before the ball was ever snapped."

Until the complexion changed from Carolina Blue to Georgia Red in the third quarter, the Tar Heels were ahead 7-0 on a four-yard touchdown plunge by Walt Pupa and an extra point from Bob Cox.

"The magnificent Tar Heel linemen had Charley Trippi bottled up," a newspaper reported. "His ground-gaining total was on the minus side rather than showing a plus. Tar Heel supporters were waving hundred-dollar bills at red-faced Georgians. Carolina was superior in every department of the game."

The Tar Heels, 14-point underdogs, seemed determined to continue driving the ball down the Bulldogs' throats in the third period. Justice faked a kick and handed the ball to Jim Camp, and the wingback rushed into Georgia territory, stopping at the 48. Justice faked a pass and squirmed to the 42. Then Ed Romano carried on an end-around play and moved the ball to the Georgia 35, lugging a Bulldog player on his back most of the way.

That was one of the last good things to happen to North Carolina that day, however, as the game's flow dramatically turned in Georgia's favor. Walt Pupa faked to Justice and threw a long pass that was intercepted by Georgia end Joe Tereshinski on the 24 yard line. North Carolina players swarmed around him as Tereshinski attempted to break free. Seeing he was bottled up, Tereshinski pitched the ball to Georgia fullback Dick McPhee.

"Georgia rooters quelled their yells," wrote Carlton Byrd in the *Winston-Salem Sentinel*. "Everyone saw it was a forward lateral. But McPhee ran and ran."

Field Judge Hill had seen the maneuver and threw his handkerchief down. Then he quickly picked it up. McPhee continued on to the Carolina 14 yard line before he was pulled down from behind by Tar Heel center Dan Stiegman. Three plays later Johnny Rauch went over for a Georgia touchdown, and George Jernigan kicked the extra point to tie the game. The

With the protection of a bodyguard, Jim Camp carries for Carolina.

Tar Heels were raging mad, howling that McPhee was in front of Tereshinski when he took the pitch and therefore it constituted a forward maneuver rather than a legal lateral.

"The Tar Heels didn't go downfield to line up for the play," Byrd commented. "A few stayed behind where the ball had been lateraled. Guard Sid Varney said one of the officials had told him the ball was lateraled illegally. But the officials went on downfield. They made no motions to indicate that the play was illegal. They allowed it to stand. The Tar Heels were demoralized by that incident. Carolina was a lost football team."

A member of Snavely's coaching staff remarked: "We weren't the same team after that disputed play. Georgia knew it and drove it down our throats. The emotional side of football wins as often as the physical side."

The injured Tar Heels fluttered to life briefly. They moved the ball deep inside Georgia territory, and Bob Cox kicked an 18-yard field goal for a 10-7 North Carolina lead. But the Bulldogs had been buoyed by their earlier touchdown and within three minutes had another score and a 13-10 lead they never relinquished. This one, too, came on a highly disputed play. There were 55 seconds left in the third quarter when Trippi threw a long touchdown pass to Dan Edwards. The play was allowed to stand despite violent protests from Carolina that a Georgia player was offsides.

"A Georgia lineman was clearly observed across the line of scrimmage before the ball was snapped," reported a newspaperman. "There was no offsides penalty called. The Tar Heels said after the game they thought anyone could see that the Bulldogs were offsides on that touchdown play. They said one of the officials blew a horn on the play, but failed to bring the ball back after the touchdown was scored."

The Sugar Bowl continued to leave a bitter taste in the Carolina camp. Another apparent injustice was piled on the others when the Tar Heels lost a touchdown in the fourth quarter. After Georgia had scored its final touchdown for a 20-10 lead, North Carolina marched to the Bulldog 20. Pupa passed into the end zone, where Ken Powell caught the ball and fell in a heap with Georgia's Rabbit Smith. At first it appeared to be a Carolina touchdown, but an official threw down his handkerchief, indicating that the pass receiver had interfered with the defender on the play. The 15-yard penalty set back any flickering Tar Heel hopes for an upset.

"Carolinians can't figure how Powell interfered with Smith, since he was standing in front of the Rabbit and facing the oncoming ball. Moreover, Powell was knocked out on the play," wrote an unbiased observer, Kris Kreeger of The Associated Press. "Many times it appeared the officials overlooked some rough stuff. Once, when Carolina's Justice had punted, Tereshinski was still rushing him after the ball had stopped rolling. Often the spectators gave voice to their disapproval of the officiating."

After the controversial game, a somber Snavely was heard to say: "We certainly won this game today. We just had it taken away from us."

Today Ernie Williamson looks back on that piece of bittersweet Carolina football history with some regard.

"From our viewpoint, Gabe Hill miscalled that lateral play," recalls Williamson, the onetime North Carolina tackle who is currently vice president of the university's Educational Foundation. "The film showed him pulling his handkerchief and dropping it and then picking it up. He never called another game after that. The humorous thing about that, of course, is that we probably got more publicity from losing the ball game with this controversy than if we had won. The newspapers down there said that Carolina won a moral victory. Well, Morris Mason, our trainer, said, 'I don't like those moral victories. I like those scoreboard victories.'" It was pointed out that perhaps overtraining as well as bad officiating cost Carolina the game.

"Snavely took the team down two weeks before the game and trained them hard," notes an observer. "In the Saturday scrimmage before the Sugar Bowl game they were fantastic. But then in the game, they were kind of flat. Snavely overdid it. Georgia Coach Wally Butts, on the other hand, had a reputation for being so tough on his players, but for this one, he let 'em go home for Christmas. And they dominated the game in the last quarter."

Confirmation of this self-destructive Carolina condition came from Hugo Germino in the *Durham Sun*: "It was in the last period that the Georgia players appeared to be in better physical condition than the Tar Heels. The Carolina boys tired noticeably. The Bulldogs got their second wind, it seemed."

A North Carolina player verifies the toughness of the pre-bowl workouts: "Everybody wanted to win it so badly. The amount of preparation put into it indicated that. We went down two or three weeks early and practiced twice a day before the bowl game. It was real work. We went into it with the idea in mind that it was a long time since the end of the season, and we had to get back into shape and really go at it."

The heralded personal battle of Charlie Justice and Charlie Trippi failed to materialize as such for the 73,000 fans in murky Tulane Stadium. Neither player scored a point, although both played nearly the full game. Trippi beat Justice in the statistics battle, as Georgia had beaten Carolina in the war. It was not much of a show, though, just 56 yards rushing for the Georgia star to 37 for Carolina's leading man. Later Justice was a teammate of Joe Tereshinski with the Washington Redskins, and they reminisced about the notorious game.

"I saw more than enough of you in that game," Justice told Tereshinski.

"That figures," said Tereshinski.

"What do you mean?" Justice asked.

"Simply that I had a job. My assignment on every play was to get to you and tackle you whether you had the ball or not."

"You did a great job," Justice said. "I spent more time with you in New Orleans than with my wife."

Coaches Carl Snavely of North Carolina and Wally Butts of Georgia had kept busy trying to outcry each other before the Sugar Bowl game. Each was doggedly determined to be the underdog, but their credentials belied their pleas. They both had fine football teams, and everyone knew it. Led by Trippi, the flashy All-American runner, and Johnny Rauch, a skilled quarterback, the Bulldogs had won the Southeastern Conference championship in 1946 with a high-powered offense that scored 372 points in 10 games. The irresistible Georgians were one of only two unbeaten and untied major teams in the country.

The Tar Heels had been tied 14-14 on opening day by VPI,

A New Orleans department store welcomes North Carolina and Georgia to the 1947 Sugar Bowl with a dressy window display. Georgia later took the measure of North Carolina, 20-10.

then won eight of their last nine games. Only Tennessee was able to beat North Carolina and then just by a six-point margin. Had not the Tar Heels been so convinced of Tennessee's invincibility, that game might have had a happy ending for them.

"Our scouting reports showed that their tackles could not be moved," Justice said at the time. "We were afraid to open with anything because we didn't think it would work against Tennessee. We were playing Tennessee most of the time with about five plays. That was all wrong, though. We found as the game moved on that Tennessee's line was about like any other line and that we were defeating ourselves because we didn't think we had what it took."

After that midseason 20-14 loss, North Carolina's players found themselves with more confidence and more victories. They beat William and Mary and then Wake Forest, a team that had taken Tennessee, and closed with easy victories over Duke and Virginia. Justice was the key, of course. Almost every game had been highlighted by some brilliant long-distance running from the Tar Heel star. He burned Tennessee with a 74-yard run from scrimmage, had a 68-yarder against VPI, 70- and 90-yard bursts against Florida, 66 against Miami, and 45 and 54 against Virginia.

Many of these runs out of Carl Snavely's single-wing power machine were sponsored by some of the best offensive linemen in the country. Justice's success was due in large part to the herculean efforts of guards Sid Varney and Ralph Strayhorn, tackle Haywood Fowle, center Chan Highsmith, and end Art Weiner. Ironically these five superb players were either missing or injured before the start of the 1947 Sugar Bowl game, giving Snavely some cause for deep concern and loading the dice and the odds in Georgia's favor.

Both Varney and Fowle, bulwarks of the Tar Heels' championship season in the Southern Conference, suffered ankle injuries in practice a few days before the game. Highsmith, the all-Southern center, hurt his back in the closing game of the regular season. Strayhorn missed most of the Tar Heels' rigorous prebowl practice because of the illness of his father. And Weiner, who eventually became an All-American, had left the team because of personal problems and quit school temporarily.

"They said when we first came down here, we had a slight advantage in reserves," said Snavely, voicing his displeasure at the time. "Now all we have left is reserves. The past few days' workouts have cost us what little chance we had of winning the ball game."

Snavely could not be blamed for wallowing in self-pity. Even on the day of the game, Lady Luck had a slap in the face for the Carolina team. En route to Tulane Stadium, the Tar Heel bus rammed a stalled taxi. End Joe Romano bruised a knee when he was pitched forward from his seat but was able to start along with the unsteady Strayhorn and Varney. Snavely expected a call any minute that the remainder of his starting team had been swallowed by the bacchanals of Bourbon Street.

Despite these obvious deficiencies, the Tar Heel players gave the brutish Georgians their toughest game of the year. The infighting had all the grace of a heavyweight slugging match. In the safety of the dressing room after the game, one of the Georgia giants, who was being treated for cuts over his eyes, commented: "It is the first team I've ever seen which could punch twice while I'm punching once."

The Best Team Stands Up

The Tar Heels listened attentively while Russ Murphy, the defensive backfield coach, went over the other team's strong points.

"You can't block this guy," he said, "he's an All-American." Silence.

"And this guy's tough," Murphy said. "You can't block him."

The Tar Heels continued to stare solemnly at their instructor.

"Now this guy's awfully mean," Murphy insisted. "There's no way to stop him."

A player raised his hand.

"Coach, is it too late to cancel the game?" he asked.

"Yes, why?"

"Well," said the player with his tongue deeply imbedded in his cheek, "if we can't block anybody, I don't see any need of going over there."

The room shook with laughter. Everyone knew the Tar Heels could beat anybody. At least that is what they felt.

The plane lazily dipped a wing and curled downward toward the Raleigh-Durham airport. A monster crowd had been keeping a vigil for its return. The roar of the motor triggered a buzz among the welcomers.

"They're here!" someone shouted.

The craft adroitly hit the landing field and wheeled toward

the terminal. The crowd surged forward, eager to catch a glimpse of the returning warriors of North Carolina's football team. As each player stepped off the plane, his ears were assaulted by ringing salutes.

"I don't think there was a dry eye on the team," remembers Art Weiner, the brilliant North Carolina end. "We looked down as we stepped off and you never saw so many people in your life. There must have been 5,000 people there to meet the team."

Ironically, this generous welcome followed one of Carolina's most inglorious defeats in the Charlie Justice era—a 34-0 thrashing at Texas. It pointed up dramatically the fever and the flavor of the day.

"We thought there was a wreck at the airport," Weiner says. "We didn't think anybody wanted to see us after that game. But the student body and the fans were so absolutely marvelous and so rabid during that period, it was unreal. I think as a result of that kind of support we went out and won every game for the rest of the year."

That is not exactly what happened. Carolina was beaten by Wake Forest the following week, but that was the last time the Tar Heels lost in 1947. Carl Snavely's magnificent single-wing machine picked up speed and ran over William and Mary, Florida, Tennessee, North Carolina State, Maryland, Duke, and Virginia and wound up as probably the best team ever constructed by the stern Tar Heel coach. As fate would have it, it was the only team during the four Justice years that did not attend a bowl.

"We should have played on New Year's Day of 1948," Justice remembers. "We should have played in the Orange Bowl, but they wouldn't give us enough tickets to satisfy the needs of our alumni and backers. We wanted 3,000 tickets. The Orange Bowl wouldn't let us have them, so the administration turned down the bowl. That was the best ball club we had in Chapel Hill in all my four years. I know we lost to Texas out there, and then we came back and lost to Wake Forest the following week. But at the end of the season I think we had the best ball club that we ever had."

After the Tar Heels had racked up Virginia 40-7 on the last day of the season, North Carolina was besieged by bowl invita-

The 1947 team was generally considered the best that Carl Snavely produced at North Carolina.

tions—nine in all, ranging from the major Orange Bowl to vastly inferior productions. A group in Boston said it would devise a new bowl and offered a blank check to the Tar Heels if they attended. An organization in Los Angeles hoped to land the Tar Heels for a late December game. But none of these winter dreams came true for Carolina's boys. It was hard to imagine that such an exquisite team should be put in mothballs so early. After kicking away two of their first three games, North Carolina quickly emerged as one of the nation's major powers. The Tar Heels hurdled the field and found themselves in the Top Ten by the end of the season, fulfilling rich promises of spring.

Many preseason assessments insisted that the Tar Heels were thoroughly irresistible.

"How can North Carolina be stopped?" asked one national

magazine. "There is no answer. Our scouts insist there isn't any. Carl Snavely's backfield, built around more and more Justice for all, with Walt Pupa, one of the tiptops in fullbacks, will be the best below the Potomac. His line, minus only two men, bulges with combat-seasoned power, plus depth. He has some of the best in Joe Romano and Ken Powell, a couple of fatalistic ends; Len Szafaryn, tackle, and Sid Varney, guard."

At the start of the season, Snavely called his team "the finest edition since I began coaching." The Tar Heels indeed seemed to be the team that had everything—depth, size, speed, maturity, and a wonderfully positive attitude. "Coach Snavely's biggest problem," noted a semi-serious observer, "is deciding which All-American to start."

Georgia, the team that had spoiled Carolina's bowl debut the year before, was the opening-day opponent. Each passing day since the Sugar Bowl had heightened the desire for revenge, and this was fulfilled as the Tar Heels beat the Bulldogs 14-7 before an excitable full house at Kenan Stadium.

Literally and figuratively up in the clouds en route to Texas for the second game of the season, the Tar Heels soon landed with the abrupt shock of a plane hitting a runway. Bobby Layne, the Texas quarterback who was to become a great pro, dominated the onesided game. The Longhorns had a 20-0 lead at halftime, while the Tar Heels were having trouble staying on their feet, no less scoring. Sickened by a bad plane ride and further tortured by the king-sized Texas heat, players indiscriminately dropped on the field. Bob Mitten, the Carolina guard, blacked out three times during the game and had to be benched.

Snavely refused to blame the plane ride and the weather on the eventual 34-point defeat. "We didn't have it," he said. "We just didn't have it." Justice, particularly, had one of his most disappointing days. And the crowd, aware of his gaudy reputation, further humiliated Carolina with the chant: "We have Layne—you keep Choo Choo."

The outrageous hostilities of Texas were greatly diminished when the Tar Heels returned home to a splendorous welcome. It began at the airport with adoring crowds and feverishly continued on to the campus.

"We went on down to the gym and there were the cheerleaders, and the band and two thousand others," reported the *Alumni Review*. "The bus was an hour late but not many left;

Man on the run: wingback Jim Camp.

the band played, people looked ahead, not back. Finally they came, they who had not conquered, and a mighty cheer went up. Carl Snavely spoke briefly, not without emotion; said that we just took a licking from a great team. He mentioned the heat and the head colds, but said that they weren't the cause...."

The week after, the Tar Heels lost a 19-7 decision to Wake Forest, causing bewilderment and shock in Chapel Hill. "We've got nothing left but our press clippings," said an emotionally upset Charlie Justice.

"Wake Forest really defeated them decisively," recalls newspaperman Dick Herbert. "They just murdered them in the first half, and then Wake Forest coach Peahead Walker called off the passing that had really killed them. Otherwise, it would have been worse."

The North Carolina morale plunged. Justice huddled with Snavely one gray day and surmised that the players "aren't giving 100 percent." Another big problem was brewing in the Carolina camp. The Southern Conference questioned Justice's eligibility, since it had been rumored that the glamour player had signed a contract with the Philadelphia Eagles when he was at the Bainbridge naval station during the war. After several days of agony, Justice was cleared of this unsupported charge, and the action seemed to spark a new life in the Tar Heels. Justice got North Carolina back on the right track with two touchdown passes and 55 yards rushing, leading the Tar Heels to a 13-7 victory over William and Mary.

"This team is going places," said Jim Camp. "We're just beginning to play the kind of football expected of us."

In fact, the Tar Heels were. Hosea Rodgers showed that there were players in the Carolina backfield other than Justice by leading the Tar Heels to a 35-7 rout of Florida with one of the best all-around performances in Carolina history. Rodgers accounted for 245 yards with his passing and running, hurled three touchdown passes, and scored once himself on a 76-yard dash from scrimmage. The fullback's shining moment was sponsored by exquisite team unity. "Vastly improved team play made Hosea's exploits possible, which may reasonably seem to be a happy harbinger of things to come," noted the *Alumni Review*. "In trouncing a spirited and well-coached Florida eleven the Tar Heels made fewer mistakes and showed their best blocking of the campaign."

Shortly after North Carolina dismissed Florida, Snavely set his sights on Tennessee, the only team to beat the Tar Heels during the regular season in 1947. "Russ Murphy says they're good and tough," Snavely noted with a trace of pessimism.

Not only would Tennessee be a challenge for North Carolina's players but also a personal challenge for Snavely himself. "I've never been beaten by a coach three times in a row—and General Neyland of the Vols trimmed me our last two meetings. I'd like to pay him back some of the anguish he's doled out."

Snavely had a lucky charm with him at the game—a loud red, white, and blue tie that had been given to him earlier in the season. "I'm not superstitious," he said, "but after losing to Texas and Wake Forest, I got this tie in the mail from a friend. I've worn it since, and we haven't lost yet. I'm not going to take it off."

Snavely's tie was the conversation piece before the game, but everybody talked about Charlie Justice afterwards. He was rarely better. He scored once and pitched touchdown passes to Bob Cox and John Tandy. And Carolina won, 20-6. "You can't ask more of a player than Charlie Justice gave today," noted Snavely.

Justice could be a threat without the ball, as the next game against North Carolina State showed. On the Tar Heels' first play from scrimmage, Walt Pupa took the ball from center and faked to Justice, then pounced through a wide hole in the line. The fullback ran 45 yards without assistance, but on the North Carolina State 25, a Wolfpack player raced to bring him down. Suddenly a Tar Heel came up to cut the red-shirted defender off his feet, and Pupa scored standing up. As the North Carolina player crossed the goal line, he looked back to see that it was Justice who had thrown the key block. Justice had another of his field days on offense as well. He rushed for 123 yards, passed for 42, and sailed punts for a 41-yard average. The result was a predictable 41-6 victory for North Carolina, a winning habit the Tar Heels followed to the end of the season with shutouts over Maryland and Duke and a 33-point victory over Virginia.

Art Weiner, now a successful businessman in North Caro-

About the only time Charlie Justice could be caught standing still was for a picture. Here Number 22 poses with another back, Billy Britt.

lina, leafed through his scrapbook of memories.

"The thing about that 1947 team," he recalls, "is that the linemen of that period in Snavely's system were very small but very mobile. The guards and the tackles on that offensive line were really one of the keys in the team's success, those pulling guards in the single wing. They were like 170, 175 pounds. You had Bob Mitten and Sid Varney, among others. They were both very small but excellent blockers. They had to do their job, and they did it well."

Justice seconds the motion.

"We had a tough start and we didn't go to a bowl game," he says, "but at the end of that year, we could have beaten anybody in the country."

Happy Ending

"I was kinda standing there waiting for him to put the ball down, because I was running in front thinking he was going to put it down and I'd have to jump and try to block it. I did get even with the guy, maybe a little bit past him as he set it down, and sat on it, and Mike Souchak kicked me and the ball at the same time, square in the pants. It was a real strange thing, and what was really amusing about it, you read so many accounts of it, they had me going through blockers. But nobody laid a hand on me."—Art Weiner.

The North Carolina players dressed in Chapel Hill and left in chartered buses at 12:30 p.m. for their 2:00 game in Duke Stadium. The procedure was thought to be best for their "nerves." But the buses got tied up in traffic, and there were few more nervous than the Tar Heels when they took the field just minutes before kickoff. Charlie Justice arrived in time to hear the "Star Spangled Banner" and embrace his teammates in the emotional, game-opening ritual.

What followed then did nothing for the Tar Heels' nervous systems or their fans' heart conditions. In one of the most frenetic football contests ever staged in the South, the Tar Heels played the Blue Devils on November 19, 1949, in a game that literally had two endings. Fortunately both were happy for North Carolina, and the Tar Heels escaped with a 21-20 decision.

"That Duke game was quite a game," remembers North

North Carolina defenders have a Duke runner bottled up in this 1949 game that ended 21-20 in Carolina's favor.

Carolina end Art Weiner, who was in on the game-saving play at the end. "It was 21-20 up to the last few seconds, and Duke was moving down the field and got the ball to about our 20 yard line and attempted a pass with about four or five seconds left. But it was an incomplete pass, and as soon as the ball hit the ground, the clock was supposed to stop. But some official inadvertently let the clock go on and then signaled the end of the game. So both teams started off the field, and it appeared that the game was over."

Mike Souchak, Duke's kicker, had been preparing for a field goal attempt when referee J.D. Rogers rushed in to indicate that the game was over.

Thousands of fans came on the field, giving the unbearably tense contest its apparent finishing touch. But the game was not over. Duke officials argued with Rogers and won their point that time could not run out after an incomplete pass play until the ball was snapped on the next play.

"It took police and grounds keepers and a frenzied appeal from the public address system about five minutes to clear the field," reported North Carolina's *Alumni Review*.

Weiner remembers, "I'll bet there was something like 15,000 people on the field. They had to go back and round up some of the players, too."

Exhilarated Tar Heel fans, who had crowded onto the field to touch the players after the apparent victory, were told by Justice: "Please, please stand back!" Then they understood that victory was not theirs yet and melted back in shocked disbelief. Their silence turned quickly to roars of pleasure, however, when Weiner streaked in to block Souchak's field goal attempt from the 20.

"In all the excitement and all the trouble of getting the field clear, they forgot to overshift and block Weiner, who was our end on the far side, and he just came in and practically sat down on the ball before Mike kicked it," remembers Justice.

"Evidently they had a mixup in blocking assignments," Weiner reflects, "because nobody even touched me. Paul Stephanz and one or two other Duke players have told me since that some of their players even left the field, as some of ours had, and when it came time to get the place-kicking team together, there was a lot of confusion, and I don't think they had their whole team lined up. Mike Souchak was to attempt a field goal from the 20-yard line. But instead of lining up for a field goal, they lined up like they would for a punt, with both of their blockers on the right side and nobody on the left side where I was. I was very, very close to the ball, and I got there so fast that I almost ran on by the guy holding the ball. Had I done that, we probably would have lost the game, but I was lucky to stop and I sat on the ball, and Souchak kicked me in the rear end."

A crowd of 57,500 had waited impatiently for the North Carolina team to arrive, and many of them were Tar Heel fans, judging from the pregame ovation.

"It was our last game at Duke Stadium for Charlie and me and some of the rest of the seniors," recalls Weiner, "and the Carolina fans got up and cheered solidly for 15 minutes when we came out on the field. They didn't sit down, it was a deafening kind of thing. It was just unreal."

The way the game started, however, it did not figure to be North Carolina's day. On the first play from scrimmage, Duke's Billy Cox stunned the Tar Heels and quieted the Tar Heel supporters with a 75-yard touchdown run off right tackle. The shock was softened a bit when Ken Powell and Ed Bilpuch broke through to block Souchak's extra-point attempt, a play that turned out to be very important later in the game. North Carolina's hopes were further crippled when Justice was carried off the field in the first quarter with a bad ankle injury.

"How does it feel, Charlie?" the trainer asked.

"I think I can move on it," Justice said, grimacing.

The pain made his eyes tear, and he hobbled over to the bench. The roars of the crowd filled his ears, and he looked down at the ankle.

"Damn!" he said, "I've got to get back in there."

Carl Snavely came over.

"How is it, Charlie?"

"It'll go, coach," Justice said, wearing a half-hearted smile.

Justice looked at the field, where his blue-shirted teammates were holding their own against Duke. The game was being played between the 40 yard lines.

The minutes ticked by; the crowd noise swelled and ebbed.

"Get some novocaine over here," a voice on the North Carolina bench said.

They would get Justice back into the game with a pain-killing drug.

"You'll be fine, Charlie," someone said.

"I know, I know."

The game had belonged to Duke before Justice came back in. Then North Carolina's lame thoroughbred showed that he was as good on one leg as most were on two—probably better. He passed to Art Weiner for a touchdown, and North Carolina had a 7-6 lead at the half. He later caught a touchdown pass from Billy Hayes and then threw another one to Weiner, extending North Carolina's lead to 21-6 in the third quarter.

Barely had the roars of North Carolina supporters died when they were drowned completely by cheers from the Duke side. It took the Blue Devils just 18 seconds to get back into the game. Tom Powers returned the kickoff 93 yards for a touchdown, and Souchak kicked the extra point to narrow North Carolina's lead to 21-13 going into the fourth quarter.

Duke held the ball for most of the last period but was unable to score until aided by a North Carolina fumble in the last minutes. North Carolina's George Verchick dropped the ball, and Louis Viau recovered for Duke on the Tar Heel nine yard line. Four plays later the omnipresent Cox went over right tackle for the touchdown, and Souchak kicked the extra point to bring Duke within one point with 2:55 left in the game.

The remaining minutes were not for people with bad hearts. Hayes returned Souchak's kickoff to the North Carolina 13, but the Tar Heels could not move the ball, and Justice punted. George Skipworth returned his kick to the Carolina 40. Cox then faked a pass and ran around right end to the 20 before being tackled. North Carolina fans breathed easier when Dick Bunting intercepted a Cox pass on the one yard line, but the insanity was far from over. Justice tried to kick Carolina out of the hole, but it was a weak effort, and Powers returned the ball to the Tar Heel 20. Cox then threw an incomplete pass as time apparently ran out. It was at this point that the fans surged on the field, only to find that Duke still had one play left. Souchak's field goal try was then nullified by Weiner, giving the Tar Heels the Southern Conference championship.

"From the standpoint of ability, this was the finest game a Duke team ever played," whispered Duke coach Wallace Wade. "Yes, the finest."

In the North Carolina dressing room, Snavely embraced Justice's gallant effort: "He played on one leg today, and he was just about the best I've ever seen. Under the circumstances, he was the greatest. I never thought he would last through the first period."

Justice had leaped from depression to euphoria in the space of one week. Only seven days before he had been kept out of North Carolina's first game ever with Notre Dame because of an injured ankle which was sprained in a 20-14 victory over William and Mary.

"I was very disappointed," Justice recalls. "You know, you always dream about playing in Yankee Stadium and playing against Notre Dame, and I didn't get a chance to. I'm not complaining, but that probably cost me the Heisman Trophy, because had I played in New York and let the New York writers see me play, I might have won it. Of course Leon Hart of Notre Dame had a real good day in New York and won it that year."

Injured ankle or not, Justice had every intention of playing against Notre Dame until Snavely made an 11th-hour decision.

Fullback Billy Hayes churns for yardage against Duke in 1949.
The Tar Heels wound up winning this thriller 21-20.

Remembers Justice:

"At the last minute the coach came up to me and said, 'We gotta play Duke the next week, and if we lose to Duke, why I'll have to pack my bags and leave town. So I'd rather have you against Duke than have you against Notre Dame.'"

For obvious reasons Justice would have embraced the challenge of Notre Dame. The Fighting Irish were football's glamour team, and Yankee Stadium was the most glittering showplace for a game. Many North Carolina students forgot about classwork that week and made preparations to accompany the team up to New York in cars swathed in Confederate flags and blue-and-white bunting. They held an impromptu pep rally in Times Square, snarled traffic, and raised several eyebrows with their undisciplined behavior. "Stop Sitko" chants could be heard at every crowded corner. They were an obvious blast at football

68

writer Grantland Rice, who had chosen Notre Dame's Emil Sitko over Justice on his All-American team.

"This was quite a thing for us," says Irv Holdash, the All-American North Carolina center. "We were in awe of this huge stadium. And Notre Dame would always out-psyche you immediately. We were down in the far end of Yankee Stadium next to those little statues of Babe Ruth and the like, and that was impressive in itself. But the best was yet to come. All of a sudden the crowd's cheering like hell, and we look up at the other end of the field and 11 players stream out in green uniforms. They came down the whole width of the field in a wave. Then 11 more would come and they'd run down the whole width of the field. And all of a sudden we caught ourselves standing there with our mouths open, gaping at this. Notre Dame must have brought six or seven teams out. It was something."

New York City was never the same after this Times Square Carolina pep rally before the 1949 Notre Dame game.

Then the game started and Holdash recalls with some amusement:

"One of the prerequisites of making a Notre Dame team was that you had to have your front teeth knocked out. It's true, really. We'd be ready in a defensive position, and they'd come out of the huddle with a growl. The guys were all ugly because nobody had any front teeth in the front line, and you'd start to shiver and shake and say, 'What the hell's going on here?' They scared the devil out of you when they came up to the line with that big roar and their mouths open and growling...."

The Notre Dame players were not all bark and no bite either, Holdash points out.

"They had a lot of finesse in their blocking. They wouldn't beat you up like Tennessee and Wake Forest and Georgia would do physically. They weren't necessarily a physical team. They'd just get in your way, you know, that type of finesse. And they had a ton of guys...."

Holdash found out that day why mountainous Leon Hart was the Heisman Trophy winner.

"In that game Hart would just run down the field about 10 yards, turn around, and throw up his hands, and they'd throw the ball to him. And all our halfbacks would get on his back, and they couldn't move him. And then he'd lateral off after all the guys climbed up his back. It's an old Notre Dame play, you know, a quick pass and then an almost immediate lateral. So I said, 'Look, I'm going to take care of that big lug.' I told my teammates to cover my area, and I would really lay into that Leon Hart. So maybe two or three plays after that, I shot across the line to the other side of the field, and Leon turned around to catch the ball, and I just let fly. I planned to cut him in half. But I got to his belt line and my whole body simply froze in mid-air, and with my arms wrapped around him I just simply slid to the ground in a state of shock. I mean, I hadn't even budged him. 'Well,' I said, 'as long as I'm here, I might as well do something.' I grabbed his foot and tried to twist it, you know, and he looked down, after he lateraled off, and he just picked up the other foot and put it right in my chest and stood on me. He growled, and I said, 'Get me out!' I didn't try to take

70

on Leon Hart anymore."

There was also Holdash's unnerving confrontation with Emil Sitko, the great Notre Dame running back.

"The sportswriters threw a tag on me," Holdash says. "They used to call me 'Six-Inch' Holdash, because I supposedly never gave up more than six inches on the line. They lied worse than I did. Anyway, when we were playing Notre Dame, they had Emil 'Six-Yard' Sitko. Of course they called him that because he gained an average of about six yards a carry. So when the writers were done with Charlie Justice and those guys, the big question of the game was: What's going to happen when 'Six-Yard' Sitko meets 'Six-Inch' Holdash? I said, 'Wait until after the game and I'll tell you.' Well, we did real well in the first half, held them to a 6-6 tie, but it ended up 42-6 in Notre Dame's favor. And the writers came around and asked: 'Say, what's the story on Sitko?' And I said, 'Listen, you can refer to that bum from now on as 'Six-Yard, Six-Inch' Sitko.'"

The disabled and dejected Justice only made two appearances on the field for North Carolina that day—once to hold the ball on an unsuccessful placement attempt and the other to argue a referee's decision. Dick Bunting played admirably in his place as the Tar Heels took an early 6-0 lead and held the

North Carolina players could not stop Emil Sitko on this run, nor could they stop Notre Dame in 1949. The Fighting Irish beat the Tar Heels 42-6 in the first meeting between the teams.

Dick Bunting scores against Notre Dame in 1949 at Yankee Stadium, the only bright moment in the Tar Heel's 42-6 loss to the Irish.

brutish Fighting Irish to a halftime tie. North Carolina still was in the game after three periods, trailing only 15-6 before Notre Dame's superior forces overran the Tar Heels in the last quarter. With Justice on the sidelines, the showing was regarded as something of a moral victory for the Tar Heels, and this was duly noted in the nation's press.

North Carolina completed the season with the dramatic victory over Duke and a triumph over Virginia to earn a berth in the Cotton Bowl, but clearly this was not the same team of earlier years. Most of the veterans, particularly in Carolina's exquisite line, had graduated. Gone, too, were backfield players of high caliber such as Hosea Rodgers and Walt Pupa.

In 1948 a handsome array of talent had carried the Tar Heels to their dizziest heights in the polls and one of their best records in history. A rout of Texas on opening day and victories over Georgia, Wake Forest, North Carolina State, LSU, and Tennessee shot North Carolina's stock way up. At one time the Tar Heels were ranked No. 1 and would have had a perfect season except for one afternoon's letdown—a 7-7 tie with William and Mary, a four-touchdown underdog. The gorgeous resiliency of the team was displayed the week after the William and Mary tie, when North Carolina rebounded to smother Maryland, 49-20. Triumphs over Duke and Virginia earned the Tar Heels an invitation to the Sugar Bowl game with Oklahoma, a game that Art Weiner likely will never forget.

Art Weiner in a familiar position: Over the goal line with the ball.

Sugar Bowl Blues

"We had about three pass plays. One we just called in the huddle 'sideline,' just square out like they do today. Then we had 129-4, that was a post, and 129-3, a corner. But most of the time with Art Weiner, we went with the sideline, when I would start the play to the right, then throw back. We could have thrown that sideline all day long because there was no way the defender could stay with Art. Anytime we wanted to, we could throw it. When Art would go down that sideline, they'd lay way back off him...."—Charlie Justice.

Art Weiner caught 34 passes in 1948, but everyone remembers the one he dropped.

"There must have been 10 million people that saw it," Weiner says, somewhat amused, "and I explain to them that the ball hit me in the head."

It could not have come at a worse time for North Carolina. It happened in the Sugar Bowl game against Oklahoma. Had Weiner caught it, it would have changed the complexion of the game. As it was, the Sooners stayed in command and went on to a 14-6 victory over the Tar Heels.

The botched play occurred in the second quarter with the Tar Heels trailing 7-6. Justice had Weiner clear in the end zone, but the usually sure-handed end misplayed what would have been the go-ahead score for North Carolina.

"Justice threw me a perfect pass," Weiner recalls. "I was

supposed to cut toward the sideline on the left. Darrell Royal—you know, now the Texas coach—was the defensive halfback, and I had to get away from him. Charlie threw perfect, but I was more concerned where Royal was than the ball, and I took my eye off the ball. Some who saw it say it hit me in the head and almost bounced up in the stands. Had I known, Royal actually fell down and wasn't even standing when I got the ball, and it was a sure touchdown which would have given us the lead then, and it may have won the ball game."

Thus Oklahoma maintained a 7-6 lead at the half and built it to 14-6 in the third period on Lindell Pearson's eight-yard smash over left tackle. Then the Sooners resorted to conservative football and sucked up the remaining quarter with time-consuming ground plays.

"Beyond their two offensive successes, the Sooners attempted nothing outstanding and were content, with the masterly quarterbacking of Jack Mitchell, to keep possession of the ball as much as possible," noted Ernest Mehl in the *Kansas City Star*. "Like a ride in a surrey with the fringe on top, the method employed by the Bud Wilkinson-coached eleven was methodical, safe, dependable."

Weiner was understandably upset over his disastrous mistake but no more self-critical than Justice. Despite several astonishing runs from scrimmage, a fistful of gorgeous punts, and a recovered fumble, the Carolina triple-threat hated himself for one of the rare things he did wrong that day. He threw an intercepted pass, and the opportunistic Sooners turned it into their first touchdown. That was unforgivable, Justice thought, and he raced into the locker room, pulled a blanket over his head, and hid in a corner for 10 minutes. When he finally came out, the bitterly disappointed Justice whispered to reporters, "I lost it—you can say that."

Carl Snavely, his coach, was in total disagreement.

"I don't see how the kid went as far in his condition," Snavely said.

Snavely's reference was to a celebrated stomachache that Justice had before the game. For several days prior to Sugar Bowl time, the halfback lived on soups and other liquids. His ailment was kept secret until a reporter stumbled on the details a day before the game, then Justice's condition got presidential treatment in the press.

"Rumors grew," Bob Quincy and Julian Scheer reported in their book, *Choo Choo, The Charlie Justice Story*. "One 'reliable source' had Charlie just before being wheeled into the operating room for an appendectomy. Another felt sure he would miss the Oklahoma game unless an oxygen tent accompanied him on the field. The frantic reporting was reminiscent of the famed Babe Ruth illness during the mid-20s."

Justice certainly did not play like a sick man, though. He had runs from scrimmage of 9, 10, 13, 25, 11, 14, and 8 yards and kicked four times for 65, 65, 57, and 53 yards.

"There's no question about Justice being a great back," Oklahoma coach Bud Wilkinson said after the game. "He was the player we feared most, and he showed it."

In 1949 the Tar Heels had lost 22 lettermen from their illustrious Sugar Bowl team. Luckily Charlie Justice and Art Weiner were not among them. Without those two, North Carolina football would have gone nowhere that season—and especially not to the Cotton Bowl. The drawing power of Justice particularly was probably the only reason that the Tar Heels were invited to a major bowl at all. They were outscored for the season and lost three games before taking a 27-13 shellacking from Rice in Dallas.

"They were just an ordinary ball club, and the game in the Cotton Bowl was the most merciful score that's ever been in football," says a North Carolina newspaperman. "Carolina was just terrible, and Rice coach Jess Neely called off the dogs, otherwise the score would have been worse. He just killed 'em in the first half, and then Jess Neely was real nice to 'em. I think Carl Snavely exchanged five movies with Neely before that game, and he watched them hour after hour, and he was delighted to discover that Tobin Rote threw to his right all the time. So in the Cotton Bowl game, he threw everything to his left and just killed them."

Behind their great passer the Owls had a 27-0 lead in the final quarter. Then Justice passed to Paul Rizzo for one touch-

Fullback Bob Kennedy takes the safest route behind two blocking behemoths, Paul Rizzo (66) and Ted Hazlewood (81), in this 1948 action.

Art Weiner, one of the big wheels on the North Carolina machine in the post-war years of the 1940s.

down and lateraled to him for another to salvage some dignity for North Carolina.

"It was so onesided," remembers the newspaperman, "that the North Carolina press delegation was actually laughing in the second quarter."

The most undistinguished team of the Justice era was clearly underprivileged but not without its highlights. There was, of course, Justice himself, an authentic folk hero. Weiner possessed an uncanny ability to seize his passes and as a result tied a collegiate record with 52 receptions in 1949. The big end averaged 13 yards a catch on a gaudy total of 762 yards.

"Justice threw a real catchable soft ball," Weiner remembers. "He had a good arm and could throw the ball; the percentages speak for themselves. I went into pro ball, and his ball was as good and as soft to catch as just about any quarterback that I played with."

Justice completed more than 54 percent of his passes in 1949, but his mastery in that department did not evolve easily, he remembers.

"The first two years we never worked on our passing at all; we had our running game. I only threw about 50 passes in a whole season, and our passing game was a waste, a total waste. I couldn't throw a lick in '46. I threw, and gosh, it was awful. Walt Pupa did most of the passing. The spring of our sophomore year we started working on my throwing. I got the idea watching the baseball catcher make the throw to second base, so I learned to get the ball up behind my ear, and I learned to set up on that low step, a step taken and a step to the left, and throwing.

"And our junior year we really spent some time. Art and I would go out 30 to 45 minutes early every day before practice, working together, me throwing the ball at the time he was breaking. I don't know how many passes we tried. And then in '49 we had to throw. We just couldn't run, we had lost the offensive line, and I was passing better."

Weiner, perhaps, would have reached more astronomical levels had it not been for Snavely's excessively conservative style. Justice points out:

"Remember, we kicked on third down. Unless we were inside the 40 on their side of the field, we kicked on third down. If we had more than two yards to go on third down at their 40, we punted. So, you see, there's another down Art missed, and this is the down where you get more passing. Weiner had deceptive speed. He had that long stride, didn't look like he was moving at all. When he made the cut, most defenders thought he was slow. He took such long steps, in a stride he took two yards, maybe more, two steps to cover five yards. I remember the last game, Virginia, I threw and hit him, and the halfback was there, too, but in two steps Art just outran him. Just ran off and left him. He ran like a big halfback."

Both Justice and Weiner were named to All-American teams in 1949, an honor also bestowed on Ken Powell, classified as "a mean end" by one sportswriter. The Carolina camp also housed another rising star, center Irv Holdash.

The scent of pessimism was temporarily dispelled at the start of the 1949 season, when North Carolina opened with victories over North Carolina State, Georgia, South Carolina, and Wake Forest. The successes ran the Tar Heels' regular season's unbeaten streak to 21 games, but few expected it to last much longer. Holdash recalls:

"Snavely would say in his inimitable fashion, 'We'll win because we're smarter!' And we did, sometimes, but gee we took a helluva physical beating. All those brutes on the other teams, they weren't any nicer to us because we were polite. We didn't have much deception, either. We'd come out of a huddle up to the line and point a big red arrow: 'We're going that way.' No deception whatsoever."

It was not a lack of deception that cost North Carolina its first loss of 1949 but perhaps the lack of a dry field. The Tar Heels saw their unbeaten streak, that had started in early 1947, come to an end in Baton Rouge, Louisiana, on a warm October night. They were beaten 13-7 by Louisiana State and some say by the underground tactics of Louisiana State loyalists. It was charged that LSU had watered the field in an effort to slow down Justice. The assertion was of course denied by the school, but a sportswriter made it a big point in his game story.

"The Bengals, who have proved good mudders in two previous home games, were aided by a mechanical 'local shower,' for when the fans appeared in the stands they were bewildered with the glistening appearance of the sodden turf," Bud Montet wrote in Sunday's *Baton Rouge Morning Advocate*. "As it hasn't rained in Baton Rouge for the last two days, the fans were mystified."

There were no excuses the following week, though, when the Tar Heels returned home for a game with Tennessee and were treated rather roughly by the Volunteers.

"That was the worst physical beating I've ever taken," Justice said after Tennessee's destructive 35-6 victory.

If North Carolina supporters needed any proof that this

indeed was the worst of the four teams in the Justice era, they got it a few weeks later when their cleated demigods fell to muscular Notre Dame 42-6 in Yankee Stadium. This monumental blow was somewhat assuaged the following week when the Tar Heels defeated Duke in a brilliantly played one-point game and won the Southern Conference championship. They closed out the Justice era at Kenan Stadium with a 14-7 victory over Virginia before 48,000 insane football fans, the largest crowd ever assembled in that park up to that point. The victory put North Carolina in the Cotton Bowl.

Charlie Justice remembers the good times.

"Fame is strange," he says. "Once you get it, your life is never your own. We always felt we belonged to the public, Doak Walker and me and the rest. People need heroes. Kids, they just gotta have somebody to idolize. At least they used to. I sure did. I remember when Frank Sinkwich won the Heisman in '42. I turned to Sarah—we were sweethearts even then—and

Carolina's Art Weiner grabs a pass against Virginia in this 1949 game. The Tar Heels endured, 14-7, and went to the Cotton Bowl.

said, 'I'm going to get me one of those.' And I should have had it in '48, too. Doak Walker won it, but he'd had a better year in '47. Forty-eight was my year. Of course, in those days there were lots of heroes—presidents, generals, movie stars, sports figures. All gone now."

He reflected on the universal condition of life, growing nostalgic.

"You know, it reminds me of an old hillbilly song that went, 'Where have all our heroes gone....'"

"But what the heck..."

In outward appearance Charlie Justice has grown old gracefully, but there has been a turmoil existing within since he stopped playing football a quarter-century ago. Justice found the adjustment hard from sports to "civilian" life after a brief career in the pros with the Washington Redskins. An oil business failed in North Carolina, and Justice stumbled often before finally landing on his feet with an insurance business in Greensboro. His checkered business career was further complicated by problems at home, where his son, Ronnie, needed psychiatric help. The inability to keep up with his famous father tortured him.

"As much as I enjoyed all that attention, I'd have given it all up if it would have helped my son, given him confidence," Justice says. "Lord knows the boy wanted to be an athlete. It got so he began thinking he was a big disappointment to me. He got so worried and upset about it that he couldn't perform at all. He'd be the first kid picked in games because of his name. But he just couldn't play up to it. Then it got so I'd try to protect him from this kind of embarrassment. I did a lot of coaching in the midget leagues in those days. Well, it turns out that protecting him was the wrong thing to do, too. The psychiatrists told me I should let Ronnie lead his own life. The poor kid was confused. He had two nervous breakdowns. It was just too much for him to live with. But he's stabilized now. Works right here in town. He's gonna be all right."

When life was beginning to feel comfortable again, business and family troubles aside, Justice suffered a heart attack and had to change his pace. But old runners have that innate ability to bounce back, it seems. Justice still tears through life with the fearlessness of a young tailback but once in a while glances over

Charlie Justice (22) and his teammates get a breather while Carl Snavely directs the North Carolina production from the side-lines.

his shoulder.

"It was a good time," Justice says of his playing days. "Everybody was respectful of one another."

The *Daily Tar Heel* once referred to the players of the 1940s as "bums," and Justice's electric reaction points up as much as anything the universal brilliance and pride attached to that era.

"Somebody wrote that Carolina was all through having football bums on campus, like the ones they had back in the late '40s," Justice says. "Now that really got me, so I just sat right down and wrote a letter to that paper. 'Bums!' I wrote 'em. 'Who are you calling bums? Why, you should have so many bums like that,' I said. Then I went right down the roster of our team: ten master's degrees, eight lawyers, seven dentists, four presidents of big corporations. I gave it to 'em position by position. Look at old Art Weiner, an All-American end. Now he's an executive vice-president at Burlington Industries. Is that a bum? Then I got to tailback. 'Here,' I said, 'maybe you got a point after all. This is the only failure on the whole damn team....'"

Justice laughs at the self-deprecating remark. He knows what all the football fans in North Carolina know—that old tailbacks never fade away, they just fade back.

What It Was, Was Football

Charlie Mangum looked up from his prone position and, for a moment, thought he was dead. Surely this must be heaven, he said to himself. Comforting him from above was a girl as pretty as an angel.

"What happened?" the football player asked.

"You're alive, all right," the girl said. "You just got a pretty bad knock on your head."

Mangum found a bump as large as a golf ball and massaged it tenderly.

"Stay there for a while, and you'll be okay," the girl said, lathering him with a sweet liquid.

"What is that stuff?" asked Mangum.

"Oh, that's our 'Fair Special' cologne. We use it to revive all the players who get knocked unconscious."

Several of them had made the trip to the sidelines to be doused by the all-purpose remedy. There is some suspicion that the players took advantage of the situation and feigned injury in order to lie in the arms of the lovely St. Mary's coeds who posed as Florence Nightingales that day.

"Practically every North Carolina player in the game made his way to the first-aid area at least once," a sportswriter pointed out.

The occasion of the girls' Christian work was the first intercollegiate football game played by the University of North Carolina. It happened on October 18, 1888, and provided a thunderous sideshow for thousands of people who had attended

Fair Week in Raleigh. They were drawn to the football field by curiosity and kept there by excitement. Before the enigmatic new game began, there had been players who told of football's wonders while the crowd listened attentively.

"This is a football," one of the players said, holding up a round, inflated leather ball.

He paused for effect.

"There are 15 men on each side...."

He pointed to the field.

"There are goalposts on each end."

After a civilized explanation of the curious new sport, the players of North Carolina and Wake Forest became uncivilized and beat each other's brains out. They kicked, crawled, pushed, pulled, fell, fumbled, and flailed at each other. It was football at its most primitive—and the crowds loved it. Mangum was just one of several battlefield casualties, and by the time it was over Wake Forest had won the war, 6-4. Goals counted two points apiece, and the contest was staged in three parts, with Wake Forest winning the match game.

The game was newsworthy enough to be printed in the *Raleigh News and Observer*, although placed inconspicuously at the bottom of the regular Fair column:

"Decidedly one of the most interesting features of the whole fair was the game of foot ball (two words) yesterday between Wake Forest and Chapel Hill, resulting in a victory for Wake Forest. The game was exciting and was played by excellent teams on both sides. It was witnessed by a tremendous crowd. The players were uniformed and were a skilled and active set of boys."

No complete lineup was recorded of this first game. Among the prominent players for North Carolina, however, were Charles S. Mangum, A.H. Patterson, J.M. Morehead, George Graham, George Ransom, J.M. Holmes, and Henry A. Gilliam. Included on the Wake Forest team were Carey Dowd, E.W. Sikes, John E. White, W.A. Devin, Hubert A. Royster, and E. Vernon Howell.

Although their presence in the barbarous affair did little to move football forward any great length, it was nevertheless a beginning. The seed had been planted, and it was further nurtured in the year when Trinity College—now Duke University—

challenged North Carolina to the more scientific game of rugby, in Raleigh, on Thanksgiving Day. Steve Bragaw, newly elected captain of the North Carolina team, pulled out his rugby rules book and did some quick homework. Trinity, though, had the advantage, because the game had been practiced there for some weeks under the tutelage of Dr. Crowell, a Yale man, and North Carolina lost, 16-0. The final score did not show it, but actually the boys from Chapel Hill had put up stiff resistance to the seasoned Trinity team. Writes Smith Barrier in his book *On Carolina's Gridiron*:

Early in the game (William) Headen (of North Carolina) wrenched his knee and had to be removed—which by the way was the only reason for substituting for many seasons to come. Logan Howell replaced Headen. The greater experience of the Trinity team was early recognized. However, for thirty minutes Trinity was held without a score, although it possessed the ball almost throughout. S. Durham scored first, the touchdown counting four points. Shortly after Daniels made a touchdown. After each the goal was kicked, counting two points each. The first half was over. There had been 45 minutes of play and the 10-minute rest between the halves was indeed welcome.

When the play was resumed for the second 45-minute period, the University showed a complete reversal of form. Improvement throughout enabled the University to hold the ball in Trinity territory most of the second half, although it failed to score. George Graham, later labeled the best kicker in the state, barely missed a field goal by dropkick, which would have scored five points. Crowell made Trinity's final touchdown.

The North Carolina players lined up in this order: rushers—Captain Steve Bragaw, Lacy Little, Henry W. Wharton, William F. Shaffner, Sam Blount, Palmer Dalrymple, and William E. Headen; quarterback—Reuben A. Campbell; halfbacks—George Graham and Henry A. Gilliam; and fullback—Edgar Love. Trinity's lineup included: rushers—Captain Johnston, R. Durham, Crowell, Fearrington, Nicholson, Crawford, and Mitchell; backs—S. Durham, Rahders, Daniels, and Sharpe.

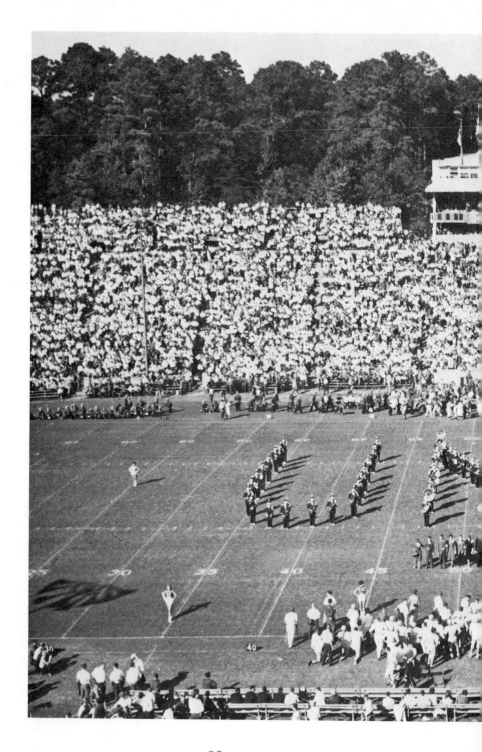

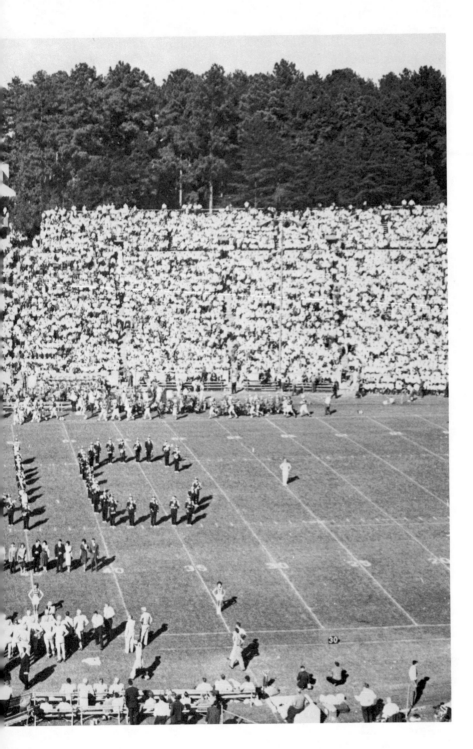

The referee was H.B. Shaw of North Carolina, and the umpire was Frank Jones of Trinity.

The *Raleigh News and Observer* had inspired interest in the game, devoting considerable space and time to its coverage. The newspaper carried a complete set of rugby rules on its front page on the Tuesday before the contest and big scoops of pre-game publicity. A crowd of 600 cash customers turned out on November 29, 1888, paying $.25 for "gentlemen" and $.15 for "ladies."

After the game representatives from North Carolina, Trinity, and Wake Forest met to organize the "North Carolina Inter Collegiate Football Association." It was the first specific step toward the development of athletics, and especially football, in the state of North Carolina.

"King Of Winter Sports"

It was a full seven days' ride from civilization, and the horsemen were tired and, worst of all, out of whiskey when they finally located the place. Eons before, the legendary Triassic Sea once washed these North Carolina foothills. But now the land was dry and clean, perfectly suited for their purpose. They got down from their horses and claimed the spot for America's first state university. The year was 1792, and the university was North Carolina.

The band of hardy trailblazers had made the incredible journey on orders from the state legislature. According to one writer, the reason for the remoteness of the school was so that "its students might encourage the development of knowledge and wisdom unencumbered by the tentacles of a corrupt world." Unfortunately, it did not work out that way at the start. When the first building, Old East, was opened to let in the 50 male students on January 15, 1795, there was no place more corrupt than Chapel Hill. Most of the students kept kegs of whiskey in their rooms and often lurched to classes under the influence. The unruly students carried their indulgences to vandalism as well. When dissatisfied with one particular university president, the students cut off the tail of his horse and overturned his privy. The president got out of town in a hurry when he got a note from the students that promised to render him "as secure as Pharoah in a hieroglyphic of feathers and a balmage, sir, of delicious tar."

There had also been several serious fights and shooting affrays among the students and "at least four cases of insanity from over-study and perhaps some deaths which might be attributed to the same cause," according to an *Alumni Quarterly* of the 1890s.

Fortunately for the university the students could also channel their voracious energies into more productive purposes, like physical activities. Walking and buggy rides were probably the most predominant exercises in the early years. In the 1820s cock fighting and horse racing took the center of attention for a brief period, although the students gradually turned to more personal physical pursuits. Sleighing was popular in the 1840s, and then ice skating became a campus fad in the 1850s. In the spring a young man's fancy turned to hunting, fishing, and swimming in Carolina's lush, natural paradise. Marbles became a pastime, along with the more rigorous arts of boxing, fencing, and a brutal game called bandy or shinny, where life and limb were imperiled by boys swinging large, curved sticks at a small ball of hard wood.

The fires of the Civil War raged in the 1860s, engulfing North Carolina among the other universities in the South, and dealt the educational as well as the sporting process severe setbacks. By 1867 the North had not only won the battle between the states but was also injecting some of its sporting blood into southern veins. Baseball, a game from the North, was introduced on southern campuses, and a group of students organized a team at North Carolina. The university closed for five years during the Reconstruction Period from 1870 to 1875, and it was at this point that a grander athletic purpose surfaced at Chapel Hill.

Baseball flourished with renewed life, and the North Carolina team, attired jauntily in white shirts, Palm Beach trousers and tennis shoes, accepted the challenges of other squads. An outdoor gymnasium went up, equipped with horizontal bars and swinging rings. And finally in 1885 a long-sought indoor gym was erected on campus after years of agitation and frustration.

The American game of football, as opposed to English-oriented rugby, had made its appearance at North Carolina in the late 1870s. The first mention of football came from this note in the April 1878 issue of the *Carolina Magazine*: "A few weeks ago foot ball engrossed the attention of the students but 'kicking a bag of wind' is no longer indulged in."

Later on, the sport became the campus craze. It had some likeness to the fast-flowering rugby game which was the basis for modern football. Charles Mangum, a member of the original North Carolina football team in 1888, once recalled for posterity:

"Previous to 1889 the game of football played at the University was a modification of the English game. The ball was round and about the size of a basketball. To win a goal the ball had to pass between the goal posts and touch the ground behind. It was a rough game. The player was permitted to advance the ball in any way he could. He could run with it, pass it in any direction, or kick it on or off the ground. Also, on defense, he was permitted to do anything he could to obstruct an opponent who had his hands on the ball. He could tackle, trip, push, block or clip from before or behind. This naturally led to many fights which frequently interfered with the progress of the game, and sometimes stopped it altogether until the matter at issue was settled."

The students needed little other than a $4.00 ball and stout heart to play, since there were no ambitious thoughts of stately uniforms or other equipment. Old clothes would do, they decided. Charles Baskerville wrote in the *Hellenian* in 1898:

Early each fall a subscription list was passed around and, as soon as the money necessary to buy a ball was subscribed, the season opened. The game was played every afternoon on the old athletic field, the present site of the Bynum gymnasium. The area of the football field assumed about the same proportion of our present ground, although the side lines were only imaginary. At each end of the field was a goal, each goal consisting of two poles about ten feet high and ten feet apart, without crossbars. The ball was kicked off from the center of the field, but as there was no such thing as lineups and line plunges, the man receiving the ball advanced it as he saw fit. It was an individual game, each man playing independent of the other.

The players not only had to be quick on their feet but also fast with their fists. Baskerville, a great Carolina runner of the 1890s, pointed out in his article:

> The minimum of players per side was fifteen, so in the afternoon, as soon as many as thirty reported, two were selected as captains and these resorted to the old country school method of choosing up. Then the game began and as fast as the others came out they were chosen on the respective sides, until each side was often composed of as many as a hundred men. With such an army on each side, and a game of this nature played under the existing rules, scraps naturally became every day occurrences. As soon as a difficulty arose, in order that all might get the benefit out of it, the game was discontinued, a circle was made in the center of the field, the contending parties placed therein and made to settle their dispute in a free-for-all and fist-to-fist scrap. The disputed question was then always decided in favor of the more valiant combatant. But no sooner was the mooted point settled, than the game was again resumed as though nothing out of the ordinary had occurred.

By 1886 football's popularity on the North Carolina campus had grown to such appealing proportions that the *University Magazine* described it as "the king of winter sports." And by 1888 the players were ready to seek lofty new levels of competition. Recalling football's intercollegiate genesis at Chapel Hill, Mangum reported in 1934:

> Early in October, 1888, the sophomore class, Class of '91, which happened to contain an unusually large number of athletes, challenged a team chosen from the three other classes of the University. The game lasted through two afternoons and the sophomores won. Flushed with this victory the team then challenged the sophomore class of Wake Forest College to a game to be played in Raleigh during the State Fair. Wake Forest won. Many years later Vernon Howell, who was a member of the Wake Forest

team and played in the game, told me that, owing to a misunderstanding of the conditions of the challenge, the Wake Forest team had been picked from the entire student body and even included a druggist from the village. This druggist was the type of man who would make a star fullback today. I do not remember his name, but I remember him. He put me out of the game. Mr. Howell himself had always thought that our team represented the whole University. In my opinion that defeat was one of the chief factors in arousing a general interest at the University in the game of football and led to the introduction of the American game before the college year ended.

The loss took none of the swagger out of the North Carolina players, and they eagerly swallowed a challenge from Trinity for a rugby game later in the year. The North Carolina team outweighed Trinity by an average of six pounds a man, 156 to 150, but could not overcome inexperience in the elegant new sport. The *University Magazine* reported with resignation after that futile contest:

"Well, we were beaten, and beaten fairly, and we say— Hurray for Trinity! Sixteen points to nothing. It's funny, but when we'd ask any one of the team about it, he'd say—'we got beat, but boys—we had the best time!' And then would come into his eyes that mellow look which fellows have when they talk about a certain class of beings."

Distressed by these two losses in the first season, North Carolina was grimly determined to make up for it in 1889. The school joined with Wake Forest and Trinity to form a state league and laid plans for a championship series of games. The tenacious students in Chapel Hill raised funds to hire a coach, and Hector Cowan came down from Princeton. He only stayed a week, but it was enough to get the Tar Heels on their feet.

That "Carolina Spirit"

The calendar read March, but February was still in the air. The wind hissed impatiently out of the north, and some of the crowd at the Raleigh Athletic Park fought off the cold with strong liquid refreshments and heavy mufflers. They had been waiting a long time in the imperfect weather for the football game to start.

On the field the North Carolina team was waiting, too. The players had arrived in plenty of time for the one o'clock game, but unfortunately Wake Forest was late.

Captain Steve Bragaw turned to a teammate.

"I hope we're in the right place," he said.

One hour went by—and still no Wake Forest. The crowd stirred. The North Carolina players worked out on the frozen tundra in nervous apprehension.

Another hour vanished without any sign of their opponents, and now the North Carolinians were beginning to work up a sweat, literally and figuratively. The 500 fans became more fidgety and began stamping their feet and clamoring for a refund of their $.25.

Finally, at 3:15, the Wake Forest team appeared and was able at last to play out the scheduled football drama. It was a long wait for North Carolina, but as it turned out, it was well worth waiting for. Displaying newly acquired skills, North Carolina defeated Wake Forest by a decisive 33-6 score to record the first intercollegiate victory in the university's history. The date was March 1, 1889, and the reason for the resounding triumph could be laid to the teaching proficiency of a Princeton football player.

"In February, 1889, Hector Cowan, one of Princeton's great tackles, came down to teach us the game," remembered Charlie Mangum, who played football then. "He remained only one week, and on two days that week 'Old Pres' (President Winston) excused the entire squad from classes. We played football morning and afternoons, on frozen ground and without pads. We had no uniforms to start with, so the experience was hard on both skin and clothes. I remember one afternoon when Mr. Cowan took the ball to show us how to carry it. He was a big man and fast. Quite a large number of spectators were present, some of them in family carriages. They had crowded in too close and as Cowan sped down the side line with the whole squad at his heels, the ladies screamed and the horses reared and plunged and tried to run away, and one old gentleman had a heart attack. An exciting event for Chapel Hill."

There were no reported heart attacks after that, but there was a broken leg and a busted collarbone. The broken leg belonged to Bragaw. The North Carolina captain suffered the injury in a 25-17 loss to Trinity on March 8, 1889. And when George Graham broke his collarbone later in the year, the trustees at North Carolina decided that football was far too savage a game for "civilized" college life and outlawed the sport in 1890. Despite this negativism, the Tar Heels had done comparatively well in 1889. Their record for the year showed two victories, one of them a forfeit by Trinity, and two losses. They had played two "seasons" during the year—one in the spring and one in the fall—and finished sharing the state championship each time with Wake Forest and Trinity.

When football was put on the sidelines in 1890, it signaled the Great Depression of athletics at Chapel Hill. The *University Magazine* reported at the time: "As it stands now, our boys have no incentive to advance athletics." And later in a review of the athletic scene in 1890, the magazine said in part: "Little interest is shown in tennis. Baseball is dead. Football— deader...." Except for Professor Horace Williams, it might have stayed that way. Williams provided a ringing voice in favor of athletics and along with two other professors, F. P. Venable and Eben Alexander, and a large group of dogmatic students convinced the trustees to reconsider their decision to kill football. The game was permitted to go on under faculty supervision in 1891. Williams, the gadfly of the movement to resurrect football, was named chairman of a newly created University Athletic Advisory Committee. And he was embraced by the athletically minded as the savior of sports at Chapel Hill.

Expressing the thought of many, football player Charles Baskerville remarked: "Our athletics owe Professor Williams a great debt of gratitude for his energy in reviving that necessary phase of college life."

The trustees might have regretted their decision to revive football, considering what happened in the first game of 1891. A North Carolina player by the name of Herbert Reeves Ferguson appeared to throttle a Wake Forest runner and kicked off a large-scale fuss. A Wake Forest tough jumped to his teammate's defense and socked Ferguson, and the Tar Heel returned the compliment. North Carolina was assessed a 25-yard penalty for this incident. That enraged North Carolina captain Mike Hoke, according to the *Carolina Magazine*:

"For throttling, the Umpire gave Wake Forest 25 yards, but refused to disqualify either Hall or Ferguson, though he saw the blows passed and though the rules provided that a player shall be disqualified if he strikes a player of the opposing team. The decision was too much for the University, so Captain Hoke threw up the game to Wake Forest. The ball at the time was on Wake Forest's 40-yard line and the score was 6 to 4 in favor of the University."

There was no doubt at this time of the serious intention at Chapel Hill to get football rolling again. William P. Graves, a Yale man, was brought down to coach the team for a season that lasted merely two games. Both were losses, but according to one player, "he laid the foundation for the success of the teams in following years."

The 1892 season brought an ambitious six-game schedule and was considered the first complete football season at Chapel Hill. Certainly, it was the most productive until that point. The university boys won five games and lost one with a 15-man squad that became known as the "Wonder Team" because of its remarkable immunity to injury. Only one substitute was used all season as the Tar Heels fulfilled promises in the student magazine that the year would "surpass any we have had in the past."

The players were small by modern standards. The starters averaged 155 pounds in the backfield and 180 on the line. Only three could be considered heavyweights—guards David "Baby" Kirkpatrick at 230 pounds and Eugene Snipes at 195 and center rush Pete Murphy, a 200-pounder.

This distinctive team, composed of future jurists, chemists, surgeons, ministers, and manufacturers, actually went beyond all expectations. Under the captaincy and coaching of Mike Hoke, the North Carolina team played with the "recklessness of a barroom brawler," according to one observer. They also played with shocking, boundless energy—at one point tackling three opponents in an exhausting five-day road trip. The North Carolina players left Chapel Hill on Tuesday, November 22, arrived in Atlanta at noon Wednesday, and beat Auburn 64-0 that afternoon. They left for Nashville after supper and beat Vanderbilt 24-0 on Thursday, then returned to Atlanta for a Saturday game with Virginia, Carolina's greatest rival at the time. The result was a ringing 26-0 victory for North Carolina and a blistering welcome-home party for the conquering heroes. One observer remembered:

"A committee was appointed to arrange for a banquet, another to decorate and send to University Station a special train to meet the players. When it reached Chapel Hill the students enthusiastically converted themselves into equines and drew the carriages from the station to the campus. President Winston, Captain Michael Hoke and Charles Baskerville, manager of the team, were in the leading carriage. The shouts of 'Rah! Rah! White! Rah! Rah! Blue! Hoopla! Hoopla! N.C.U.!' rang out on the campus until a late hour."

A 30-18 loss to Virginia earlier in the season had established the character of the team, one newspaperman pointed out: "The Virginia defeat in 1892 might well be termed the beginning of the 'Carolina football spirit,' for after that game the team 'felt tears in their hearts' and resolved to remove them by victories. Thus in 1892, the Carolina spirit was born."

The 1892 Carolina team was distinctive for another reason. The university assumed the name "Carolina" in interstate competition for the first time, dropping the "University" and

North Carolina's 1892 football team—Front row, left to right: Louis Guion, Alfred Barnard, William Augustus Devin, Charles Baskerville. Middle row: James Biggs, Michael Hoke, Pete

Murphy, William Merritt. Back row: Benjamin Stanley, William Wooten, Norfleet Gibbs, David Kirkpatrick, William Snipes, George Little, and James Pugh.

"Chapel Hill" sobriquets from athletic teams.

The players wore jaunty new football uniforms with "NC" emblazoned in front and soon were able to purchase monogram sweaters, officially approved by the Athletic Association in 1893. The success of the 1892 team obviously had inspired such progress, and later teams of the 1890s continued to build on that foundation. The "Gay '90s" was not only an appropriate term for the country but for football at Chapel Hill as well.

Football in the South during this time began to take a distinctive shape with the formation of the Southern Inter Collegiate Athletic Association. Initiated by the University of Virginia, the group was formed to fix a universal set of rules and establish means to select a champion of the South. North Carolina joined Virginia, St. Johns, Johns Hopkins, Wake Forest, Tennessee, Sewanee, Alabama, and Vanderbilt in this venture.

North Carolina, meanwhile, did not confine its activities solely to the southern world. The Tar Heels traveled to New York City during the 1893 season to play Lehigh, thus becoming the first southern team to play there. They were beaten 34-0, but made a good showing, according to the *New York World*: "If these Southern men had any scientific knowledge of the game, they would have easily beaten Lehigh. All their gains were made by sheer force and brute strength...."

The loss to Lehigh dramatized the need for good and regular coaching at Chapel Hill, and Vernon Irvine, a Princeton man, was brought in to dress up the ragged Tar Heels. The result was a 6-3 record, a second- place finish in the South, and the state championship in 1894. The 1895 season was even better, and it took another Princeton man to do it. "Doggie" Trenchard brought both science and sympathy to the job. He established a paralyzing defense that scored six shutouts and held the opposition to merely 17 points for the year. His unique defensive setup consisted of a 10-man line with one back utilized as a safety man for quick kicks. North Carolina, meanwhile, rang up 146 points and completed its most exquisite season until that point with a 7-1-1 record. Even the one loss to Virginia at Richmond was suspect. The Tar Heels lost a 6-0 decision, but the pro-Virginia crowd had a lot to do with it, twice running on the field to block Carolina runners on their way to touchdowns.

Trenchard's team made a distinguished road trip in 1895.

Fifteen North Carolina players left Chapel Hill in the afternoon on October 26 and arrived in Atlanta the next morning. They beat Georgia that Saturday, then took Vanderbilt in Nashville on Monday, tied Sewanee at Sewanee on Tuesday, and then returned to Atlanta, where they again beat Georgia on Wednesday. Trenchard doubled as a trainer on the train ride back to Chapel Hill, unceasingly massaging his players with liniment and hot water.

"It is said that this was the tiredest group of football players in the United States," an observer noted.

The first game with Georgia was significant in that North Carolina supposedly threw the first forward pass in football history. Relates Bob Quincy in his book on North Carolina athletics, *They Made The Bell Tower Chime*:

John Heisman, a noted historian, wrote 30 years later that, indeed, the Tar Heels had given birth to the forward pass against the Bulldogs. It was conceived to break a scoreless deadlock and give UNC a 6-0 win. The Carolinians were in a punting situation and a Georgia rush seemed destined to block the ball. The punter, with an impromptu dash to his right, tossed the ball and it was caught by George Stephens, who ran 70 yards for a touchdown. Perhaps Heisman knew more than the Tar Heels. There is always the chance of historical exaggeration. Stephens, on being quizzed about Heisman's recollections, couldn't remember the play. He did score a touchdown on a 70-yard sprint.

Heisman wrote he was at the game standing near the action on the sidelines. He is emphatic that Pop Warner, who was coaching Georgia, protested to the referee to no avail. And he adds he personally wrote Walter Camp, the final authority on football, of the possibilities of "the pass" making football a new and more exciting game. Accounts of the game make no reference to a forward pass. A double-lateral, however, is mentioned. It seems if George Stephens did cradle the first pass he was unaware of it—and that it was illegal.

It is appropriate that Stephens was connected with that

piece of significant history. He was one of the best of the early backfield players at North Carolina and in later years earned recognition on a consensus "all-University" team of the 1890s and early 1900s. An informal committee selected Hunter Carpenter of the 1904 team to run in the dream backfield with Stephens. Joel Whitaker, a player of later years who picked the team after consultation with "10 old University men" came up with this all-star lineup in a 1910 article: Edwin Gregory, left end; Bob Wright, left tackle; Louis Guion, left guard; Herbert Cunningham, center; "Bear" Collier, right guard; Romy Story, right tackle; Herman Koehler, right end; William Jacocks, quarterback; Stephens, left halfback; Carpenter, right halfback; and Arthur Belden, fullback.

North Carolina continued to look to Princeton for leadership, and that famous northern university ceaselessly fed the Tar Heels with sublime young coaches. By the late 1890s Will Reynolds arrived to become somewhat of a fixture at Chapel Hill. He coached for four years at North Carolina from 1897 through 1900 and had a strong record of 27-7-4, including the only perfect season in North Carolina history. Reynolds' exquisite 1898 team outscored opponents 201-8 and included seven shutouts in victories over Guilford, North Carolina A&M, Greensboro Athletic Association, Oak Ridge, Virginia Polytechnic Institute, Davidson, Georgia, Auburn, and Virginia. The starting lineup for that early classic team usually consisted of Herman Koehler and Edwin Gregory at ends; Samuel Shull and Frank Bennett at tackles; R.S. Cromartie and Ike Phifer at guards; Mink Cunningham at center; Frank Rogers at quarterback; Vernon Howell and James MacRae at halfbacks; and Ernest Graves at fullback.

Reynolds continued to have good records, although game officials seemed bent on discouraging him. In 1899 North Carolina had a 7-3-1 mark, but it would have been better had some atrocious calls not gone against the Tar Heels. In one game against North Carolina A&M, the Tar Heels had the ball on their opponents' half-yard line and one timekeeper said there were 17 seconds left in the game. North Carolina's players lined up and carried the ball across the goal line, only to be told by another timekeeper that the time was up before the play. That touchdown, if counted, would have given North Carolina a victory.

As it was, the Tar Heels did not claim the touchdown and wound up with an 11-11 tie. Against Sewanee that year Ernest Graves scored a touchdown, but Sewanee was offside and the play recalled. Then Herman Koehler drove over the goal line and yelled "Down," but the referee said he did not hear him. The result was a 5-0 victory for Sewanee.

By 1900 North Carolina had a new athletic field, but for the most part, it just sat there while the team moved around the countryside. The Tar Heels wore pseudonyms of the "Tired Heels" and the "Well-Worn Heels" while tramping through the South to stops including Nashville and Knoxville, Tennessee; Atlanta, Georgia; Raleigh, North Carolina; Norfolk, Virginia: and Washington, D.C. It was a credit to Reynolds and his indefatigable crew that North Carolina finished the season with only one loss.

Handsome varsity sweaters are modeled by this early North Carolina team.

The 1905 team had everything—beautiful varsity sweaters and the ball from the 17-0 victory over Virginia.

The Best Of The Good Old Boys

It had all the finesse of a kick in the pants, but Romy Story had an idea how to stop Virginia's virulent "Flying Wedge."

"Watch this," he told his North Carolina teammates.

Virginia's thundering herd rumbled down the field like heavy armored tanks, and North Carolina's tough guy backed away to get a running start. He put on a full head of steam and took off like a broad jumper, his knees doubled up as he flew through the air with the greatest of ease.

He slammed against the chest of the Virginia player leading the "V" formation. The wedge shivered and collapsed.

"Hey, you'll kill somebody," a Virginia player growled.

"I'll quit if you stop using that 'V' wedge," Story shouted back.

Virginia refused and continued to drive the wedge into North Carolina's belly. And North Carolina met Virginia's challenge head on, or actually in Story's case, feet first. Neither team scored much in that barbaric contest. But in later years oldtimers remembered the bizarre picture of Story leaping into the Virginia shock troops, blood streaming down his face....

It was a game made for boys but played by men. Recalling those flaming 110-yard wars of the early 1900s, Louis Graves observed 50 years later: "Football has gone through a lot of changes since my time. Perhaps the most important change is that football today is much faster than it was in my day, but not nearly as rough."

In his retiring years Graves could observe football from a safe distance. It made him wonder aloud why he nearly killed himself playing for North Carolina from 1900 through 1902, in the prehistoric period before the more civilized rules changes of 1906.

Graves, an underweight quarterback who played in a forest of giants, shuddered and told an interviewer: "The 'Flying Wedge' was used by all teams back in those days. The team would form a V-shaped formation to protect the runner who stayed within the formation. Brute strength instead of skill was the main qualification then. The 'Flying Wedge' was one of the many reasons so many changes have been made in football. We suffered many injuries back then, and it was not unusual to have players killed, although I don't believe we ever suffered a death here."

Brutality in football at the turn of the century was so shocking that movements were afoot in many states to outlaw the sport. An effort was made to do the same in North Caro-

The 1904 Carolina team lines up under the watchful eye of Coach Robert Brown. Oh, how they played the game!

lina's legislature.

"Much of this roughness was due to the fact that no whistle was used in the game, and a play was finished only when a player was willing to yell 'down' or when the ball had touched the ground," Graves remembered.

Perhaps the term "Iron Men' was no more appropriate. Very few substitutes were used in a game, and the team would struggle through a taxing season that often included three games in a week.

"We boarded a train Tuesday night, October 30, 1900, for a three-game trip with Tennessee at Knoxville on Thursday, Vanderbilt at Nashville on Saturday, and Sewanee at Atlanta on Monday," Graves observed. "We won the first two games, had a scoreless tie in the third. When we got to Charlotte, November 7, the porter brought newspapers on the train showing that McKinley had defeated Bryan for the Presidency of the United States. This seemed very unimportant to me beside the fact that we had got to Sewanee's three yard line and couldn't score."

The exhausting schedules and treacherous play explained the off-beat method employed by coaches to juice up team spirit. Remembered Graves: "Many coaches carried whiskey with them for the players. When enthusiasm ran low among the players, a hearty drink was served to all who cared for it."

There were no high-powered recruiting methods for hot prospects in Graves' day. In fact, players came to North Carolina without prior knowledge of football, since it was not played in high school and prep school at the time.

"Of course, football players were given financial assistance then just as they are today," Graves noted. "About the only difference was that we had very few, if any, players come to us from any place except North Carolina. Out-of-state players were rare. Then, too, freshmen were allowed to play on the varsity team, and many of the university's professors played. I played on the team while being a member of the faculty in 1902."

When Graves played, the field was 110 yards long, and the goalposts were on the goal line. He was a quarterback, and a good one at that, guiding North Carolina teams to a 16-4-6 record in his three years. The Tar Heels played before appreciative audiences, he remembered.

"A city like Atlanta, for instance, would draw a crowd of

about 8,000 persons for an outstanding game, and the price of admission was about $1.00 per person."

The outrageous violence of the game dictated changes after the 1905 season, when an unusual number of football players were either killed or injured. The game, on the verge of being knocked out by a nationwide backlash, was dramatically overhauled with safety first in mind for the players. It was still impetuous after that, although not as deadly. William Ferguson played in this period at North Carolina, from 1908 through 1910, and saw the birth of the forward pass and the kicking game.

"They had what they called a side kick at that time," he recalls. "They kicked it to one side, somewhat like a forward pass. The ball was kicked over the line, and it counted two points when it was kicked into the end zone."

Ferguson found football "a good, hard game as it is today.... I believe they were even more aggressive tackling in my day. Back in those days they would dive at a man from some distance, and if you could catch his legs, that's all they wanted to do."

Ferguson was a lineman but admits that he had it easy compared to the job of the quarterback.

"The quarterback, I think, had it pretty tough because they called on him in defense to dive into the melee wherever it was. If they were coming through the line, why, he was to dive right into it, to try to stop the advance."

The North Carolina team gained mainly through "line plunges," but occasionally opened up their offense under Coach Arthur Brides. The Tar Heels played out of a T-formation.

"We depended on gaining principally through the line," says Ferguson, "but we also went around end. Around end was a very popular play...throwing the ball to the end and letting him make the end run."

Ferguson played under two coaches, Edward Green in 1908 and Brides in 1909 and 1910. Both had moderate success, and Brides gave way to Branch Bocock in 1911, who only stayed one season and in turn left in favor of William Martin. By 1913 "Doggie" Trenchard, a well-known football player and former Carolina coach, was brought back to Chapel Hill and wasted little time in meeting his extravagant goals. He wanted a

112

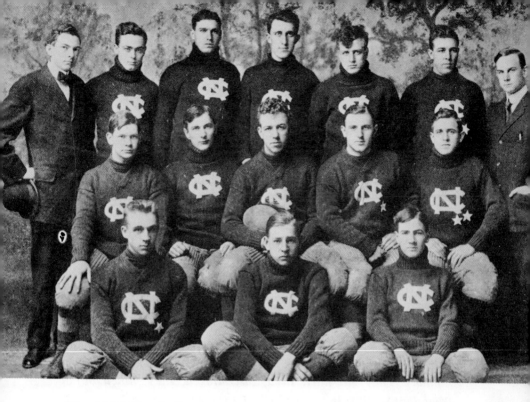

The 1908 North Carolina football team played in an era of significant rule changes and saw the birth of the forward pass.

great football team in a hurry, and he got one in the 1914 season, when the Tar Heels had a 10-1 record and scored an astronomical 359 points to only 52 for the opposition.

When the call was issued for the 1914 team, more than 60 players reported to Trenchard. But before the first practice, some 20 of them had gone off by themselves to train at nearby Lake Kanuga. This early training paid dividends during the season, when the Tar Heels, led by captain Dave Tayloe, ran up the following scores in the first six games: 41-0, 65-0, 53-0, 48-0, 41-6, and 40-0. The Tar Heels' only loss came to arch-rival Virginia on the last game of the season, and it was a bitter defeat. It was particularly galling to Trenchard, whose inability to beat Virginia eventually cost him his job. The Tar Heels had not beaten Virginia since the 1905 season, and it would not be until 1916 that they could conquer their No. 1 enemy. It was truly a blue-letter day in North Carolina history, but unfortunately Trenchard, who had recruited some of the best players in the South for Chapel Hill, was not there to see it.

The Virginia Game

"I am proud of just one thing about that Thanksgiving Game. I found that those Virginia fellows were just ordinary humans. They got hurt, tired, discouraged, they pulled bonehead plays, they fell down when they hit somebody or when somebody hit them, just like ordinary folks. Right along in the first of the game I blocked a little fellow, and when I hit him, he grunted just like a Wake Forest man would do. It surprised me and delighted me, so I cut him down again just for fun. Some nineteen others found out that they grunted, too."—a North Carolina player.

Thomas Wolfe wrote about it, football romantics sang about it, but all North Carolina men did was cry about it until 1916. Then they cheered about it, because that was the first time the Tar Heels had beaten Virginia since 1905. By then the "Virginia Game" had become more than just a matter of football, it had become an impassioned vendetta. The extraordinary rituals following North Carolina's 7-0 victory over Virginia testified to its significance for the Chapel Hill gang.

"Our fans carried us around the field at Richmond on their shoulders," remembers Raby Tennent, who played in the momentous game. "That was a rough ride, I'll tell you, but very sweet. Then they took the town. Nobody could do anything wrong, nobody got put in a paddy wagon, they just captured Richmond. They were 10 deep at that round bar in Murphy's, drinking up firewater and just having a grand time. And when we got to Chapel Hill, fans met us at the bottom of South Hill, and for two miles they shouldered us up that hill. It nearly killed us. We were ridden all the way up to Emerson Field. There, a gigantic pile of material piled around a 55-foot-high-frame upon which rested a coffin draped in Virginia colors of blue and gold was ignited."

The long-awaited victory over North Carolina's chief nemesis provoked unusual generosity from the school. For the first time in history, Tennent recalls, the athletes were given sweaters. And each of the North Carolina players was also gifted with a brass football as a souvenir of the consequential event.

Wolfe, the renowned author who was graduated from North Carolina, took a page from "The Game" and inserted it in one of his books, *The Web and the Rock*. In his fictionalized version, North Carolina became Pine Rock, and Virginia took the role of Madison. Tennent became an easily recognizable character called Raby Bennett, while Bill Folger had the part of Jim Randolph, and Macon Williams wore the name Randy Sheppardson.

This rare immortalization of a football game perhaps showed more than anything the significance the Virginia series holds in North Carolina football history.

"In the first quarter of the 1900s and earlier in the Gay '90s, the annual game with Virginia was 'The Game,'" says Spike Saunders, author of a column called "Views of a Wayback" for Carolina's *Alumni Review*. "'On To Richmond' was a Carolina battle cry. The Virginia Game...those three words for old-timers carried an unusual depth of significance. Win, lose, or draw, it was a season's high spot."

The first game in the series was played in Charlottesville on October 22, 1892, and was won by Virginia, 30-18. The next year the game was moved to Richmond to accommodate bigger crowds. There, 18 games were played with North Carolina winning merely three—in 1898, 1903, and 1916.

A humiliating 66-0 defeat by Virginia in 1912 forced North Carolina to reconsider the direction of its football program. The Tar Heels had suffered through their second losing season in three years and decided to rebuild under a new coach, "Doggie" Trenchard.

"By 1913, Carolina alumni had gotten pretty well fed up with the situation," remembers Tennent. "It was then that a determined effort was made by certian loyal alumni to start recruiting promising athletes, hire a coach under contract, and produce a winning team. Meaning, of course, to beat Virginia, that was the game of games. Although I never saw a copy of the contract that Trenchard signed, I know it was for three years with a provision that a winning team be produced. And I suspect that a further provision in it was that he had to beat Virginia."

Tennent was among the first players ever recruited at North Carolina. He recalls that the school made somewhat feeble attempts at romancing athletes in his time.

"There was no actual money or scholarships available," Tennent says, "but there was something called 'self-help' promised by the university. This meant waiting on tables, marking tennis courts, running special clubs, selling apples from back home from barrels. Board at the university was only $8.00 a month. So you can see the effort far outweighed the food."

From his first step on campus, Tennent was brainwashed against Virginia. "Virginia was our main target," he says. "Win the game with Virginia...and nothing else mattered."

The esteem in which the game was held was underscored by a rule at North Carolina that required a player to start against Virginia in order to win his letter for the season.

"It was a very narrow and unfair rule, of course," Tennent points out. "Trenchard continued this rule, and it worked an unfair condition on rookies trying to oust the holdover favorites. I considered myself among those hurt by this rule. I tried the line in 1913-1914 and then end in 1915. I played in most games but never was a starter against Virginia."

After losing three straight years to Virginia, Trenchard's contract was not renewed.

"Thomas Campbell, a Harvard All-American, became the new coach. He immediately set to work to correct the errors of the past. A general shuffling of players took place. I was assigned the fullback job on offense and linebacker on defense," Tennent says.

The arrival of Campbell brought a dramatic change in coaching style and a marked change in personalities as well.

116

"Trenchard was pig-headed and tough," Tennent notes. "I think the men respected him for his ability, but he was awfully hard on them. I don't think he got the best out of a man. Tommy Campbell was a different type. He got the best out of everybody, and he put everybody where they belonged."

Campbell's magical ability to squeeze blood from a stone was evident in 1916 when only four lettermen returned from the 1915 team, yet the Tar Heels were able to manufacture a winning season and collect the state championship for the sixth straight year. The crowning achievement, of course, was the victory over Virginia. A crowd of 15,000 was on hand in Richmond to watch North Carolina's revenge victory, fashioned on a slippery, wet field. Because of the conditions, the Tar Heels missed three scoring chances in the first half. Then early in the second half Bill Folger ran through right tackle for 52 yards, and it was the only touchdown in the game. George Tandy kicked the extra point to complete the sweet victory.

Edward Reid dialed a number from his memory bank, something that had been deposited there about 60 years ago.

"Virginia's players were the finest, cleanest men you ever played," he said. "I loved to play 'em. We'd want to play Virginia more than anybody else for that reason."

He does not have such fond memories of Wake Forest, however.

"They were a dirty team. We hated them. Lord, they were the dirtiest players in the South. They would twist your ankle or do any damn thing to get you out of the game."

Reid had the pleasure of playing Virginia's teams but never the pleasure of beating them. He was at North Carolina from 1913 through 1915, before the euphorious "V-Day" in the 1916 season emancipated the Tar Heels from Virginia's bondage. Reid describes himself as "a plunging fullback" who was used only for short-yardage situations.

"I couldn't run more than about seven yards and I'd fall down," he says. "I could always make about five or seven yards, and then I'd just fall flat on my face. I always ran off-balance."

Kicking was more of Reid's game. "Oh, I guess I was the best on the team...they had to have some punter."

The anatomy of North Carolina's home field gave him

After World War I, football made a comeback at Carolina with the 1919 team.

problems, though.

"Emerson Field wasn't entirely level," he says. "I know down in one corner it was maybe two feet lower than the rest of the field. I remember I always hated to punt from that low corner. You felt like you were punting uphill."

Enthusiasm never ebbed at Chapel Hill. While the players drilled, Reid remembers, the students would have "cheering practice" once or twice a week on the sidelines.

This vibrancy and vitality carried over to the games, and soon it was evident that Emerson Field was not large enough to hold the growing football audiences that swelled Chapel Hill. When the capacity of the permanent concrete seats was exhausted by spectators, temporary wooden seats were built on one side and at the ends of the field. But even this was not

enough, and by 1921 the university was turning away thousands from North Carolina's home games. It was obvious that a new football arena was needed to feed the hungry populace, but it took five more years before one was built. Kenan Stadium literally was a sight for sore eyes in 1927.

Team Of A Million Backs

Marion Alexander called them "The Team Of A Hundred Backs," and time served to embellish that colorful sobriquet. It became the "Team Of A Thousand Backs" and finally the "Team Of A Million Backs."

It actually was a team of 17 backs, but obviously it was more than enough. Like a prizewinning chemist, Coach Chuck Collins mixed the explosive parts with potent results. This genius for mixing and matching talents resulted in one of the best football teams in North Carolina history, the fabled 1929 squad.

"He used his backfields more or less interchangeably," remembers Alexander, who handled sports publicity in those days. "Each of those backfields was as good as the other; there wasn't much to choose between them. Collins had two lines, too. The first line was very good on both offense and defense. The second line was pretty good on defense and fair on offense."

Among the famed backfield players of the day were Johnny Branch, Chuck Erickson, Jimmy Ward, Pete Wyrick, Jim Magner, Jimmy Maus, Strud Nash, Phil Jackson, Henry House, Pap Harden, Yank Spaulding, and Rip Slusser.

"They did a lot of fancy running," recalls Alexander, "and each backfield had a passer who could hit someone on the fly with a 50-yard pass. There was Jimmy Ward in the first backfield, Jim Magner in the second, and Jim Mause in the third. Chuck Erickson, who was later athletic director for many years,

The "Team Of A Million Backs" had a coach of a hundred skills, Chuck Collins.

was halfback on the third string, but he was one of the best broken field runners in the group. The other leading broken field runner was Johnny Branch. He was a little jackrabbit, about five feet, six inches tall. He weighed only 165 pounds but had legs like a 200-pound tackle. You just couldn't catch him or pin him down. That was quite a fine team. That was the best team that the college ever had, in my opinion."

Scoring was no problem for this machine-like team. Neither was playing defense. The 1929 Tar Heels chalked up

The 1922 North Carolina team won a lot of games and a lot of fans. A school record of 68,500 watched the Tar Heels that season.

346 points, second highest in the school's history, and allowed only 60 in 10 games. The "Million Backs" team won nine games, most of them by lopsided scores, and was beaten only by Georgia by one touchdown.

"I figured up after the season that the average scoring dis-

123

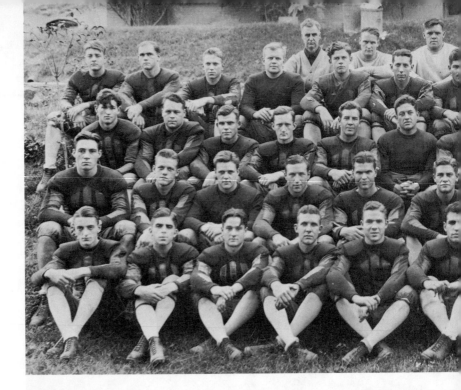

The 1926 team was the first under Chuck Collins. The best was still to come.

tance of our plays was 20 yards," recalls Alexander. "They had so many long runs for touchdowns, it was unbelievable. It was one of the highest-powered offenses of that day."

The Tar Heels of 1929 were so complete, they even had a kickoff specialist named Ezra Rowe. It was a luxury for the time.

"He got so used to kicking off and doing nothing else that one time he kicked off and instead of going down the field with the rest of the team, he just ran for the bench," laughs Alexander. "I think he was the first of the specialty men."

Collins' superb backfield players were complemented by a group of skilled and powerful linemen led by Ray Farris, the All-Southern guard who made lasting impressions on newsmen and opposing players alike.

"Every game was a World Series to Ray," says columnist Bob Quincy of the *Charlotte Observer*. "He keyed himself to a feverish emotional pitch, crying at times and challenging his teammates to a superior effort in the name of the school colors. No one had to get Ray 'up' for a game. They had to get him

down. Ray was a 'triple threat' guard, if there ever was such a
denizen. He was an excellent blocker with a solid 190 pounds
on his 6-1 frame. He ramrodded the linebacking. He punted—
and occasionally passed on a trick play."

Farris, who started his football career in high school as a
halfback, moved to end as a freshman at North Carolina and
finally was shifted to guard, became the shaker and mover as
captain of this famous team. Among the prized linemen along
with Farris were Don Holt, Bill Koenig, Ned Lipscomb, Ellis
Fysal, Bud Eskew, Fenton Adkins, and Julian Fenner.

The 1929 team was clearly the high-water mark of Collins'
eight-year coaching career at North Carolina. He had played
football at Notre Dame and come to Chapel Hill in 1926, taking
over the Tar Heels from the brother coaching team of Bill and
Bob Fetzer.

"Chuck had one of the quickest, keenest football minds of
any man I ever knew," notes Alexander. "He's the only man I
ever knew that could watch two teams run a play and immediately after he could tell what each man did, right or wrong, on
that play. I never saw anyone else who could do it. Collins was
so quick and so keen that in his latter days, I would say that
things that were obvious to him went over the heads of some of

his players. I sat in on some of his lectures, and he'd be talking over their heads and over my head as well."

Erickson found Collins to be "a good, smart innovator" who was perhaps ahead of his time and certainly ahead of his players.

"He had a very agile mind, but the thing about him was that his players didn't have as quick a mind as he did," Erickson reflects. "He expected them to pick up things fast, and when they didn't, he didn't have any patience with them. Collins had ideas way ahead of everyone else. He was the first fellow I saw that started to use defensive slants. We went down to play Tennessee once and he wanted to stop their plays, so he put the big tackles on the outside, jamming in, with the ends floating on the outside and crossing up all their blocking. He originated things."

Collins got some of his ideas from Knute Rockne, whom he played under at Notre Dame, and instituted them at North Carolina. Erickson remembers one such definite Rockne touch.

"In the spring, Collins would divide us into separate teams and have us play games with one side acting the role of one of our opponents for that year, say Georgia Tech."

The idea, of course, was to familiarize the North Carolina

The "Team of a Million Backs" gave Carolina followers a million thrills in 1929.

Jimmy Ward of North Carolina getting away on a long run against Georgia in 1929. The 19-12 loss was the only one for the Tar Heels' "Team of a Million Backs" that year.

team with the style of the individual opponents for that year.

"Boy, those games were tougher than the real games," Erickson recalls. "You'd run back to catch a punt, and they would come charging like they were going to knock your head off. They were rough, tough practices, I'll tell you, and that's the way Collins liked 'em."

Collins, known for a cutting wit, likes to emphasize that he was part of Rockne's herd, but a black sheep in his family.

"I was the only one that Rockne didn't get a coaching job for," Collins remembers. "Maybe he didn't think I was coaching material. Everybody else got a job through Rockne. I asked Rock about it and he said, 'You go into business...sell frozen fish or something.'"

Collins dismissed Rockne's fatherly advice and eventually found his way to Chapel Hill by a series of side roads. Collins had a tough act to follow at North Carolina. The Fetzer brothers had produced several good Tar Heel teams, including the sparkling 1922 squad that won nine of ten games.

The Fetzers were the entire athletic staff at North Carolina

127

when they came to Chapel Hill in 1921. The university dismissed an old policy of one-year contracts and awarded Bill and Bob Fetzer with a long-term position. They followed Myron Fuller's disastrous 1920 season with a winner in their first year on The Hill, then produced a team in 1922 that won the South Atlantic championship and tied for the title of the newly formed Southern Intercollegiate Conference. The SIC consisted of 16 teams, or just about all the major institutions in the South.

The only defeat administered to the 1922 Tar Heels was an 18-0 whipping from all-powerful Yale at New Haven, a game that was the subject of heated controversy. North Carolina's Red Johnston led a drive to Yale's one yard line, and the Tar Heels punched the ball over three times, only to have the plays recalled by penalties. Fred Cochran, who played for North Carolina in those years, says the officials definitely favored Yale at home.

"We played Yale four straight years, and they beat us every year," Cochran remembers, "but the 1920 team scored two touchdowns that they took back from us for some reason. The official was a Yale man. I remember he said, 'Hell, if you boys had more beans, maybe the South would beat the North.' He was obviously prejudiced."

Bill Blount, who played in the 1922 Yale game, says, "It was the only game I played in where I felt I was robbed. The field judge was calling penalties from all out of position and everything else. He just didn't want Yale to lose. It was really taken away from us. We should have beaten them...we had a better football team than they did."

North Carolina, ranked No.11 in the country by an intercollegiate magazine, had better luck with the other teams on the 1922 schedule. The Tar Heels, with such players as Blount, Johnston, Suey Cochran, Pierce Matthews, Grady Pritchard, C.C. Poindexter, Herman McIver, Casey Morris, Monk McDonald, Fred Morris, and Allen McGee, knocked down all challengers in the South, including powerful Tulane. The Tar Heels played before a total of 68,500 fans during the season, a school record to that point.

Pritchard, the captain, points out that the success of the 1922 squad was fashioned by speed and agility rather than brute force.

"It was a light team. We didn't have a man that weighed 200 pounds in the starting lineup. I was among the heaviest of the starters, and I weighed only 190 pounds. But we had a very quick, fast team."

The single wing was in vogue then, and the Fetzers utilized this as their principal offense, perhaps throwing in more passing than any other teams in the South.

"Monk McDonald and George Sparrow did most of the passing," Pritchard remembers. "And of course we had a great open-field runner in Red Johnston. He had that elusiveness. He was probably the greatest running back we ever had."

The Fetzers, while not especially innovative, attacked football with a zeal that quickly translated to their players.

"They were two fine men to work with, and they really knew their football," reflects Cochran, an end under the Fetzers. "They had a group of men who had pretty good high school and prep school training for those days. They had a very aggressive line. They weren't 220- and 240-pound men that you find today in the pros, but they were good, raw-boned boys and they played their hearts out."

"They were good disciplinarians, and they kept after you," points out Blount, who played center on the Fetzer teams. "They concentrated on execution and fundamentals. Nothing fancy—we ran the regular old single wing with the end around and guards running out and that kind of business. The Fetzers knew how to handle people—and had a very good fundamental team."

The Fetzers never had a better team than the one in 1922, nor one that was any more courageous than the 1925 edition. That year an unreasonable amount of injuries hit the Tar Heels, but they were still able to compile an admirable 7-1-1 record and win the state championship. The Virginia game that year, which ended in a 3-3 tie, attracted 16,000 spectators to Chapel Hill's Emerson Field, which had a seating capacity of only 2,400.

The passion attached to Carolina football during this period was evident. Vic Huggins, the head cheerleader in 1924, introduced the school's first mascot, a ram called Rameses who was purchased for $25.00 and shipped in from Texas. The animal became a crowd-pleaser and an instant legend when Bunn Hackney rubbed Rameses' head for luck before taking the

Kenan Stadium before and after. At left, workmen clear the forest for a dream. Below, the dream becomes a reality.

field, then kicked a 30-yard dropkick to help the Tar Heels beat the Virginia Military Institute, 3-0, in 1924. Two years later Carolina's most famous cheerleader, Kay Kyser, was inciting the fast-climbing crowds with his antics. Kyser, later to become a show business star, led a popular cheering group called the "Carolina Cheerios" on the sidelines, and their fast-paced tempo matched the football pulse of the day.

The biggest news of the time, however, was the birth of Kenan Stadium, a football arena that was long overdue. It was obvious that Emerson Field no longer could hold the burgeoning crowds, and an alumni committee met for the first time on May 24, 1926, to lay plans for a more appropriate arena. Their work came to a head on November 13 of the same year when William Rand Kenan, a well-known engineer in New York City and a North Carolina football letterman of 1893, walked into the office of the president and handed over a $275,000 gift check for a new stadium. Kenan's only request was that the stadium serve "as a memorial for my father and mother."

Davidson visited Chapel Hill on November 12, 1927, and played the first game in North Carolina's gleaming new showplace. The Tar Heels celebrated the occasion with a 27-0 victory before 9,000 fans. The stadium, framed in heart-breaking pine trees, was officially dedicated on Thanksgiving Day two weeks later, and 28,000 spectators watched North Carolina win an appropriate 14-13 decision over ancient rival Virginia.

By the time the 1929 "Million Backs" team came around, 139,500 people watched North Carolina play football, establishing an all-time attendance record for the Tar Heels. Led by charismatic Johnny Branch, one of Carolina's most exciting runners, the Tar Heels not only presented power on the field but strength at the gate. Branch's electrifying punt returns were the talk of the town. His most famous run was a 96-yarder that pulled out a 28-21 victory over Maryland in 1930. No North Carolina player has topped that feat yet.

"I was standing in the end zone, planning to play it safe," Branch recalled in later years. "The punt first hit about the five, but instead of bounding forward, it flipped high and sidewise. I looked up the field and saw the defense closing in—and my instinct told me to grab the ball. I cut through to the right, then back inside. By the time I reached the 40, I was alone."

Locomotion

If ever a game symbolized the death of a football era, it was the "Battle of Kenan Lake." North Carolina and Duke closed out the 1930 season with a scoreless tie in a sea of mud at Kenan Stadium, and the Tar Heels continued to have unsteady footing the next few years. The Depression forced North Carolina to tighten its money belt, and as a result Coach Chuck Collins had no bait with which to lure fresh talent. The teams also became worse, and so did the records under the frustrated Notre Dame man.

"We started playing students," Collins remembers. "Students are the loveliest guys in the world, but they aren't football players. They just went through the motions."

When his barber began telling him how to run his football team, it made his hair stand on end. And when he heard more outspoken sideline criticism from other quarters, he saw the handwriting on the wall. Collins had some suspicion that he would be released after his second straight losing season in 1933, and this was confirmed on December 10 after a long meeting by the university athletic council.

The choice for North Carolina's new coach was a quiet Dutchman who had made a brilliant record for himself at Bucknell, Carl Snavely.

Considering the circumstances when Snavely arrived, he did a remarkable job of turning the North Carolina football program around. University president Frank P. Graham was on record publicly opposing any privileges to athletes, and this

133

Before a face-lifting that added a second deck, Kenan Stadium looked like this in the good old days.

A full house in 1935. Naturally, it was the Duke game.

immediately put the new coach in the back of the recruiting class. But despite Graham's roadblock, Snavely was able to manufacture a winning team in his first year. The Tar Heels had an admirable 7-1-1 record in 1934, led by an outstanding guard and linebacker by the name of George Barclay.

"When Snavely first came there, he took on a pretty good bunch of sophomores, and with these five or six players, we filled in the places we needed," reflects Barclay. "Snavely was very thorough, and it turned out to be a very well-coached football team."

In the second game of the season, the Tar Heels led General Robert Neyland's monstrous Tennessee team by a 7-6 score at the half. But a lack of reserve strength cost North Carolina the contest, 19-7, and that turned out to be the only loss of an otherwise beautiful season lighted by Barclay's brilliance.

"George at guard and at linebacker was a ball of fire," remembers a sportswriter. "The 5-foot-11, 185-pounder was a downfield blocker and a tackler of extraordinary talent. His keen desire carried over into the practice sessions. When the whistle sounded, likable George went into his other world. He demolished people. Virginia fans remember George quite well. In 1933 he intercepted a Cavalier pass and galloped 35 yards for a touchdown. In 1934 he opened the scoring with an interception of 55 yards as Carolina won, 25-6. It was an identical theft."

Barclay tells a story attached to that second touchdown run.

"A friend promised me a fine suit of clothing if I would score against Virginia my last year. I anticipated a pass on the play, moved back and out from my linebacker's position, and, sure enough, they threw a pass, hitting me in my mid-section, and I ran for the touchdown with no one in front of me. The next day, the newspaper wrote an article about 'George's interception and beautiful run for a touchdown.' It spoke of how I dodged, sidestepped, and set up my blockers to make the score when actually, all I had to do was run straight down the field, because no one was in front of me. My only thought was the promised new suit! I received my blue flannel suit two weeks later."

Barclay was nicknamed "King George The First" by one

writer, since he was North Carolina's first All-American football player. Teammates loudly seconded the motion by several All-American teams, including The Associated Press.

"George was so good, one group (the All-America Board) picked Barclay at tackle," said Charlie Shaffer, who played wingback and tailback on Snavely's first Carolina team. "That

George Barclay: A touchdown won him a blue flannel suit.

shows you how versatile he was. In my book, Barclay was as good as any in the country at that time. He was the greatest diagnostician of plays I've ever seen. George called the offensive plays in the huddle. I gave the starting signals at the line of scrimmage, but we were running George's plays. He put a lot of pep into the team. He was a great inspiration. He didn't give me much work to do as a defensive halfback, either. And on offense, old George would just knock 'em one way, and I'd run the other. No worries. George was fast, a good runner of interference, and an exceptional blocker."

Snavely's dramatic success continued into 1935, when the Tar Heels had an 8-1 season, losing only to Duke in the next-to-last game.

"Maybe we weren't quite as prepared as we should have been for Duke," reflects Crowell Little, a North Carolina tailback of the day. "We thought we should have beaten them. We did get some bad breaks. We got a punt that was fumbled by them on a tackle, and we got penalized 15 yards, and we really recovered the fumble and that seemed to be the turning point in the game. And they played a pretty smart, heads-up game, and they beat us. The day was dreary, cold, and wet. We moved the ball very good on the ground, though. I talked to Wallace Wade, the Duke coach, years afterward and he told me jokingly enough that they knew they were going to beat us. I said, 'Coach, there's no way in the world you could have known that.' And he said, 'Yeah, you all weren't as good as you thought you were, and we weren't as bad as our record showed.'"

The 25-0 loss was considered a blow to the Tar Heels' Rose Bowl hopes at the time, but actually there would not have been a trip to California anyway, owing to the whims of North Carolina president Frank P. Graham. Graham, outraged by high-powered recruiting methods and the increasing amount of money spent in amateur athletics, mounted a movement to deemphasize sports. Graham was quite plainly against bowl participation, and his well-known "Graham Plan" was adopted by many university presidents in the country.

Graham pursued his purge of athletics with a witch-hunter's zeal. Remembers Steve Maronic, an All-American of the 1930s:

"President Graham called players into his office and tried to break us down to tell him that we were getting something from the school. He once grilled me for an hour and a half. I don't think a murder trial would have been any worse. I'm not a liar, but that's one time where I couldn't tell the truth. He wanted me to admit that I was on a scholarship. I don't know what the hell would have happened if I told him I was on it. He was against any athlete getting help. A man in New York already had given my father enough insurance so that I'd get a four-year education at North Carolina...."

This sports deemphasis explained the departure of Snavely after the 1935 season, according to Barclay.

"It didn't look like they were going to be able to recruit at all. Snavely got a little upset about it and left for Cornell. He had an offer from Cornell which he might not have taken but for the Graham Plan. He had enough good football players at Carolina then, had he stayed and fought it out with Graham, everything would have been all right."

North Carolina, which traditionally had looked north for coaching help in the past, found a brilliant leader in the Southwest. Ray "Bear" Wolf, a successful line coach at Texas Christian University, was hired to coach the Tar Heels in 1936 in the midst of Graham's handicapping purity campaign. His appearance literally had the North Carolina football team up in the air. Wolf was one of the nation's foremost exponents of the forward pass, and his wide-open style of football was a dramatic change of pace from Snavely's rigid conservatism. Minus many of the great players that helped rank North Carolina among the nation's top teams in 1935, Wolf guided the Tar Heels through a strenuous 10-game schedule in 1936 with only two losses, to Tulane and Duke.

In 1937 North Carolina under Wolf lost only one game, to Fordham, and eventually claimed the state championship and the Southern Conference title. Wolf lost an All-American and seven all-Southern Conference performers in 1938 but still put out a strong Tar Heel team that had a 6-2-1 record. One of the losses was a 17-14 thriller to Tulane, a game that could have gone either way. The Tar Heels claimed a moral victory over Fordham that year, holding the favored Rams to a scoreless tie. In 1939 the Tar Heels were one of the most successful and

Ray Wolf: His productions were always wide open, exciting, and winning.

exciting teams in the country, with a series of breathtaking fourth-quarter rallies that produced victories over New York University and Penn and a tie with Tulane. North Carolina had an 8-1-1 mark that season, losing only to Duke by a 13-3 score. Wolf's fifth year, 1940, produced a modest 6-4 record, but it was more impressive when one looked behind the statistics. Two of the losses were by only one point, and the season included impressive victories over Duke and TCU.

"I think he is one of the great coaches that the game has produced," says Little, who played tailback for Wolf in 1936 and 1937. "He was tough, but he was fair. He was an innovator. He came into our area from the Southwest, where they threw the ball a lot, and he brought in the double wing formation, and we played a really wide open brand of football."

Wolf was fortunate to have players that suited his team's flamboyant personality. From 1936 into the 1940s, such dynamic performers as Little, Maronic, Andy Bershak, Jim Lalanne, Paul Severin, George Stirnweiss, and Gates Kimball helped establish one of the most consistent football periods at Chapel

Fordham's Pete Kazlo (47) is being tackled by North Carolina's Art Ditt in this 1937 game after just having received a 10-yard pass from Ed Granski. Dominic Principe of Fordham (25) looks on.

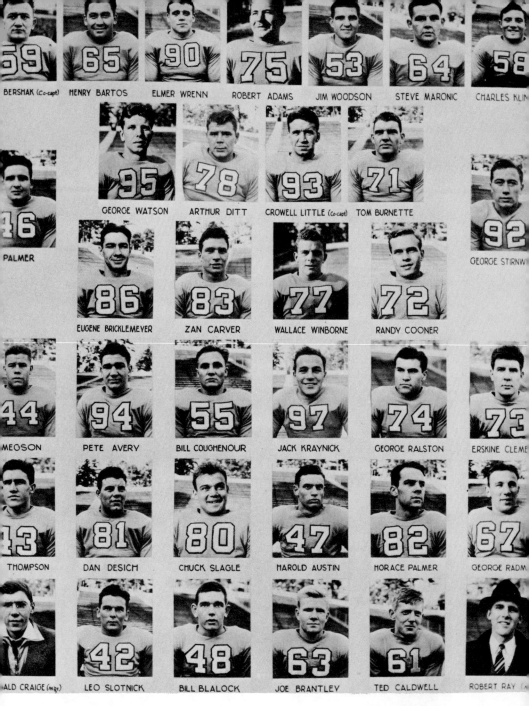

BERSHAK (Co-capt)   HENRY BARTOS   ELMER WRENN   ROBERT ADAMS   JIM WOODSON   STEVE MARONIC   CHARLES KLIN

PALMER   GEORGE WATSON   ARTHUR DITT   CROWELL LITTLE (Co-capt)   TOM BURNETTE   GEORGE STIRNW

EUGENE BRICKLEMEYER   ZAN CARVER   WALLACE WINBORNE   RANDY COONER   GEORGE STIRNW

MEGSON   PETE AVERY   BILL COUGHENOUR   JACK KRAYNICK   GEORGE RALSTON   ERSKINE CLEME

THOMPSON   DAN DESICH   CHUCK SLAGLE   HAROLD AUSTIN   HORACE PALMER   GEORGE RADM

ALD CRAIGE (Mgr)   LEO SLOTNICK   BILL BLALOCK   JOE BRANTLEY   TED CALDWELL   ROBERT RAY

These faces on the field brought smiles to the faces in the stands at Kenan Stadium in the 1930s.

141

Hill. Before World War II put an end to Wolf's winning ways in 1941, his teams posted a 35-10-3 record in his first five seasons. The Tar Heels under Wolf were a marvelous blend of balance, whose defensive heroics very often matched the dazzling accomplishments of the offense. In both 1937 and 1938 North Carolina's opposition scored under 40 points for the season, and in the latter year the Tar Heels pulled off six shutouts.

The combination of Lalanne at quarterback and Severin at end gave the Tar Heels an irresistible passing game in the late 1930s and early 1940s. Lalanne introduced the jump pass to North Carolina and had an arm as accurate as any in the country. Wolf once called Lalanne the greatest player he ever coached, and after watching him perform one year against Penn, one would have to believe him. Penn led 6-0 going into the

Wartime recruit Tom Young spent one year (1943) as coach of the North Carolina Tar Heels.

second half before the Tar Heels scored 30 points behind their explosive back. Lalanne ran 50 yards for one touchdown, hit three TD passes, and moved the Tar Heels into range for Harry Dunkle's field goal, all in six minutes. This expatriate from Louisiana performed similar feats of heroism against other teams, earning him the nickname of "Sweet Lalanne." Lalanne had the good looks of a movie serial hero and the dashing ability to escape similar perils on a football field. "He could emerge from a muddy pileup and look as if he stepped out of a village haberdashery," commented one sportswriter.

Severin was Lalanne's favorite target but earned an All-American shield with his defensive as well as offensive performances. Severin is perhaps remembered most for a touchdown-saving play he made against Duke in 1940. He was knocked on his back, yet managed to scramble up and catch a runaway halfback 40 yards downfield and prevent a touchdown. The Tar Heels eventually emerged with a 6-3 upset in one of the more magical moments in their history.

"Severin was a two-time All-American at Carolina," remembers newspaperman Orville Campbell, "and he really made the All-American team in 1940 because he caught Steve Lach from behind on that great play in the Duke game. Steve had run around Severin's end, and Severin had been blocked out of the play. But he got up and began chasing Lach across the entire football field. Lach was a good back, but he was a little slow, and Severin caught him from behind in the open field."

This was the game which inspired a "Touchdown for Dunkle" war cry from the Carolina fans. Harry Dunkle, the Tar Heels' halfback and punter, had been injured and carried from the field early in the game. Throughout the contest, the Carolina students repeated their touchdown plea, which was finally answered when Lalanne flipped a scoring pass to Joe Austin late in the fourth quarter.

"We went about 75 yards in 16 or 17 plays to score that touchdown," recalls Campbell, "so it was a tough drive. We never gained more than seven or eight yards on any one play."

Remarkably, North Carolina used just 13 players in that memorable game, either a testimony to Tar Heel energy or lunacy. "That's probably the last football game where Carolina ever used so few players," Campbell points out. "The only two

Gene McEver was caught in a revolving door of coaches at North Carolina during World War II.

replacements that were made were for players who were injured and had to be carried off the field."

North Carolina was not so fortunate against Duke the following year, nor did the Tar Heels fare as well against other teams on their schedule. Stunned by wartime depletions, the Tar Heels lost more games than they won for the first time under Wolf, finishing with an inglorious 3-7 record in 1941.

North Carolina not only lost games but its coach as well. Wolf joined the navy after the 1941 season, opening the door for a merry-go-round of one-shot successors through World War II. Jim Tatum, a onetime star tackle at North Carolina, succeeded Wolf for one year and was followed in turn by Tom Young and Gene McEver. Finally, Carl Snavely came back to North Carolina in a surprise return visit in 1945. In the 1930s he had only spent two years at Chapel Hill, leaving in a huff over school policy on recruiting athletes. This time, however, he planned a longer stay.

"King Carl"

"Backing up a line against a single wing always reminded me of a fellow caught in a thickly wooded area in an earth-quake...these trees, these legs and arms and bodies...to get to the ballcarrier you had to go through this mass of people. I always felt that the field would sink a bit. Everybody was on one side of it. They'd run for 40 yards and make one yard. It was just terrible, what an old system. But when it worked, well, it was a thing of beauty."—Irv Holdash.

Carl Snavely was up before dawn, making coffee while Bernice stirred in bed.

"Carl?" she said through half-closed eyelids.

"It's all right," he said. "I've got to get there early."

He pulled on a pair of gray pants and a shapeless sweater with the letters "C.A.A." printed across the chest and snapped a long-billed khaki cap into place on his head. Armed with sheafs of papers, he kissed his wife goodbye and went out into the near-dark.

Snavely approached the morning ritual in his office with soldier-like precision: meeting with assistants, watching movies, thrashing over the coming week's game. By afternoon he was out on Navy Field, squinting pale blue eyes across a sea of sweating football players. In the background a loudspeaker belched out the steady beat of a metronome, which Snavely used to perfect timing. Snavely howled out occasional instructions as he walked from group to group.

145

Carl Snavely (hunched forward) directs the Carolina show from the sidelines. On his left, sitting cross-legged, is line coach Max Reed.

By nightfall the players had retired, but Snavely had not. He sent an assistant out for ice cream and told him, "I'll be watching game movies tonight. Don't disturb me."

He watched movies deep into the night until his eyes blazed. Very often he was late coming home....

Carl Snavely will always be remembered by football historians as the king of the single wing, the trailblazer of game

146

movies, and the architect of North Carolina's golden era. But his players will always remember him as a regal martinet, a nobleman, a religious abstainer of alcohol and tobacco, and a man who loved vanilla ice cream almost as much as football. These strong personal flavors emerge from former players and obervers of the Carolina scene.

Charlie Justice, Snavely's most famous player at North Carolina, recalls that the Tar Heels' successful coach "was a real disciplinarian and very hard to get to know. But he was fair with everyone. Regardless of who you were or the position you played, everyone was treated equally. His main love was football, and he was always adding new wrinkles to the single wing."

"He was a perfectionist," says Mike Rubish. "He was an excellent coach. He worked us hard during practice. We'd run wind sprints until we were blue in the face. At times we longed for a game. It was easier. He had only one vice. That was vanilla ice cream. He was crazy about it. I guess that was next to football."

Joe Augustine found Snavely to be "a fantastic football mind. I don't know anybody who knew the game any better. He'd get so involved in coaching he'd lose track of time. The assistant coaches had to tell him at times when to quit. We were thankful for them."

Snavely was not a totally heartless creature, though, Augustine says. He remembers the team getting an invitation to the Snavely home for "ice cream. He sure loved vanilla ice cream. He had a freezer full. He ate and slept football, but he sure loved his ice cream." Augustine also recalls a time that Snavely stopped by his house to give him a ride to Kenan Stadium. "How many coaches would do that for a player? He was always willing to help."

To Art Weiner, Snavely was "a great coach. This was proven by the fact that he was successful everywhere he went. He was extremely dedicated, there was no limit to the amount of time he put into his job. He was very well organized, and his practices and preparation were second to none. He was a real stickler for detail. He demanded and got full cooperation from the players. There was no disrespect for Coach Snavely. He fit into the same mold as Duke's Wallace Wade and Tennessee's General Robert Neyland. He was a disciplinarian. He was a gentleman, too, and when he said something he meant it. He was a credit to our society. He was hard to get to know, but everybody had a great deal of respect for him."

Snavely, a teetotaler and non-smoker who demanded that all of his players abide by his lifestyle the year round, was respected but obviously not loved by all. Ken Powell, one of Snavely's better ends at Carolina, says today: "I didn't like him when I was in school. He was not a likeable person. But he had tremendous integrity, and I thought he was an excellent coach." Other observers, especially reporters with whom Snavely was consistently unfriendly, echo Powell's sentiments.

Snavely did bring winning football to Carolina, however, and no one could criticize him for that. Recalls author James Street:

"UNC gave him a free hand when he returned to Chapel Hill in 1945, meaning he was absolute chief. After the war, he designed a team to fit his particular formations, and with the wealth of returning GI talent he had little trouble recruiting platoons tailor-made for his system. All-American Charlie Justice, for example, was a hell of a punter, and quick. Snavely turned the quick kick into an offensive weapon and won many games and scored many points by quick kicking on second and third downs from short punt formation. This accounted for those long punting averages by Justice. Opposing teams grew so fearful of the quick kick that Snavely developed a shift to draw them offside when he needed less than five yards for a first down. This chicanery was later outlawed, of course, but Carl had a field day with it until then."

Snavely's cold dignity hardly lent itself to color, and there were very few of the anecdotes and legends attached to him that usually surround great coaches. However, a sportswriter once told a story that revealed the fire behind Snavely's stoic manner.

"Judge Ben Egan, the noted eastern referee, had brought a speaker to the annual dinner of the Football Coaches' Association," remembers the writer. "He was one of these professional pests who berates celebrities at the table and spills soup on them, you know. Well, he did an imitation of a professor who was investigating college football, and everyone in the room knew that the recipient of his barbs was Gloomy Gil Dobie, the

Cornell coach. The speaker laid into Dobie and Cornell with a vengeance. Dobie saw through the hoax and remained unmoved. However, when the speaker retired to the lobby, he was followed by one of the younger coaches. When discovered, the younger coach was handing this guy the beating of his life...and only a hurried explanation stopped it. The young coach who had gone to battle for Dobie was Carl Snavely."

Snavely was doubtlessly influenced in his coaching techniques by Pop Warner, one of college football's illustrious

Carl Snavely: His deft touch turned football programs to gold.

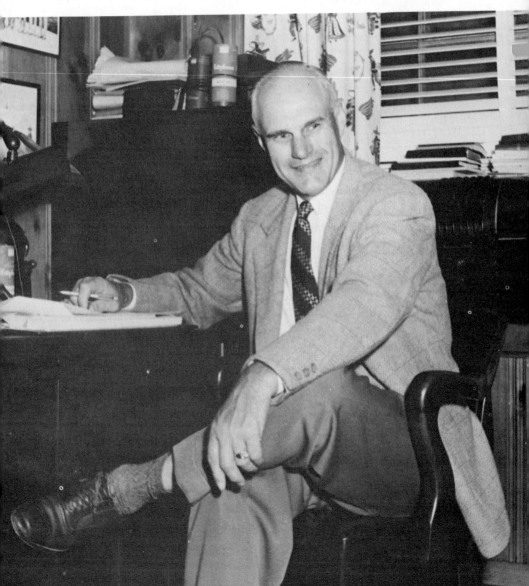

names. Snavely used a modified Warner system, featuring single wingback formation and triple-threat plays from punt formation. Each year at North Carolina saw the installation of a more deceptive attack of reverses, intricate end-round plays, and laterals. And each year saw new successes through the glamorous 1940s, a period when Snavely led North Carolina to three major bowl games, rubbing elbows with the nation's football elite.

During his time at North Carolina Snavely earned several appropriate titles. The most obvious was "King Carl" for his haughty, royal demeanor, but others such as "The Gray Fox," "The Dutch Master," and "Mr. Single Wingback" clearly reflected the man's approach to football.

"He had one of the greatest minds in the game," says Jim Camp, who was a wingback and an assistant coach under Snavely. "He handled everything from the bench, not like they do today. He was in complete control of himself and the team."

Snavely's deft touch turned football programs to gold wherever he went. In a 32-year career which carried him to Bucknell, Cornell, North Carolina twice, and Washington University in St. Louis, Snavely compiled a 180-96-16 record. Included among his achievements were two Sugar Bowl teams and a Cotton Bowl team at North Carolina, three Ivy League titles in nine seasons at Cornell, and an unbeaten year at Bucknell. Despite all of these accomplishments, Snavely remained a cockeyed pessimist throughout his career.

"He views every game with alarm and pretends that he never expects to win," a writer once said of him.

Snavely, the son of an Omaha, Nebraska, minister, grew up in Pennsylvania, where he attended Lebanon Valley College and won letters in baseball, basketball, and football. He played two years of professional baseball, but dropped his glove and began picking up the threads of a hugely successful coaching career. Between 1915 and 1927 he coached football and taught some courses at high schools, prep schools, and small colleges in Ohio and Pennsylvania. His work at Bellefonte Academy, where he won national championships in 1924, 1925, and 1926, was a stepladder to Bucknell. There he had a 42-16-8 record in seven years and won the Eastern intercollegiate championship.

In later years Snavely was to gain greater fame, but it is quite possible that he never got as much satisfaction as he did from his first Bucknell team. His squad beat Penn State for the first time in 40 years, and the winning play was imprinted in Snavely's memory for the rest of his life. Bucknell had taken an early lead only to have Penn State tie it and hold on until the last minutes. Then a Bucknell back shook loose down the sidelines for 55 yards and the winning touchdown. One of his most amusing recollections also remained from his Bucknell days, and this, too, involved Penn State.

"In those days, every substitute had to hand the umpire a piece of paper with his number written on it as he ran onto the field," recalls a writer. "Snavely had been watching the play intensely and jotting down a corrective note. Once he jotted down: 'Tell that end to quit breaking so deep.' He thrust the note to a substitute and told him to remember it. When the sub ran onto the field, instead of his number, he handed the umpire Snavely's note. The bewildered ump called time out and went into a huddle with the referee. The result was a 15-yard penalty against Snavely's team for 'coaching from the sidelines.'"

Snavely, an amateur photographer, began taking movies of his players at practice to detect Bucknell's strengths and weaknesses. The movie-making became a standard practice at games as well, and Snavely eventually became the pioneer in the use of football films for coaches. At one time later in his career, he spent an average of $5,000 a year making upwards of 40,000 feet of film each season.

Snavely was brought to North Carolina in 1934 to revive a dying program and applied remarkable surgical skill to the sick Tar Heels. In 1933 the Tar Heels had suffered their second straight defeat from Duke, an unbearable blow for most alumni, and wound up with a discouraging 4-5 record. Snavely beat not only Duke but just about everyone else in his first year at Chapel Hill. North Carolina's 1934 team won seven games, tied North Carolina State, and lost only to Tennessee. By 1935 North Carolina's winning ways triggered Rose Bowl talk until an upset by Duke in the next-to-last game of the season.

About the same time that Snavely was enjoying his success, North Carolina president Frank P. Graham was lowering the boom on athletics. He proposed his famous "Graham Plan" to eliminate preferential treatment for athletes and touched off a virtual civil war among alumni and football fans. Dr. Graham's purity campaign, which eliminated grants to athletes, hit Snavely where it hurt—in the recruiting system—and eventually caused his premature departure from Chapel Hill. Snavely was quoted by one reporter as saying: "Under the Graham plan, I do not believe I could put on the field a team that would beat Raleigh high school."

Snavely obtained release from his three-year contract and headed back north, where he signed up with Cornell for its "exceptional opportunities." Some sportswriters said that the "exceptional opportunities" at Ithaca comprised a $2,000 raise, but be that as it may, Snavely showed what he could do without the "Graham Plan" and with good talent. His Big Red teams won 46 games, lost 26, and tied three, going undefeated and untied in 1939, when Snavely was frequently mentioned as "coach of the year." Brud Holland, Bill McKeever, Nick Drahos, and Hal McCullough were among the all-star players Snavely produced at the Ivy League school.

Snavely's brilliant teams gained him national prominence, but it was ironically a game he forfeited that made his name even more well known and exemplified his shining ethics. Trailing 3-0 against Dartmouth in 1940, Cornell scored the game's only touchdown when referee Red Friesell erroneously awarded the Big Red a fifth down. When Snavely reviewed films of the contest afterward and discovered that the referee had made a mistake, he wired Dartmouth coach Earl "Red" Blaik immediately to inform him that "Cornell relinquishes claim to victory and extends congratulations to Dartmouth." The famous "Fifth Down" Dartmouth game stayed with Snavely throughout his career.

By 1945 Snavely had the same kind of problems at Cornell that he had faced at North Carolina. The school seemed uninterested in recruiting replacements for his generation of pre-World War II All-Americans. He began looking for another job and was lured back to North Carolina by a salary offer of $12,000 a year and a promise that the "Graham Plan" was a thing of the past. There was some suspicion that Snavely preferred Chapel Hill all along, even though he had departed angrily a decade before.

The return of Snavely brought Carolina football its golden era, in terms of artistic as well as financial accomplishments. The 1944 team had won only one game, but in Snavely's first year in 1945 the Tar Heels had a 5-5 record with modest talent. The next year the celebrated Charlie "Choo Choo" Justice headed a class of gifted athletes who rocketed Carolina to the stars. From 1946 through 1949 North Carolina had a 32-9-2 record on the field and a record to match at the box office. In 1949 Carolina games drew 513,000 spectators, and when the Justice teams had gone, they left a reminder of their stay, a huge surplus of cash. Surprisingly, the university did not use any of this to help Snavely in the post-war years, and the football program suffered in the 1950s as a result of it.

Snavely was caught up in the inevitable coaching cycle after a class of great players graduates. The caliber of players depreciated along with the lack of money spent on recruiting.

"The athletic department and the university had been real fortunate in the 1940s because these boys had been on the GI Bill and as a result, the program was not costing them much,"

Jim Mutscheller clutches a pass from Bob Williams (9) for a Notre Dame touchdown in 1950. It proved to be the winning margin as the Irish beat the Tar Heels 14-7.

says onetime player Ernie Williamson. "Well, in 1950 when most of the veterans finished school, then you had an entirely different group which you had to pay for. So in my opinion, the university had to make one of two decisions: to either go out and raise money to maintain the same level, or cut back. They elected to cut back, and they cut Snavely to 18 scholarships a year. They didn't have a chance to win with the teams they were competing against."

Snavely, who had lived by the single-wing formation, vowed to die by it. But he was not even given that dignity.

"There was a lot of pressure from the outside and from the university to a certain extent for him to change to the T-formation," Williamson remembered. "He could stay if he changed to the T, see, because everybody said, well, the single wing is outmoded. He changed, but Snavely later told me that this was the biggest mistake he ever made, because he didn't know anything about the T. He knew the single wing, and he should have continued with it."

North Carolina's Frank Wissman (63) connects with Jeff Newton on a touchdown pass in the 1951 Georgia game. The score did not help the Tar Heels win, though, as the Bulldogs took a 28-16 decision.

Snavely's transformation to a T-formation coach brought him failure in capital letters. He had three straight losing seasons in the early 1950s and was eventually eased out after the 1952 season.

"It was hard to fully understand," notes North Carolina newspaperman Orville Campbell. "It was just like two people who were married to one another. They got a divorce, and it was all over...and Snavely could never put it together again."

Snavely was obviously wounded over his split with North Carolina. He wrote to a friend at the time of his dismissal: "I hope to remain in football, but frankly the circumstances and developments here have brought so much discredit upon my standing and reputation as a coach that I anticipate difficulty in finding an acceptable position in the coaching field."

"Snavely became one of the most bitter men that you have ever known," reveals an intimate. "He had great bitterness toward North Carolina University...and it was many years before he decided to come back for a reunion."

Snavely found a quiet Shangri-la at Washington University in St. Louis, away from the pressures of big-time football.

"The emphasis on winning was too great at North Carolina," he said. "You're still confronted with a game every week here at Washington University, but you don't have the desperate, absolutely unyielding demand for victory. A defeat here is not a financial disaster. No alumni with private interests in the team present a problem."

Time at last healed his wound, and Snavely eventually made a triumphant return to North Carolina for a dramatic reunion with his players and peers.

"Art Weiner and Charlie Justice met Snavely at the airport," noted a friend. "His wife, Bernice, was in a wheelchair, and they escorted the two of them around the campus. It was all very sentimental and a lovey-dovey get-together. All the by-gones were by-gones."

While coaching at low-key Washington University, Snavely became an outspoken critic of big-time football. He maintained its only justification was "the fact that many boys who otherwise wouldn't get an education got one on a football scholarship." And he pointed out, "If all schools played football the way Washington University does, college football would be

Georgia back Fred Bilyeu picks up a yard but is turned on his back by several North Carolina players in this 1951 game. On the bottom of the pile is Tar Heel end George Norris (69).

wonderful."

Snavely finally broke off his romance with football after the 1958 season, retiring to go into a car-wash business. He made rare public appearances after that, surfacing in 1965 to be inducted into the National Football Foundation Hall of Fame. He preferred obscurity and lived quietly until the summer of 1975, when he died of a stroke in Kirkwood, Missouri.

Snavely's death jogged memories at Chapel Hill.

"He was probably one of the biggest factors in my life," Charlie Justice said. "He handled me in a way that I didn't get spoiled."

"He made a great contribution to football in this area," noted Chuck Erickson, the onetime North Carolina athletic director. "He did a great job with the talent he had here."

And what talent he had. It was called the "Charlie Justice Era," and when Snavely appeared at Kenan Stadium that August of 1946 to ask for players to report to the south end zone, it seemed the field would tilt. The names eventually became household words in North Carolina: Justice, Hosea Rodgers, Art Weiner, Ernie Williamson. Walt Pupa, Bob Cox, Jim Camp, Bob Mitten, Len Szafaryn, Emmett Cheek, Sid Varney, and Ralph Strayhorn, to name a few. For four years the Tar Heels walked with the giants of the football world. Seventeen of 21 games at Kenan Stadium were sold out. The pictures of North Carolina players adorned national magazine covers; the players were picked for All-American and All-Star teams, and continually made the Top Ten ratings and trips to bowl games . They called it the "Charlie Justice Era" but it was the Carl Snavely era as well. Few at North Carolina have forgotten.

Going Back
To Rabbit Patch

"Had he gone into the automobile business, Jim Tatum would have been president of General Motors. He was that kind of guy."—Orville Campbell.

Jim Tatum played a round of golf and packed it in for the day.

"Let's go to the club, Orville," he said to Orville Campbell, the publisher of *The Chapel Hill Newspaper*.

Campbell noted that his friend looked under the weather.

"I don't feel good," Tatum said.

At the club he had a drink.

"I feel so awful, I just have to have one."

Then he got up from his chair.

"I've got to go home," Tatum told Campbell. "Would you drive me?"

That was the last Campbell saw of Tatum. The North Carolina football coach was taken to a hospital shortly thereafter and soon died of a rare disease some diagnosed as Rocky Mountain fever. Others suggested that Tatum literally drove himself to death by an exhausting work schedule.

"There was suggestions that the rare virus which struck him down did so because he had been too demanding of his vital organs," said Bob Quincy, a columnist with the *Charlotte Observer*. "It is true that Tatum was perhaps the hardest worker in sports, but that was simply the way that Jim Tatum challenged life. Jim was always trying to prove you could wring 26, maybe 28 hours from a 24-hour day."

Jim Tatum: A Carolina blue blood.

Tatum died in July 1959, just three years after he had returned to his alma mater as head football coach. Tatum was a brilliant tackle at Carolina in the 1930s and coached the Tar Heels for one year during World War II before embarking on a majestic career at Maryland, where he produced three 10-game winners, five bowl teams, and a national champion. When he had the opportunity to return to Chapel Hill, he was exquisitely happy to be going home.

"I'm like an old br'er rabbit going back to the briar patch," he said in 1956. He continually referred to his alma mater as the "rabbit patch."

This "patch," though seemingly had a lot of thorns in it. When Tatum took over the head coaching job at Carolina, the Tar Heels had suffered six straight losing seasons, including the last three under former All-American George Barclay. Tatum gauged the remnants of the Barclay teams and the backbreaking schedule, then announced cheerily: "I'm going to try to win 'em all."

A tense moment has Tar Heel Coach Jim Tatum up on his feet along with his players.

Tatum did not do that exactly in his first year. In fact, he did not even win half of them. But his bubbling enthusiasm and cockeyed optimism had been translated to his players, and by 1957, his second year at Chapel Hill, Tatum produced a winner. In 1958 the Tar Heels again had a winning season, and Tatum appeared on the verge of plowing into the football stratosphere when he died quickly and mysteriously one month before practice opened in 1959. Tatum's wife, Edna, hovered near death with the same raging temperature that had assailed the football coach, but she rallied to survive.

Tatum's death brought a choking pall to the Carolina campus and especially to the Carolina players.

"He was like a second father to me," says Al Goldstein, one of Tatum's greatest ends. "It took a lot out of me, losing a man like that. Tatum was probably one of the most inspirational men in my life."

Goldstein has cause to revere Tatum. The coach had pulled him through one particularly agonizing period of life and restored his dignity. Goldstein remembers:

"I tore a ligament, and I had two of the greatest ortho-

pedic men, one from Duke and one from North Carolina, operating on me. I was an expensive piece of property, I guess, so they really did a job on me. Two days after the operation, they came in and told me I wouldn't play again. They told me I'd be lucky if I walked right. It was quite a shock. But the third day, Tatum came in with his own barrage of coaches. He told me I'd be at Chapel Hill for the summer and that he was counting on me for next year. I stayed there and lived with the trainer all summer. In the middle of the summer, Tatum had all the photographers out and they took pictures of me. Then he timed me, and I had everything back."

Goldstein repaid Tatum's faith by becoming an All-American in 1958.

"The best thing I can say is I hope my son can play for a coach like that one day."

Other players also recall Tatum with warmth and reverence.

"He never got mad at us for losing," says Jack Cummings, a quarterback under Tatum. "After a loss one time to Notre Dame, he said, 'They were good up there.'"

"He knew our mistakes," notes Dan Droze, "and we always knew that he knew of them—but he never got mad at a boy. He never fussed."

Wade Smith recalls with some nostalgia: "I remember he said we'd have a better chance against Tennessee if it rained...so he wore a raincoat to practice every day. And do you know it rained? We won 21-7."

Goldstein, Cummings, Droze, and Smith remember Tatum, as others do, as a stalking sideline giant who not only coached but led the cheers. Pacing nervously in front of his bench during a game, Tatum would grab players by the arm as they came off the field.

When a player came off the bench, Tatum was there to whisper words of encouragement into his helmeted ear and give him a hard slap on the legs as he sent him winging into the game. Tatum's success was due in large measure to the respect and admiration he earned from his coaching staff and players.

"No one could get out of people what Tatum did," Goldstein points out. "I remember in the Duke game of my senior year, we were 13-point underdogs and went out and beat them

Al Goldstein repaid Coach Jim Tatum's faith by becoming an All-American in 1958.

solely because Tatum had gotten us so sky-high. It was one of the most emotional games that I ever played in. The guys held

Duke scoreless into the fourth quarter, all on emotion."

Tatum was a master of locker-room language and very often achieved his purpose by a malapropism. One time at Maryland, when his team had done poorly in the first half against a mediocre opponent, Tatum was enraged. He met with his players and gave them a verbal lashing for their lukewarm performance.

"You're not hustling," he snapped, "you're not trying. You don't look like a football team. Are you afraid?"

He paced up and down in front of his tense players, then faced them straight away.

"Tell me," Tatum shouted in a challenge, "what are you—men or mices?"

This misuse of words brought smiles and then titters to the players. Tatum blinked. He had broken the tension, and the Terps eventually won the game by four touchdowns.

Tatum could be compassionate one moment and tough the next, as one of his players found out after North Carolina lost to Maryland in 1957. The game was played before the Queen of England, who was a special guest during her American visit. The winning coach was to have the honor of visiting the royal box at the conclusion of the game, and Tatum was enormously disappointed that he missed this opportunity. In the hotel lobby a player who had not performed up to expectations approached Tatum and asked him if he could drive home with his parents instead of taking the team bus back to Chapel Hill. But Tatum glared at him and responded: "No sir. You stay with the rest of the team. Remember, everything for the winners...nothing for the losers."

Tatum's capacity for work was nearly superhuman, and his devotion to his sport was downright religious. Even in his death-bed delirium, it is said, he talked football. Tatum was completely oblivious to everything else once he got on his favorite subject, and this passion almost got him killed in an auto accident once, according to a friend. Don Faurot, a coaching colleague of Tatum's, tells this story of a wild ride through Missouri's back roads:

"He was trying to explain a defense to me. We approached a little shanty on the side of a curve. Tatum was so busy talking he didn't realize he was going at a pretty good clip, nor did he see the curve. People were sitting on the porch in horror. Tatum's car left the road, and I knew our doom was sealed. We went into the yard, under a clothesline, over a ditch, and bounced out on the other side of the curve, miraculously back on the same highway. Jim never once changed the subject or the tone of his voice. He never noted, as far as I can tell, our narrow escape. His defense, incidentally, worked."

Tatum was celebrated for two prime abilities as a football coach—his skill at devising defensive tactics and his machine-like efficiency at organization.

"Every small detail got proper attention," notes Dick Herbert, the longtime columnist of the *Raleigh News And Observer*. "The organization work at Carolina took most of Tatum's time. As one of the top recruiters in football, he was completely aware of the importance of the alumni that provided the needed scholarships. He worked tirelessly and with effect in the growth of the North Carolina Educational Foundation, which sponsors athletic grants-in-aid."

"Tatum built up alumni support to its most enthusiastic and spirited pitch in history," pointed out another observer.

While building strong outside support with his indefatigable efforts, Tatum was also building strong football teams despite discouraging odds.

"Tatum faced many problems on his return to Chapel Hill, one of which was a defeatist complex that had come upon the Tar Heels following a cycle of lean seasons," wrote Jake Wade, the one-time sports publicist at North Carolina. "He was entirely successful in a campaign to get rid of that. He won the affection and respect of the campus faculty and administration with a new high level of relations between football and the university."

Because of his own experience as a tackle, Tatum always built his teams with that position in mind.

"My theory is that a good football team MUST have experienced tackles," he said. "A tackle must protect much ground defensively, and he's in position to take the brunt of the offense pitched in his face. He can be run at, run around, faked at, and blocked from different directions. On offense, his moves set up the blocking key or running path for the ballcarrier. He must be smart and rugged. A green operative is lost as a tackle in a good

165

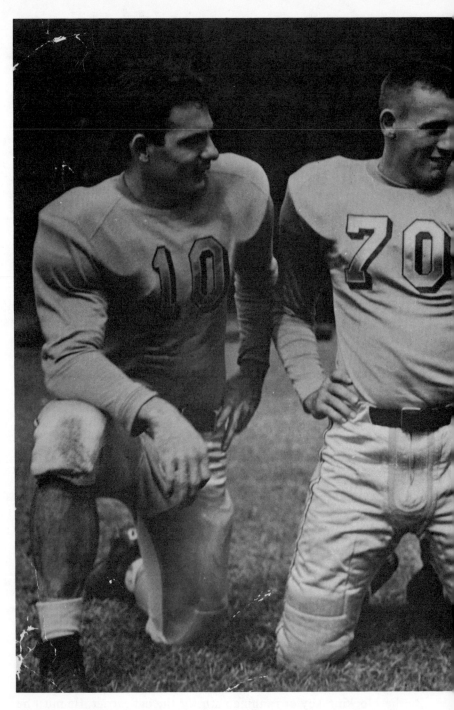

While Joe Austin (10) and Freddie Marshall (66) look on, Coach Jim Tatum ribs Chan Highsmith (70): "That pass you inter-

cepted was fine, but why didn't you run it back for a touch-down?''

football game."

He approached the passing game with caution. "Just because a pass is called doesn't mean it should be thrown. Movement of the ball is the big thing. A passer must decide quickly, then execute the proper move. A ball isn't to be tossed in the air just because it is light and will float."

Tatum was weaned on athletics so he had more than just a passing knowledge of football. All his brothers were big names in southern sports, and young Jim followed their tracks through McColl High School in South Carolina, where he captained the team in his senior season. Tatum was equally as proficient at baseball as he was at football, but it was as a tackle under Carl Snavely at North Carolina that he built a reputation as a dedicated, fierce competitor. One of the most revealing stories of Tatum's total devotion emerged during a game with Wake Forest. Both the Tar Heels and Deacons were grinding each other to dust in vain efforts to make headway when a teammate finally drew Tatum aside.

"Jim, you love North Carolina, don't you?"

"With my last drop of blood," Tatum said.

"You'd make sacrifices to see her win?"

"I'd give my right arm."

"We won't ask that now, Jim, but listen. That big brute playing opposite you is a hot-headed Southerner, a real firebrand. Next time we line up, you call him a dirty name. He'll slug you, I know, and they'll be penalized half the distance to the goal line, and we'll go over from there."

Tatum obediently assumed his stance in the line, looked his adversary square in the eye, and said, "You —— —— — —." The next thing Tatum knew, the trainer was throwing water in his face. Jim opened an eye and felt his jaw aching.

"What happened?" he said.

"You did it, Jim, old boy," Tatum's teammate crowed. "The referee saw him slug you, too. But, Jim, on that play we completed a pass for a touchdown and had to decline the penalty."

Tatum had his eyes wide open for the Duke game in 1934. In that one he made one of the biggest plays of his career, blocking a punt that eventually led to a 7-0 Tar Heel victory and a big future for Tatum.

"I'd like to see you enter coaching," Snavely told Tatum. "I have a spot on my staff. Do you want it?"

Tatum joined Snavely with unsuppressed glee and eventually followed him to Cornell when he left North Carolina in 1936. During the summer months Tatum played baseball in eastern Carolina and figured in one of the most unique trades in professional baseball history. Tatum's manager, Peahead Walker, appreciated his prospects as a catcher but found that he was overloaded at his position.

"I had to make a trade, and I couldn't get any money," Walker said. "Finally I told a rival owner I'd give him Tatum for a tie and a turkey. That was the deal. I lost in every way. Tatum helped the other club. The tie was stolen from me, and the turkey ran away."

In 1939 Tatum returned to North Carolina to coach the freshman football team but had more lofty objectives, according to one sportswriter. "Jim came home and was determined that someday he would be head coach at Chapel Hill." When "Bear" Wolf went into the service, Tatum took over the Tar Heels in 1942 and immediately reversed their losing record of the previous year. This would be a Tatum thumbprint throughout his illustrious career.

By 1943 Tatum found himself in the navy but not out of touch with football. While stationed at Iowa Pre-Flight, Tatum formed a close friendship with Don Faurot, the Missouri coach who had devised the split-T formation. Tatum and Faurot spent their off hours thinking up new ways of perfecting the attack, and by the time the war was over, Tatum was using it successfully at the University of Oklahoma. After one season at Oklahoma, Tatum was offered the Maryland job and accepted with the note that the road to College Park brought him closer to the Carolinas. It also brought him closer to football immortality. Tatum faced an awesome rebuilding task at Maryland but cut it down to size in little time.

"Tatum's work at Maryland much parallels the building of Miami Beach," noted a sportswriter. "Both were wastelands until construction began. Both became monuments—one to football, the other to architecture and leisure. The transformation was rapid and complete."

Tatum's record at Maryland was 73-14-4 and only one sea-

169

Carolina's Jack Cummings (14) intercepts a Duke pass and returns it 15 yards to the Blue Devil seven-yard line. It set up a Tar Heel touchdown in this 1958 game in Chapel Hill.

son did the Terps lose more than two games. He was named "Coach of the Year" in 1953, when Maryland won the national championship. His decision to leave the football-rich Terps in 1956 came as a shock to most of the sports world, especially since the team had won 10 games the year before and was tagged as a sure-fire national power for years to come. But Tatum was magnetized to Chapel Hill by a deep love for his alma mater and a new professional challenge. As one observer explained: "If he produced a winner at Maryland for the next

10 years in a row, it would only be what was expected of him. Maryland is now a championship factory. But Big Jim will be starting at the bottom of the ladder at Chapel Hill. He will inherit a team that has been kicked around in recent years. If he can produce a winner, he will be the rave of the nation."

While most of the old graduates cheered Tatum's return to Chapel Hill, there was some concern on campus from the intellectual set that the high-powered coach would turn North Carolina into a football factory.

"All I want to do is win," Tatum said in answer to his critics. "I can't see how success merits criticism—providing we abide by the rules."

Tatum, who had bathed in nothing but glory before, found out how the other side lives in his first season back at Carolina. Left with an undistinguished group of ballplayers, Tatum suffered through a dismal 2-7-1 year—the only losing season of his career. His second year was better, though. Observers had picked the Tar Heels to win five games at best, but Tatum won six, including a 13-7 thriller over Navy and a 21-13 decision over Duke that were counted among Carolina's most treasured victories. Before the Navy game, Tatum had said in a press conference: "Navy passes too much. When a team puts the ball into the air that much, we figure it belongs to us just as much as to them." The Tar Heels intercepted five passes and scored one of the year's biggest upsets. Navy won every other game that season, including the Cotton Bowl. In the Duke game the Blue Devils had taken a 13-0 lead and threatened to fly away from the Tar Heels at the outset. But Jack Cummings' passing arm carried Carolina to a major upset.

In 1958 Tatum could see even more improvement, even though the victories were the same number. Led by Cummings, whom Tatum called the best quarterback he ever coached, the Tar Heels scored more points and allowed less. With Cummings, Al Goldstein, Rip Hawkins, and Wade Smith serving as the nucleus, Tatum hoped for a national powerhouse in 1959 but never lived to see it. Emmett Cheek, Tatum's first assistant, fully recalled the circumstances of his death. Tatum reported to work on Wednesday, July 15, feeling "punk," Cheek noted.

"I knew he wasn't feeling well on Thursday. He reported to the office and said he ached from his head to his toes. But he took his children downtown to some of the merchants' special bargains that morning and went to Hope Valley Thursday (July 16) for a round of golf with Carrington Smith, Vic Huggins, and Orville Campbell. Edna and two daughters, Becky and Reid, left for a beach vacation, planning to stop by her home in Ayden.

"Jim planned to stay behind with Jimmy, 12-year-old son the Tatums, because he was scheduled to play in an All-Star :tle League baseball game Saturday. They were to drive to the beach to join the rest of the family after the game. But Coach

Coach George Barclay hands the ball off to Ken Yarborough, captain of the 1953 North Carolina team.

Tatum went home Friday and went to bed, he was feeling so bad. He called Edna and told her he and Jimmy wouldn't be down until Saturday. Then Saturday he got to feeling so low he called Edna again, she returned home, and they put him in the hospital that day. He thought it was a 24-hour virus and he could shake it off. But they couldn't get his temperature to stay down.

"Tatum called the office here three or four times Tuesday, he was feeling so good. But Wednesday he was a little irrational at times and Thursday he went down fast. I was afraid of what was going to happen Thursday at noon, and I started crying...."

Massacre
In Methodist Flat

"The score was 50-0. Please do not take the comparison as being in bad taste, but I'm sure the residents of Hiroshima were no more surprised with the atom bomb's destruction than those who witnessed what happened here."—Bob Quincy.

"Coach, let us go back in there."

Jim Hickey blinked in disbelief at the suggestion from Don Stallings. He sized up his overzealous tackle and thought a minute.

"Okay," he said finally. "You seniors can go back in there, but I don't want you to score. We have enough points already."

While Duke's attack stuttered, assistant coach Ed Kensler hastily rounded up all the seniors on the Tar Heel bench. Before sending them back into the game, they were warned by Hickey: "Remember, I don't want you to score. Just sneak the ball."

The return of the seniors not only bewildered the large crowd and the national television audience but enraged Duke coach Bill Murray.

"What is he doing?" he thought aloud. "Hell, he's already winning by 50 points!"

Jack Cummings, the North Carolina quarterback, took the snap from center, pitched forward a yard or two, and then fell on his belly. Before the next play was able to get off, the referee's whistle had mercifully brought an end to the game. Hickey was hoisted on the shoulders of his players and carried over to Coach Murray on the Duke side of the field. The two

Jim Hickey: "Football games aren't won simply by throwing the ball."

men shook hands, but it was obvious that Murray was distressed.

"You sure wanted that last touchdown bad, didn't you!" he snapped, then stalked away.

Hickey, stunned by the comment, took off after Murray and caught him on the run.

"Bill, you've got it wrong," said Hickey, putting his arm around the unhappy Duke coach. "I sent my seniors back in there and told them not to score. I didn't want any more touchdowns. I simply wanted my first team to finish the game."

Later, in retrospect, Murray decided that his behavior on the field was hardly gallant. He called the Hickey household and apologized to the North Carolina coach, noting that there were "no hard feelings." But if the two had kissed and made up, it is likely that Murray never forgot that 50-0 beating administered by North Carolina in 1959. And it is probable that Hickey never will forget the ride to euphoria he took after that incredible game in Durham.

"Everything happened right for us that day," Hickey recalls. "They still talk a lot about that game, and I can remember it vividly. We scored the first time we had the ball, and then Duke took the ball right down to our goal line, and we had a kid who made a good play on a pass in the end zone to keep them from scoring. Had they scored, well, you don't know what would have happened. But everything crazy happened in our favor after that."

At the half, North Carolina led 28-0 over a Duke team that was favored by six points, and the 33,000 fans on hand at Duke Stadium had trouble believing their eyes, not to mention millions more who watched on national television. The most spectacular play of the game came just after intermission, when North Carolina fullback Don Klochak took the second-half kickoff at his seven yard line and galloped up the middle on a 93-yard touchdown run, the second longest in Tar Heel history. After the first six touchdowns, Bob Shupin had converted tidily on placekicks but after the seventh, the Tar Heels wanted an even 50 points and got them when Ray Farris plunged over for a two-pointer.

"Carolina just took the ball and ran over us," Murray said bitterly. "There wasn't anything we could do about it. This was the kind of game that goes to the aggressor and Carolina was the aggressor. Nothing we did was right, that's all."

Duke captain Mike McGee banged his helmet hard on a bench as he came into the Blue Devils' dressing room. Then the good-natured giant thought a while and grinned.

"It was like being in a one-hour defensive scrimmage with the other team having the ball all the time," he said.

Cummings, voted the game's most valuable player for his exquisite leadership, revealed afterwards that the Tar Heels had played with religious fervor, owing to a melodramatic pep talk by Hickey.

"All season long, we had made a particular point of not mentioning Coach Jim Tatum's name," Cummings noted. "It wouldn't have been fitting. Before Duke, it was brought up. We knew we had to get this one for him. I've never heard a more stirring talk than Coach Hickey made to us prior to the game. Hickey told us this was the one for Coach Tatum—this is the one he would want. We also wanted this one for Coach Hickey and ourselves. It was the Gettysburg Address, you might say. Anyone who wasn't moved by it has no feelings. We came out to play a ball game."

It might have had a ring of corn to it, but there was nothing phony about Hickey's request that they "win one" for the North Carolina coach who had died so shockingly the summer before the season.

"I think the boys wanted to win it for him, "Hickey said, "more than they did for me. I wanted it that way, too. To me he was the greatest while he lived. It is difficult to say, but we wanted to give him something from our season."

This outlandish victory was a fine graduation present for the seniors on Hickey's team and an even better present for Hickey, who had walked a tightrope between misfortune and mediocrity through most of 1959. When Tatum died in July, Hickey was thrust into the position of head coach and attempted to rally a team swept by tragedy.

"That was an experience I do not want again," Hickey says. "There were no personality problems or anything like that, but the whole thing had such an unsettling effect on the staff, the fans, the players, and everyone else. It's not the type of situation where you go in and become a taskmaster. You've got to pretty much use the staff and the players in the way that Tatum had planned to do it, or you were wrong. That's the way I looked at it, and I wouldn't have done it any differently."

Actually, Hickey was not even thinking about coaching North Carolina at the time. "I was actually interested somewhere else when Tatum died." But Hickey, who had produced superlative teams at Hampden-Sydney College and was brought to Chapel Hill by Tatum in 1956, was generally acknowledged as Tatum's logical replacement.

"There was no question when Tatum died, nobody on the coaching staff, from stem to stern, ever thought he had a chance at the job, and they all rallied behind Hickey," remembers newspaperman Orville Campbell. "Hickey was appointed within

177

A tense moment on the field has the rapt attention of Carolina's Al Goldstein (81), John Schroeder (88), Ray Farris (12), and Moyer Smith (23).

48 hours."

Hickey was burdened right from the start, he remembers. "Tatum was a great optimist, you know. He always believed in overselling the team. And he did a good job of that the year before. Of course he thought he was going to be coaching, so it didn't make any difference to him." It did make a difference to Hickey, though. He could not match the great expectations, especially in a situation like that.

"Tatum's death happened a few weeks before practice was to start," Campbell recalls, "so you can imagine what this would do to a football team."

The young successor went along with the plans Tatum had made before his death. He played the same players that Tatum had placed on the No. 1 team and used Tatum's offense. The result was an opening day loss to Clemson and a bad beating from Notre Dame.

"Hickey told me later that the first serious mistake he made was trying to be another Jim Tatum when his name was Jim Hickey," Campbell recalls.

After the first two games, Hickey broke away from Tatum's posthumous hand and began to make his own decisions and make up his own starting lineup. Wrote sportswriter Bruce Phillips in the *Raleigh Times*:

"Hickey tried everything—from benching his stars to altering his entire offensive and defensive schemes—to pull the Tar Heels out of their tailspin. It didn't take him long to realize that the super-stars Tatum talked about were only human and subject to error. Calling on all his coaching knowledge, he switched players around until he got his best group together. He then made a smart defensive move—playing his slow-footed tackles at guard on defense. These renovations worked wonders against Virginia (near the end of the season), although the Cavaliers fielded a team of much lesser caliber than other schools on the Carolina schedule. Nevertheless, the Tar Heels began to show some unity. This was further established against Duke, a game they played to perfection."

The victory over Duke in the last game of 1959 provided North Carolina with a 5-5 season, below the goals of rabid alumni but somewhat satisfactory in Hickey's eyes. "We were only expected to win another game or two," he remembers.

179

Illusions of grandeur followed in the wake of that monstrous victory, but these were quickly dispelled on opening day in 1960, when the Tar Heels were shut out by North Carolina State. Incomprehensively the Tar Heels fumbled and stumbled to a 3-7 season, although they did manage to beat Notre Dame that year for the first and only time. The Fighting Irish were below par, but that did not detract from the significant triumph, recalls Mike Greenday.

"We really felt we had beaten a good team when we beat Notre Dame," he says. "Any Notre Dame team is good. We were keyed up for them. Notre Dame is No. 1 in reputation, and we knew a lot of guys on their team. They had beaten us my sophomore and junior years up at Notre Dame, but we felt we could beat them if we got them at home. We played well defensively, but our offense was poor that day."

Greenday, a big end from Pennsylvania, was raised from obscurity to Tar Heel immortality with one play that secured a 12-7 victory for North Carolina. With the Tar Heels leading 6-0, Greenday intercepted a pass and ran 42 yards for a touchdown, and this proved to be the winning score.

"I probably could have been elected governor of North Carolina that day," Greenday recalls with amusement.

The fact that Greenday was in the right place at the right time was no accident. "Notre Dame went into a formation that they had been in only once before, and on the earlier play they had thrown a halfback flare pass to the other side," Greenday remembers. "In the second quarter when they went into the same formation on my side, I played the halfback in the flat, looking for them to throw to him."

The Irish did throw—but the ball was intercepted by Greenday.

"I had a clear shot to the end zone but I was never the fastest man afoot. The thing I remember most was when I got into the end zone, I dropped the ball. Then I thought about it twice and jumped on the ball. I don't think I believed I had scored. I didn't want to catch hell if it wasn't a touchdown and I had fumbled. It was a different experience crossing the goal in college."

The 1961 season was a series of crazy bounces for North Carolina. The Tar Heels had a 5-5 record but lost two games by

Restless Jim Hickey exhorts his young warriors from the sidelines.

three points and wound up with one of their most exciting one-point victories ever, a 22-21 decision over Tennessee. The Volunteers seemingly had the game won with a 21-14 lead and only 81 seconds left. But quarterback Ray Farris guided the Tar Heels down the field, with the help of a 15-yard penalty against Tennessee. Escaping a number of fatal situations, Farris completed the dramatic drive with a touchdown pass to Ward Marslender. Then, as the Carolina crowd yelled, "Go for two! Go for two!" the Tar Heels lined up in T-formation, Farris ran the option play and hit Gib Carson in the end zone with a bullet.

The North Carolina fans were infected by the raging Tar Heel spirit and at the breathtaking finish took the field by storm and swallowed up everything in sight. Hickey was hoisted aloft like a toy.

181

Amid a machine-gun burst of newspaper superlatives, Bruce Phillips described the uninhibited scene as well as any in the *Raleigh Times*: "It was like Mardi Gras in Kenan Stadium. The delirious mob gushed on the playing field like a river over-flowing its banks. They embraced their happy, dirt-smeared, dog-tired warriors and rode Coach Jim Hickey on their shoulders. Even the steel goal posts fell before their ecstatic hysteria."

"That was the most fantastic ball game I've ever been connected with," Hickey says. "I always remember Bowden Wyatt, the Tennessee coach who was a good friend of mine, came walking across the field and said: 'Jim, that's the damnedest finish I've ever seen.'"

The Day Of The Gator

Junior Edge stretched out in the rear of the bus. He had chosen an outside seat, near the window. Next to him was a chunk of white canvas.

"Goal post pad," he said, grinning. "Fellow out there (pointing to the field) tore it off and gave it to me. This is something I'm going to keep with pride."

The canvas was part of the goal which had been cleared by Max Chapman's kick, a 42-yarder that provided North Carolina with a stunning 16-14 victory over Duke in 1963.

The bus moved slowly toward the exits of Duke Stadium while the Carolina fans cheered and waved. The players, almost too tired to wave back, acknowledged their greeting. There was a delay as the driver of the Tar Heel bus found the narrow gate almost impossible to maneuver.

"Hey, driver," shouted a player. "Make Willard get out and run through the fence."

Halfback Ken Willard would be too exhausted for that, of course. He had run hard and successfully against Duke, outgaining the Blue Devils' Jay Wilkinson for the Atlantic Coast Conference rushing title.

Bob Lacey, the Carolina end, was up front next to the driver, his face grim.

"How's the knee?" players kept asking.

"Dunno," replied Lacey. "It felt like it went out when I was tackled on our final drive. I'm just hoping it will be all

right."

Now the bus was out on the open road, sliding easily through traffic. A white station wagon pulled up alongside in the double lane. The exuberant driver, forgetful of safety, blew kisses with both hands to the North Carolina players.

Tackle Gene Sigmon, squeezing his fist into a ball and raising his left arm, shouted, "Yippee!" Several other players echoed his exultation.

Suddenly, Sigmon turned to the back of the bus with a look of disappointment.

"Junior, Junior," he shouted to Edge. "The game ball. We forgot the game ball."

"Take it easy, Sig," Edge replied. "I got it right here. First thing I did when the gun sounded. I made sure I'd get the ball."

Before the 1963 season started, North Carolina coach Jim Hickey was one of the Sunshine Boys.

"We should have a fine football team," he told the world.

Why the outrageous optimism, he was asked. The Tar Heels had won but three games the year before.

"Because," Hickey explained, "we have more lettermen (29) than ever before. We have four fine tackles—and tackles help make a team solid. We are determined to improve our blocking, running, and defense."

As enthusiastic as Hickey was, even he did not expect the miracles that followed. The mechanized Tar Heels blasted out a 9-2 record, including an impressive 35-0 victory over a strong Air Force team in the Gator Bowl. This was clearly Hickey's best team at Chapel Hill and probably his favorite.

"I think the senior leadership was the best I've ever encountered," Hickey says. "Spirit was tremendous. We had one poor showing all year against Michigan State. After that game, the kids buckled down and got to work. Our teamwork in our win over North Carolina State was a highlight of the year. We won that one, 31-10, and we've never played finer football, defensively and offensively. We didn't fumble, we didn't bust plays, we did almost everything right."

The victory over Duke on the last game of the season was even more satisfying, though. It earned the Tar Heels the Gator Bowl bid and ranked high among Carolina football thrillers.

"We won it, we lost it, and then we won it again," Hickey remembers. "It took immense determination by the members of the squad to pull that one out."

North Carolina had taken a 13-0 lead on touchdowns by Ken Willard and Eddie Kessler and appeared to be on an easy road to the Gator Bowl. But Duke came back with a 70-yard scoring pass from Scotty Glacken to Billy Futrell and then went ahead 14-13 on a 24-yard TD run by Jay Wilkinson. In the last two minutes North Carolina quarterback Junior Edge catalyzed the Tar Heels.

"I had confidence all along," he said later. "I told them in the huddle, 'Boys, we've got more than a minute and 20 seconds. We can do a lot of scoring in that time.' I just knew we could do it."

Edge swiftly moved North Carolina into field-goal range

The drama of the 1963 Gator Bowl game captures the attention of North Carolina players on the sidelines. They enjoyed the show, for the Tar Heels disposed of Air Force 35-0.

and with 33 seconds remaining, Max Chapman kicked the ball through the goal posts for a sweet 16-14 Tar Heel victory.

"This was more pleasing than 1959," Hickey said later, referring to the 50-0 victory over Duke that year. "This one had everything."

In preparation for the Gator Bowl, Hickey and his staff were careful not to warp the sharp edge gained through a classy 8-2 season.

"At their training camp in St. Augustine, Florida, the Tar Heels took it rather easy," points out newspaperman Bob Quincy. "The Carolina staff saw to it the men were in shape, but no lengthy scrimmages were held. The Tar Heel strategy was to seek and hope for a mental and physical peak. The team was housed in a plush hotel and had great accommodations and food. The Carolina team perhaps had the best rooming situation anyone ever did."

While the North Carolina players were being treated like kings, the Air Force players were being treated like troops—literally.

"They put the Air Force players into an Army base near Orlando," Quincy recalls, "and they were really unhappy about this situation. What reporters could get to them, they let them know about their feelings. They didn't have a Christmas vacation to play, and they were being treated like GIs, where the Carolina guys got this lush place. It was a situation where the psychology seemed to favor Carolina. Had the Air Force kids had first-class accommodations, they might have been in a better frame of mind to play football."

Willard's wicked runs set the tempo of the game early. The brutish back plowed through the Air Force team almost at will and went over for the first score late in the opening quarter. Quincy recalled:

"Once they got behind, Air Force just didn't have any fight. I guess they felt, 'What the hell, they didn't treat us right. We're not going to treat our coaches right.' We scored early on them and just completely mastered them, and Carolina players were telling me later there was no problem at all to block the Air Force players. They were really stunned that it was so easy. Air Force had one top-flight back that started off real well and could have made the difference. But they went on one pretty

186

*Coach Jim Hickey and Chancellor William Aycock hold on to
something good—the 1963 Gator Bowl trophy.*

decent drive about 60 yards and got bogged down. And after
that it became a completely one-sided game."

Willard gouged out 94 yards behind thunderous blocking
and wound up with the game's Most Valuable Player trophy. It
was altogether fitting that Willard should receive the award,
since he had been Hickey's most durable runner and one of the
main reasons for the team's meteoric rise from the ashes of
1962. In his junior year the 6-foot-2, 230-pounder whacked out
648 yards on the ground to win the Atlantic Coast Conference
rushing title. He realized his potential only because of an intelligent decision by the Carolina coaching staff in 1962. Willard
had been a fullback as a sophomore, but Hickey and his assistants made a decision near the end of the season to place both
Willard and his understudy, Eddie Kessler, in the same backfield. This provided Willard with an excellent blocking partner

and eventually paved the way to national recognition in 1963.

"Kessler was a devastating blocker at fullback, and he helped spring Ken many times as a halfback," Hickey says. "Kessler, too, could run. Thus we had two boys weighing 220 or better. They provided an abundance of power for our attack."

Using those two sticks of dynamite, the 1963 Tar Heels blasted 12 school records during the regular season, including the standard for total offensive yardage. The storied 1948 team, led by players such as Charlie Justice, Art Weiner, and Hosea Rodgers, had accumulated 3,245 yards in 10 games. The 1963 team amassed 3,414 on the strength of good balance behind quarterbacks Junior Edge and Gary Black. The year before, the

The scoreboard only tells half the story. It was 20-0 in favor of North Carolina at this point, but the Tar Heels eventually wound up with a 35-0 decision over Air Force in the 1963 Gator Bowl.

Tar Heels had relied heavily on their aerial game but found the skies unfriendly. In 1963 Hickey decided that the ground was a safer place on which to travel, and as a result the running game took precedence.

"Passing is spectacular, and the fans love it," he said. "But football games aren't won simply by throwing the ball. We had to energize our running."

Instead of the passing game setting up the running, it was the other way around, and the consequence was a delicately balanced attack of 1,809 yards rushing and 1,605 through the air. Bob Lacey, the All-American called by Hickey "the best receiver I've ever coached," complemented the strong running game with 48 catches and 533 yards during the regular season.

North Carolina's Gator Bowl team also had four outstanding tackles, of which Cole Kortner was probably the most consistent. The others included Gene Sigmon, Vic Esposito, and John Hill. Chris Hanburger, a one-time end, was shifted to center and became a "real headhunter," according to observers. Jerry Cabe's talents at guard further fortified a line glutted with skill.

"The team itself was not real big," points out Quincy. "The speed was good but not exceptional overall. The team just managed to get places and do things it had to do. And you had players like Willard, Hanburger, and Edge who always got their job done. Willard was just a steady workhorse—a rock 'em, sock 'em football player who'd get you that four, five, six yards when you needed it. Hanburger was a quiet sort of guy, but everybody was either scared to death of him or he had that naturally acquired leadership. When they had to get things done, Hanburger was the guy that got to them. I know one time they were down near the goal, he said to Willard, 'If you don't get that damn ball down in there this time, you'll have to handle me after the game.' That's the kind of player he was. He played center, but he was as fast as any back we had. Edge was not regarded highly at the start of the season. Everyone thought he moved too slow. But he came up with the runs when he had to have them, and he turned into a good clutch passer."

Edge, especially, was a favorite of Hickey's. "I had other quarterbacks who were flashier and could make the big play," Hickey remembers, "but none of them had the stability of

Junior Edge. Edge was just a consistent ballplayer. He was a big, fat, balding country kid who looked funny but could get the job done. He understood football.''

Edge was not back in 1964, but most of the other talent was, and this gave rise to wild optimism for the season. Inexplicably, however, the same chemistry did not happen, and the Tar Heels wound up with a mediocre 5-5 record despite the presence of Willard, Hanburger, and Company.

"We felt that 1964 would be a better season, but we managed to lose a couple of crazy games," Hickey says. "Otherwise we might have been 8-2 that year. I know we lost one game to Maryland on what we thought was a goofy ruling at the time."

The 1964 Tar Heels lost two games by one point, including that 10-9 decision to Maryland, and one by four. But they did manage to upset Michigan State, 21-15. Willard, becoming Carolina's all-time "Iron Horse" with 228 carries for 835 yards, was the second busiest back in the nation. Assured that he would have to see Willard no longer in the Carolina backfield after the 1964 season, Clemson coach Frank Howard conducted a special ceremony in the Tar Heel dressing room after a 29-0 beating sponsored by the great back.

"Where's that Willard?" Howard growled as he entered the celebrative locker room.

There was a sudden hush as the Clemson coach looked around the room for the Carolina star. Then he spotted Willard and walked over to his dressing stall and planted a kiss on his cheek.

"Ah allus kiss the good ones goodbye," he said. "Goodbye, boy, and git out of my way."

Howard's goodbye kiss to Willard not only gave the back a big sendoff but also appeared to have a trace of symbolism attached to it. Howard was not only kissing Willard goodbye, it seemed, but also waving goodbye to the last of Hickey's great teams. Despite an electrifying performer in quarterback Danny Talbott and some remarkable victories over Ohio State in 1965 and Michigan in 1966, the North Carolina football team displayed a wholly eccentric character. The Tar Heels had a 4-6

Coach Jim Hickey and one of his most electrifying players, quarterback Danny Talbott.

190

In the fall these young men's fancies turned to football. This was the 1965 North Carolina team coming out of the Kenan Stadium field house.

record in 1965 and then experienced their worst season under Hickey in 1966, winning but two games in 10.

"That 1966 season was a total disaster," recalls Jack Williams, the one-time North Carolina sports information director. "Hickey was ridiculed by the fans, and a lot of people clamored for him to be released. He was a great, great offensive football coach, I thought, but never did put it together defensively. Funny thing, the 1966 team started off great, and everyone thought they were going to be a great football team. They lost their first game to Kentucky and then won two in a row, beating North Carolina State and then Michigan at Ann Arbor. But in the Notre Dame game they lost two quarterbacks on successive plays. Danny Talbott had part of his ear ripped off, and then they put in Jeff Beaver, who had come to Carolina with a great reputation, and he went down on the very next play. Alan Page got to him and hurt his knee, as I recall. They were down to a third-string quarterback, a big, blond kid named Tim Karrs, who really had no ability to speak of. I will never forget how I admired his guts. He stood there all afternoon throwing passes, with Page and a bunch of other brawny guys on his neck every play. But the rest of the season was a disaster without direction from the quarterback. Talbott came back but never got back into top form until the end of the season. I used to walk off the field with Hickey, and the fans said just awful things to him."

While his team was going nowhere, Hickey had other plans for himself.

"The University of Connecticut wanted Hickey to become their athletic director," notes newspaperman Orville Campbell, a close friend of the coach. "Hickey had accepted the job as athletic director before his last year at North Carolina and was going to leave after 1966. Everyone in Chapel Hill basically knew this. I had the story confirmed, but I never broke that story because I didn't see where it would do the university any good to announce in August that this was Hickey's last year. I just kept it to myself, and he was asked a question at every press luncheon about his status, and he would say, 'Gentlemen, you'll have to ask the University of Connecticut about that. I'm coaching the North Carolina football team this year.'"

As North Carolina continued to lose in 1966, Hickey's noncommittal response to questions about his position wore so thin that people soon saw through it. Hickey finally confirmed everyone's suspicions by leaving after the lame-duck season.

Time Out: Bill Dooley

"Maybe I would make more money somewhere else but would I have the kind of alumni, fans, school, community that I have here? The money and the football program at Notre Dame would be nice but who the hell wants to live in South Bend, Indiana? It's not that I'm lacking ambition. Chapel Hill is a good place."—Bill Dooley.

Two big-play games underscored the bold character of the 1971 North Carolina football team. Twice against Wake Forest, the Tar Heels found themselves, ankle-deep in mud, defending a 7-3 lead inside their 10 yard line in the dying minutes. Facing the Deacons' horrifying triple-option offense, the Tar Heels held their ground with notable heroism. Lou Angelo stopped one drive with a pass interception, and another was snuffed out when Bud Grissom made a tackle inches short of a first down on the five yard line. In the William and Mary game, also played on a field resembling a Florida swamp, Paul Miller herded the Tar Heels on a 75-yard touchdown thrust in the last minutes. The quarterback then threw to Lewis Jolley for a two-point conversion and a 36-35 victory.

"Confidence became the easiest noun in town," a writer said in a smartly turned phrase.

This apparent self-reliance was undetected in Tar Heel teams of the late 1960s before Bill Dooley showed up at Chapel Hill. He had set foot on a wasteland that provided continual fodder for jokes.

Two big men in North Carolina athletics, longtime athletic director Chuck Erickson and football coach Bill Dooley.

"Carolina was in such a bad way," cracked one sportswriter, "that the alumni and fans used to meet on the field and tear down goal posts after a tie."

When Dooley first alighted in Tar Heel country and observed the remains of the 2-8 1966 season, he was known to tell close acquaintances, "I knew it was bad, but I didn't know how bad."

The Tar Heels had not only come off one of their worst seasons in history but had fielded only three winning teams in the previous 17 years. One was Jim Hickey's fine Gator Bowl team of 1963, but the last badge of greatness was worn by the immortal Charlie Justice teams of the 1940s. Dooley, who had served as a successful assistant coach at Georgia and Mississippi State, was distressed at the football poverty level he found at Chapel Hill.

"The few football players who were here in 1967 were awfully slow," he remembers. "The level of talent was way below what I had been used to at Georgia or Mississippi State. Right there at the first I was wondering about winning a game, any game."

But Dooley had been asked "to build up the program," and so he rolled up his sleeves and set about doing just that with religious fervor.

"We set our goals to recruit the outstanding high school players in North Carolina and Virginia," he notes. "To sell our program. We had great academics. A beautiful campus. And we sold the promise that we would build a winning football team. We intensified recruiting in this part of the country beyond anything that had ever been done before. Every possible opportunity I flew into towns and cities and talked to players personally. Many of them had never seen a head coach before. Certainly not in their own home."

But getting the athlete was one thing. Making him play great football was another.

"I'll never live long enough to forget the day in 1968 we lost to South Carolina, 32-27. We had taken a 27-3 lead with 13 minutes to play. We protect the ball. Play a little defense. There is no way we can lose it. They scored. We fumbled the kickoff. They scored. We fumbled again. They made two other perfect scoring drives. You could see it in the faces of our players; they were trying, but they believed that no matter what they did they could not escape defeat."

Dooley declared war on pessimism at North Carolina and stamped out all negative feelings before long. The Tar Heels increased in confidence under their swaggering new leader.

"Native North Carolina boys like tailback-fullback Lewis Jolley and quarterback Paul Miller and tackle Bud Grissom paid the price in practice and began to believe that no matter what happened in a game, we would find a way to win it," Dooley

Bill Dooley: "Chapel Hill is a good place."

says. "And we were fortunate to get some great players from out of state, such as Don McCauley, who helped turn things around."

Dooley's program got better with age, finally reaching its vintage year in 1972, when the team known as "The Cardiac Kids" carved out an 11-1 record, including an inspiring 32-28 victory over Texas Tech in the Sun Bowl. The period from 1970 through 1974 was Dooley's Camelot: four bowl games, two Atlantic Coast Conference titles, a 15-game winning streak against ACC foes, national ranking, and more winning seasons (four) than Carolina had in the previous 22 years. Dooley's heavenly rise not only uplifted the Tar Heels but the entire ACC as well. Explains one ACC coach:

"The ACC is tougher now than it ever has been. I hate to admit it, but Bill Dooley is responsible for it all. He came into the league and worked around the clock to build a winner. Now everyone has started working that hard, and it has made the league far better than ever in history."

Dooley's drive to the top has not been without curves and crashes. At the beginning his program came under heavy criticism for allegedly stepping over the boundaries in recruiting and practice procedures. These charges were never proven, though. Dooley has also been a marked man because of the style and methods of his teams—rarely imaginative on offense and hardly frightful on defense.

"Three yards and a cloud of dust is great when you win, but it's the worst offense in the world when you lose," says a newspaperman close to the Carolina scene. "Hell, when my wife can call the plays from the stands, I think it's time for Dooley to change it."

But winning has generally assuaged the sharp feelings of the grandstand quarterbacks. Dooley, who might be termed a method coach from the old school, continually defends his offensive intentions. "As a team," he says, "you are nothing if you can't run the football on an opponent."

Further explaining his offensive philosophy, Dooley will tell you: "People have the misconception that I'm entirely against the forward pass. Which I'm not. I feel that you have to be able to throw well in order to win. The key is the word 'well.' My basic philosophy is you have to be able to run the ball first. If you can run, it is so much easier to throw the ball well. We do recruit to develop a good running game first. We look for the big running back, the quick, fair-size linemen who can do the job blocking, and for what we call a run or pass-option quarterback. We're not looking for the quarterback who is going to drop back and throw the ball.

"It's funny. Not only some of our alumni think we can't pass. Some of our opponents have fallen into the trap of believing it themselves. Then when we grind the ball and grind the ball, and come up second down and two yards to go for a first down and throw the ball for a touchdown, they are as surprised as some of the fans in the stands."

While Dooley might have enemies in the stands, his players rush to defend him on the field. "We don't go in for pageantry or glamour, and maybe the fans would like more of that,"

Bill Dooley's practice sessions: A model of tortuous consistency.

quarterback Nick Vidnovic once remarked. "We're looking for wins, and the system has paid off."

"It wasn't the most exciting football in the country, but it got the job done," says guard Ken Huff. "Dooley was a fair and an honest guy and was able to get his philosophy across to the players. People knew exactly what we were going to do, but very often they couldn't stop us from doing it."

Dooley's success has been honed not only out of a shatter-proof offense but also a unique quality of toughness translated from the coach to his players.

"I remember the first spring Coach Dooley was there as being very rough," recalled defensive back Dave Riggs. "You could play football if you really wanted to, but the people unsure had to make up their minds. He drew a line, you either wanted to play badly enough to work for it, or you didn't want to play badly enough."

Dooley's practice sessions have been a model of tortuous consistency, harsh enough to warm the cockles of a drill sergeant's heart.

"Dooley was a very strict disciplinarian," recalls Ron Rusnak, an All-American guard on the 1972 team. "He set the rules, and you had to follow them—or else. I remember I was really scared to talk to the man when I played for him. Like someone would say, 'Coach Dooley wants to see you,' and I'd always get a lump in my throat. Of course after I graduated, I found him to be a very sincere, warm person."

Dooley's tough fiber is a fabric woven out of childhood. Growing up in the hard times of the Depression in Mobile, Alabama, he learned discipline and respect for authority at a young age.

"The Depression was tough on everybody," he remembers. "We all had our jobs to do. There was no complaining or griping, everybody just chipped in and did it."

There were times for games, too, but these were as robust as the young toughs who played them.

"I grew up in a rough neighborhood," Dooley says. "We played a lot of football on asphalt. I remember we had a game, throw and grab it. About 20 of us would gather around, somebody would throw the football up in the air, and somebody else would catch it—and run for his life."

Young Bill Dooley not only had to run to keep up with the other kids on the block but also had to follow a fast pace set by his older brother, Vince.

"I don't think Bill and I were as close then as we later became," says Vince Dooley, now the coach at Georgia. "We were very competitive then, and Bill was the youngest. We had the normal squabbles over who got the little red fire truck, who would wash the dishes."

Vince was two years older than Bill and a few yards ahead in football ability. Both attended McGill Catholic High School in Mobile, but Vince was an all-state quarterback, while Bill plugged away as an obscure but determined lineman under Ray Dicharry.

"He came along kinda in the shadows of Vince," remembers Dicharry, who not only coached the Dooley boys in high school but also gave them counsel after their mother died prematurely. "Bill was the quiet one. I remember he used to keep me after practice to make me prove something to him. Like a block. He tears everything apart to see why it does the way it does."

Vince, generally acclaimed and heavily recruited, received a scholarship to Auburn, 'one of the highly prized Southeastern Conference schools. Bill, unheralded and uninvited, wound up with little fanfare at Berkingston Junior College in Mississippi.

"I wasn't recruited by SEC schools," Bill Dooley notes. "I guess they thought I was too small. At Berkingston I played for a man everybody called 'War Daddy.' We opened scrimmages with 50-yard sprints. He got the nickname because you went to war every day. You knew you'd better button that bonnet everytime you stepped on the field. If we lost, we practiced Sunday mornings."

Bill Dooley began making waves himself, even if it was in a smaller pool than his brother's. He was named an all-state player at Berkingston and then heard the siren calls of larger schools, particularly from the prestigious SEC. Dooley, although forced to undergo surgery for a shoulder separation, took a shot at Mississippi State. He reported to Darrell Royal, a 29-year-old who was just starting to make his mark on the college coaching world.

"Coach Royal told me he hadn't recruited me—or anyone else on the team," Dooley remembers. "We were all in the same boat that spring. Shoulder or no shoulder, I had two weeks to make the team."

Royal, the now-famous Texas coach, found a diamond in the rough when he uncovered Dooley.

"He was a fighter," Royal recalls. "He had no trouble establishing himself on a football field despite his size. He was a player's player. He had this tremendous desire, aggressiveness, this want to. He was a fierce competitor and one of the most outstanding players I can recall coaching. When I think of Bill Dooley, I think of that year we played Miami in the Orange Bowl. He was playing for a losing football team that night. But in all my experience I don't ever recall a defensive player receiving the ovation he got from those people in the Orange Bowl when he left the field that night. He was that determined a young man. It was an amazing performance, especially for a 182-pound linebacker. I knew there was a lot to him as a youngster."

From the shadows of obscurity, Dooley was now racing

Bill Dooley: "Never a day passes that I don't think about football."

through the limelight—established as an all-Southeastern Conference guard-linebacker. He played in the Shrine Bowl in Miami amid the college stars and later was requested by Royal to become a graduate assistant in football. Dooley worked under Royal and Wade Walker before joining former North Carolina star Jim Camp at George Washington in 1961-62. Dooley returned to Mississippi State as an offensive line coach and helped guide the Maroons into the Liberty Bowl against North Carolina State. At this point he hooked his star to his brother's wagon. Vince was the newly named coach at Georgia in 1964 and enlisted Bill to join him as head of the offense.

"At first I told him I couldn't come," Dooley says. "Things were going well at State. But he came up to me and put his arm around me and said, 'Look, I'm in this thing, and I'm either going to sink or swim. I want you to swim with me.'"

Contrary to most nepotism, this situation had favorable results. Reunited, the brothers restored the Georgians to prominence.

"I was harder on Bill than anybody else in the program," Vince recalls. "I expected that much from him. But through it all, he was the best coach I had ever seen. He has the ability to teach. That's the most important thing a coach can have. He got down there with his boys, and they listened, and they learned. And they performed."

Dooley's growing reputation as an offensive magician was an irresistible attraction for North Carolina, which needed a Pied Piper in the late 1960s. Dooley had his choice of three head jobs but chose North Carolina for aesthetic as well as pragmatic reasons. He admired "the campus...the beauty of it...." He also appreciated "the facilities...the tradition, being the oldest state university in the country; the fact that good football has been played here in the past."

The most appealing aspect, though, was the mountainous challenge.

"I guess of all things, the program was on the ground, and I was asked to build it up," he says.

Dooley first had to clear the deadwood, though, before he could construct a kingdom out of a disaster area. "I couldn't believe that a major university, with North Carolina's reputation, just didn't have any football players," he said incredulously.

While Dooley was appropriating the proper sort of young thoroughbreds to pull the team forward, he endured the agonies of losing seasons his first two years. By 1969 he had the team up to .500, and this, most conceded, was the turning point in the Dooley era. It subsequently led to an 8-4 year in 1970, then 9-3, and finally 11-1 in the glamorous 1972 season. Dooley, it was discovered, became the only coach in the country to improve his record for five consecutive seasons.

"The hardest thing we had to do," Dooley reminds you, "was get across the idea to the players that they could win, turn it around, and say 'We're going to win' instead of saying, 'Well, the inevitable is going to happen, and we're going to get beat somehow.' When we came in we knew the program was down, but we didn't realize how far down it was until we got out on the field. Our record (2-8, then 3-7) indicates how far down it was. My first goal had to be recruiting when I saw the material we had. My next goal was to win the Atlantic Coast Conference championship or be a contender for it every year."

The ACC's Holy Grail secured a couple of times, Dooley can dream of standing on holier football ground in the future.

"My job is a job that lasts 11½ months a year, and you can make it 12 if you want to," says Dooley, seized by overflowing ambition. "Never a day passes that I don't think about football, and hardly ever will one pass that I don't do something about it."

Beat "Dook"

"In the fall of 1941, we were on duty in the navy. This Carolina man and I were discussing the coming Duke-Carolina game, which neither of us would be able to attend, to our bitter regret. We were hard at it, speaking well above a whisper, when a high-ranking naval officer stepped up and said, 'Are you discussing The Game?' The accent was definitely on 'The Game,' and he definitely meant the Army-Navy game. To which my Carolina friend said, and I quote: 'Hell, yes, we're talking about The Game...The Only Game...The Duke-Carolina Game.' The remainder of the story cannot be told. You would have to see the brass hat's face. That's the way it is in this area. This is the Army-Navy, Yale-Harvard, Georgia-Georgia Tech games, and all the rest of the nation's celebrated football rivalries rolled into one."—Ted Mann, sportswriter.

The Duke-Carolina series has been a rivalry made in heaven and richly appreciated by just about everybody but the management of the old Washington Duke Hotel. For many years that was the focal point for student celebration and sabotage. Once after a particularly exhilarating North Carolina victory, the Tar Heel celebrants in a fit of joy hurled all the furniture that was not nailed down from the mezzanine into the lobby. This was an unusually lusty group. Usually, the most dangerous flying objects around the hotel were eggs, rolls of toilet tissue, and paper bags filled with water. Naturally, the Washington Duke Hotel was forced to redecorate each year.

If the divine series between the close North Carolina neighbors has brought out the best in the players, it seems to have brought out the worst in the students through the years. Hotel vandalism was tame compared with other pranks pulled off by the spirited partisans. The 1930s were perhaps the Golden Age of this frolicsome off-the-field rivalry.

The statue of Old Man Duke on the Women's Campus in Durham and the Old Well and Silent Sam in Chapel Hill were the main targets of student raiding parties in the old days. The object was to paint Old Man Duke Carolina Blue. The Duke students set up elaborate defenses to protect the statue. One year they surrounded the place with a board of nails to discourage cars and a firehose to discourage raiders. If anyone got through the first two lines of defense, there would always be a cordon of young toughs around the statue, waiting with sand-filled socks. Anyone attempting to deface North Carolina's prize landmarks

Game day at Kenan Stadium, and somebody lets the balloons out of the bag.

faced the ordeal of kidnapping and a shaved and painted head.

A day or so before the game, each student body would pile up a heap of rubbish on the other's campus and set off a bonfire ahead of pep rally time. The bonfire sites were usually well guarded, and a small riot would ensue when raiders met the guards.

Rameses, the Tar Heel mascot, was usually a sure bet to be kidnapped and released the day of the game, swathed in a paint coating of Duke Blue. The Victory Bell, symbolic trophy passed to the victor each year, was never safe, no matter on whose campus it stood. And even those not directly involved in the emotional series got a taste of the flavor. Movies in Durham were continually interrupted by demoniacal Duke students, who shut off the projector, flicked on house lights, and chanted "Beat Carolina" from the stage.

In later years the partisanship passions became more intellectual and less physical, but just as emotionally unstable. The mascot and Victory Bell continued to be stolen, the Heel Howl made thousands roar, the "Beat Dook Parade" lit up the town, and there were innumerable toasts to the Tar Heels.

On the field, the action has been equally as intense and unpredictable and immeasurably more vicious. A classic rivalry because the schools are only eight miles apart, the Duke-Carolina series has been one of streaks and sputters. Carolina won nine straight games between 1894 and 1929. Duke won four straight beginning with two games in 1943. The Tar Heels won four in a row during the Charlie Justice era (1946-49), and then Duke won seven straight in the 1950s. The Bill Dooley teams of the 1970s ran off three in a row over Duke and for the most part have dominated Carolina's most traditional rival, a fact that has put him on solid footing with the powers at Chapel Hill.

"Interestingly, Dooley has had more success against Duke than probably any other coach here," points out Rick Brewer, North Carolina's sports information director. "Even when Dooley was going through his bad early years, he was able to beat Duke."

Dooley's tyranny of Duke includes a 59-34 aberration in 1970, something that will be remembered at Chapel Hill as long as Don McCauley's records stand—which should be quite a

The best place to be at Chapel Hill on a Saturday afternoon in the fall— Kenan Stadium.

while. McCauley was Dooley's blunt instrument against bedeviled Duke that day, hammering for 279 yards and five touchdowns in a glorious record-smashing game. Called by Dooley "the greatest football player I've ever seen," McCauley finished his last game at Kenan Stadium owning 23 records. His most prestigious achievement was a 1,720-yard season which broke O.J. Simpson's single-season rushing record at Southern Cal.

On the eve of his biggest day in college football, McCauley was kept awake by recurring nightmares, all with the same theme.

"I had trouble sleeping," he says. "I was scared to death, thinking about this being my last game at home and everything. Going into the game I wasn't even thinking about records. I remember there was a writeup the night before saying this was one game I wasn't going to break any."

But not even Choo Choo Justice in his finest hour ever received the thunderous ovation that McCauley did in his last game at Kenan Stadium. For the last several minutes the 48,000 fans chanted, "We want McCauley. We want McCauley."

"It sounded exactly like somebody trying to stampede a national political convention," remembers a sportswriter. "If the voting age were lowered a trifle, and maybe even without the edge, Don McCauley could have been elected governor of North Carolina."

The adoring fans could not wait until the final gun to get their hands on Carolina's All-American player, who had carried the ball 47 times—13 more than the entire Duke team. Three times they flooded the field while the game was still going and had to be pushed back across the sidelines. At the finish McCauley was swept up by admirers and carried across the field on a wave of humanity. A Duke backer later confessed that he, too, was inspired by McCauley: "I quit pulling for a Duke victory about midway through the third quarter. I just sat there and marveled at that guy running with the football."

As holy as his gigantic, single-season yardage figure was McCauley's mark for consistency. He became the first man in

North Carolina's Don McCauley gets some of the yardage that helped him break the single-season national collegiate record in 1970.

210

211

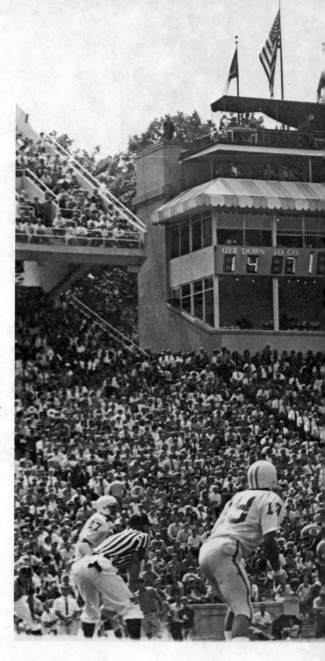

Paul Miller holds and Ken Craven kicks against Kentucky in 1970. The Tar Heels started out the season on the right foot with a 20-10 victory.

National Collegiate Athletic Association history to carry the ball over 300 times in one season (324) and average better than five yards a carry (5.3).

Ironically, McCauley was not a highly advertised product when he came to Chapel Hill from Garden City, New York.

"He played defensive back in high school and averaged carrying the ball only about five times a game," notes Dooley. "We thought he was a good athlete, but we had no idea he was super."

McCauley, though, felt "confident I could make it on

offense." This was proven right away in McCauley's freshman year, when he carried the ball for 705 yards. As a sophomore, he alternated at tailback with Saulis Zemaitis and was not able to take wing until Zemaitis was moved to fullback in McCauley's junior year. He benefited doubly from the intelligent move by the Tar Heel staff: He got good blocking from Zemaitis and more opportunities to run. And McCauley did run.

"McCauley would take the football behind the line of scrimmage and glide for a few steps like a deer looking for an opening in a forest fire," says an observer. "When the opening developed, McCauley would jet through with the force of an enemy tank. Durability was McCauley's forte. At 200 pounds, he had the strength to carry the ball four or five times in a row without asking his quarterback for time off for good behavior."

Quarterback Paul Miller, who teamed with the Magnificent McCauley, remembers: "He was beautiful. He took all kinds of punishment but he never said a word, and he never got angry. Even after he'd carried four or five times in a row, he'd still run again if I'd ask. And in the clutch situations, he'd always get the yardage."

As a senior McCauley enjoyed his most extravagant success. He was the cornerstone of an 8-3 season and the reason that the Tar Heels found themselves in the Peach Bowl against rugged Arizona State in 1970. Led by McCauley, the Tar Heels collected 3,137 yards rushing, or an average of 285.2 yards a game during the regular season. Miller, an exquisite ballhandler, gave the Tar Heels a brilliant short-range passer to complement McCauley's running talents. Halfback Lewis Jolley and fullback Geoff Hamlin lent McCaulley support in the backfield. The offensive line, described by Clemson coach Hootie Ingram as "one of the best I've seen in football," was led by Paul Hoolahan, a 230-pound tackle who ranked as one of the best blockers in Tar Heel history. Among the leaders of a defensive unit that was especially tough against the run were guard Bill Richardson and tackle Flip Ray.

The 1970 season exploded with flashes of brilliance, although there were some lapses—a three-game losing streak in the middle and a 48-26 defeat by Arizona State in the Peach Bowl. There were extenuating circumstances, however.

"All three losses during the regular season came in very

close games," Dooley says, "and we had a good chance to win them all. The thing that hurt us in the mid-season slump was an injury-riddled defensive secondary. We lost some key men back there, and we got hurt by the bomb."

The Peach Bowl game hit Carolina's defenders more like an atomic explosion. Had it not been for McCauley's high-powered day, the score would have been even more lopsided in Arizona State's favor.

"McCauley had a fantastic game," recalls former North Carolina sports publicist Jack Williams. "Carolina seemed to be out of it in the second quarter and rallied for all 26 points late in the second half. McCauley scored three or four touchdowns, broke away on several long runs, and drew raves from newsmen and Arizona State players as being the best back they had seen that year."

Because of McCauley's lack of color, he never inflamed public passion the way Charlie Justice did in the 1940s. But his prodigious appetite for running put him as close to Choo Choo's stature as was possible in Tar Heel affection. Where Justice's fame was loud, McCauley's was more subtle. It reflected the man's restrained character, never typified more than in his quiet exit from Chapel Hill.

"One thing I can't get over about Don McCauley," says Williams. "The same guy walked out of Ehringhaus Dormitory who walked in four years before. He just came by the office and shook hands and said, 'Thank you for everything you have done for me,' and got in his car and drove off. Simple as that. I wanted to stop the town. Or ring down the chimes in the Bell Tower. Or get the band. But this quiet, young, decent man just walked out by himself without knowing, and I don't think he will ever know, how great he was. Or what a place he made for himself in the history of this school."

Battle Of The Brothers

"I personally came into this game mad. Everybody was talking about how big Georgia was, how they were going to blow us out. Well they sure didn't blow us out. They were bigger, but they didn't push us around at all. The papers wrote this was going to be a mismatch, a stinker bowl. They said we were dog meat. Well, I guess we showed 'em different."—North Carolina linebacker Jim Webster after the 1971 Gator Bowl game.

It was about as big as a family argument could get. When they were younger, Bill and Vince Dooley used to fight over who kept the little red wagon, who fed the dog, who did the dishes, and who washed out the bathtub. But now they were trying to settle who had the better football team.

The occasion was the 1971 Gator Bowl game in Jacksonville, Florida—one of the most emotionally devastating matches in college football. It pitted Bill Dooley's North Carolina team against Vince Dooley's Georgia squad in an unprecedented bowl matchup between brothers.

"We never thought that we would be competing against each other," Bill Dooley reflects, "because football schedules are made 10 years in advance, and our schools were not even scheduled. All of a sudden here we are in a bowl game, and you have to get ready to play against your brother's team. It didn't concern me too much playing against my brother, but it concerned me quite a bit playing against his team. I knew what tal-

216

ent he had. I had visited his spring practices. In fact, our two offenses were practically identical. He even had my old offensive line coach, Jimmy Vickers, on his staff."

Bill Dooley, of course, had been an assistant to his brother at Georgia, and it naturally followed that the styles of their teams would be strikingly similar. They were—down to the warmup drills.

Precisely at 1:35 p.m. both teams sent their backs and ends onto the bright green Gator Bowl field. Then the linemen raced in at 1:42, the red-clad Bulldogs from one side of the field and the white-shirted Tar Heels from the other. Both sound defensively, the teams battled through a scoreless tie in the first half. Finally late in the third quarter, North Carolina's probes began to find running room on the left side, and the Tar Heels took the ball into field-goal range for Ken Craven's kick. But Georgia had the last score, Jimmy Poulos carrying around his left end for a touchdown and a 7-3 Bulldog victory.

"It was almost like playing against yourself," said Georgia's defensive end, Chuck Heard. "Carolina's offense was so much like ours."

The teams even had the same number of rushing plays—51. But the Bulldogs made better use of one of theirs when Poulos ran 25 yards for the game-winning points. Andy Johnson had kept that drive humming with a 31-yard pass to Lynn Hunnicutt.

"I thought we played well enough to win," Bill Dooley says. "Georgia had an outstanding football team. We had some opportunities if we could have taken advantage of them and gotten some points on the board. I think we each knew what the other was going to do offensively, so it made for an outstanding defensive ball game."

Carolina, despite a strong start and finish in 1971, a 9-2 record, and an Atlantic Coast Conference championship, was installed as a 12-point underdog to Georgia. Some pregame publicity declared it a mismatch, but the Tar Heels found at once that they belonged on the same field with the Southeastern Conference team.

"I really was afraid we might go out there and get embarrassed," noted North Carolina defensive end Bill Brafford. "But when the game started, I felt we could play them down for

down. Later on, I thought we'd win it. If we played them 10 times, we'd win five. We're that much alike."

The Tar Heels, who had worked up various stages of rage and outrage while swallowing the pregame disparagement, were convinced afterwards that the better team had not won.

"We're just as good as Georgia," said Lewis Jolley, Carolina's most dangerous runner that day with 77 yards. "We didn't play as well as usual on offense today, but our defense was tremendous. The defense stuck it to them all day. We just made too many mistakes. If we'd scored that touchdown to go ahead 10-0 early in the second half (it eventually wound up as a missed field goal), we would have won."

Both teams had the chance to put the game away early, but the Tar Heels' offensive mistakes were the most noticeable. The game could have been tidily wrapped up for North Carolina in the third period. Leading 3-0, the Tar Heels had a first down with the ball on the Georgia 28. Jolley tried left end on the first try and gained no ground. On the second, quarterback Paul Miller let the snap from center slide through his hands, and he had to fall on the ball for a loss.

"It was so humid, my hands and the ball were so wet, it just squished right through, and I hardly felt it," Miller said afterwards, his face twisted in disgust. "I think the play would have gone."

Georgia halted the Tar Heels, took over, and drove for the winning touchdown amid the roar of 71,000 fans. Poulos broke off the touchdown run when the North Carolina defense got caught inside on a blitz.

"We missed some tackles on that play," noted North Carolina linebacker Jim Webster. "Poulos is good. He's not so powerful, but he's awfully quick."

At the end, the teams looked more alike than the brothers that coached them.

"They've got a helluva football team," conceded Bill Dooley, "but we've got a helluva football team, too. All we had to do to win was cash a couple of scoring opportunities."

The Carolina coach sighed. "I'm awfully proud of them. The effort was great."

Lewis Jolley runs against Georgia in the famous "Battle of the Brothers" 1971 Gator Bowl game.

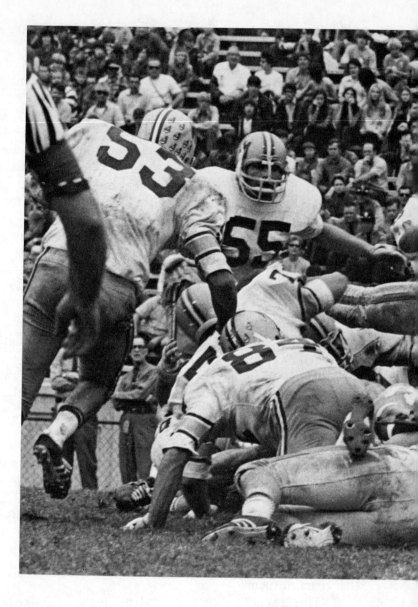

Tim Kirkpatrick dives for a touchdown against William and

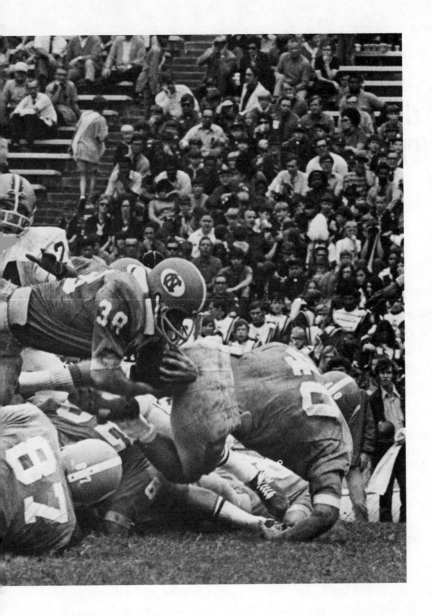

Mary in 1971. North Carolina won a squeaker, 36-35.

Adventures Of "The Cardiac Kids"

"You're a bunch of damn cardiac kids who don't know the meaning of the word quit. You've done a good job...a damn good job. You're free until we leave tomorrow. Take care of yourselves. And now, let's have one more cheer for the seniors."—Bill Dooley in the dressing room after North Carolina's 32-28 Sun Bowl victory over Texas Tech in 1972.

The Poseidon Adventure was a popular movie of the early 1970s about a luxury liner and its panic-stricken passengers going under in the middle of the ocean. It might easily have reflected the chill-a-minute 1972 North Carolina football season where almost every Saturday was a game of survival and a day of adventure. Significantly, just when the ship seemed to be going down, someone threw out a raft or a rope. In the case of the Tar Heels, it might have been a big pass by Nick Vidnovic, a key reception by Ted Leverenz, a timely fumble recovery by Jimmy DeRatt, or a dynamic run by Ike Oglesby.

Last-minute heroism was the name of the Tar Heel game in 1972, leading Coach Bill Dooley to christen his team "The Cardiac Kids." It was not a team for fans with weak hearts or nervous stomachs.

Against Maryland in the second game of the season, North Carolina endured 31-26 only after DeRatt's fumble recovery killed a Terrapin scoring threat with 35 seconds left. In the North Carolina State game, Bill Hite scored the winning touchdown with 58 seconds remaining after another DeRatt fumble

222

Ken Taylor hung onto his ball for a touchdown catch against North Carolina State in 1972, and the Tar Heels managed to hang onto a 34-33 victory.

recovery, and Carolina held on to win 34-33 despite a last-second Wolfpack score. Against Florida, Sammy Johnson bolted six yards for the go-ahead touchdown with just 1:41 left. Then the Gators drove to the North Carolina nine but could not score in four downs, and the Tar Heels hung on with their fingernails, 28-24. In the frenetic Sun Bowl game with Texas Tech, Vidnovic threw a 12-yard pass to Leverenz with just one minute left for the winning margin, and then Ronnie Robinson wrapped it up moments later when he tackled a Tech runner in the end zone for a safety.

When Dooley was presented with the flashy, golden Sun Bowl trophy in the North Carolina locker room, all he could do at first was sigh an audible, "Whew." Then he admitted, "My heart can't take too many more of these games." He was as worn-out as the phrase, "Cardiac Kids."

While squeezing the Sun Bowl hardware, Dooley also was holding a piece of Tar Heel history in his hands. The victory had been North Carolina's 11th in 12 games that season. No Tar Heel team before had won that many. And no Tar Heel team had provided as many thrills, either.

"We're 11-1," Dooley said in the jubilant locker room, "and I don't know how many times they've come back like that—State, Maryland, Florida, Tech—it seems like most of the games we've played. I know they're worn-out phrases, but this football team is just not going to be beat. They show more determination, courage, and confidence that they're going to win somehow, some way...that's the winning edge as far as this team is concerned."

Before the start of the season, Dooley showed no such confidence and in fact tended to lean more in the direction of pessimism. The 1971 season had been a trying one for Carolina's young head coach, even though the team had fashioned a glamorous 9-3 record. The year was disturbed by the shocking death of Bill Arnold, a player who had succumbed from a heat stroke suffered in practice. Arnold's death after three lingering weeks in September not only brought down widespread wrath on Dooley but did little to help his recruiting program. For years afterward Dooley was a marked man, and his practice sessions were usually policed by a swarm of doctors. The season ended on a sour note with the loss to Georgia in the Gator Bowl.

Eight of the 11 starters from the Gator Bowl team were graduated after the 1971 season, leaving Dooley with a rebuilding job and an inferiority complex. But this lasted only as long as the first game. Lou Angelo had a brilliant day in the secondary to help the Tar Heels defeat Richmond, 28-18. The defense became better in subsequent games and by the end of the year proved to be the keystone of the Carolina success.

"This team had better defense than any others Dooley coached at Carolina," points out Jack Williams, the one-time North Carolina sports information director. "In later years, Dooley had problems with his defense, but that 1972 team was hard-nosed. It had really good linebackers. Guys like Mike Mansfield, Ted Embrey, Mark DiCarlo, Steve Early, and Jimmy DeRatt."

Fullback Dick Oliver scores a touchdown against Texas Tech in the 1972 Sun Bowl. North Carolina's "Cardiac Kids" won this one 32-28.

The offensive line was another heroic feature of the team. Led by All-American guard Ron Rusnak, it featured some of the most outstanding blockers in Tar Heel history. With their help, Vidnovic was able to complete 69 passes for 1,096 yards and 10 touchdowns, Oglesby was able to run for 707 yards, and Jimmy Jerome was able to catch 22 passes for 326 yards, a 14.8-yard average, during the regular season.

Carolina's Sun Bowl victory seemed to synthesize the whole season. The Tar Heels were often criticized as being too conservative but managed to score in every manner conceivable in El Paso, Texas: two touchdowns by air, two by land, a one-point conversion, a two-point conversion, a field goal, and a safety. They also managed to wring every drop of drama out of the proceedings. Down by 12 points in the third quarter and trailing once again by four with less than three minutes to play, the Tar Heels never once seemed to doubt the inevitable outcome.

George Smith, who had helped Texas Tech rally from a 9-7 halftime deficit with touchdown runs of 65 and 46 yards that gave the Red Raiders a 21-9 lead in the third period, produced another crucial touchdown dash in the final quarter. This five-yard blast into the end zone provided Texas Tech with a 28-24 lead in the closing moments before Vidnovic rallied the Tar Heels on a crisp 37-yard drive. Vidnovic, who completed 14 passes for 215 yards that day, picked up a critical first down on a fourth and one situation and then completed two straight tosses to Leverenz. The last one was good for a touchdown and a 30-28 Carolina advantage.

To make it interesting, Ellis Alexander missed the extra point. Dooley said later in a swaggering but obvious joking tone: "We never kick 'em unless we need 'em." He must have known what was going to happen next. Seconds later, Ronnie Robinson and some of the other toughs on Carolina's defensive line grounded Texas Tech quarterback Joe Barnes in the end zone for a safety that put the Tar Heels ahead, 32-28, and gave them the ball with which to kill the clock.

The game not only had anything anyone could ask for but also something that nobody expected—a furor surrounding a penalty that cost Texas Tech a crucial touchdown. The controversy centered around a blocked North Carolina punt which was run back for an apparent Texas Tech touchdown in the second quarter. However, Tech was flagged for "unsportsmanlike conduct" when one of the Red Raiders' coaches went on the field during the runback by guard Donald Rives. The touchdown was called back, and Tech was assessed a 15-yard penalty. Texas Tech coach Jim Carlen had plenty to say about it to the officials during the game and more to say to reporters afterwards.

"It was an unusual call," he said, seething. "If it had been a clipping call, I wouldn't have questioned it. The officials said it was one of our coaches who stepped on the field during the play. I didn't see it. I spent a good deal of my time trying to avoid a cameraman wearing a red jacket. It is the first time I've had a chance to see a bunch of kids penalized for being enthusiastic."

Dooley entered the celebrative North Carolina dressing

room, and the Tar Heels cheered loudly. He held the Sun Bowl trophy aloft. More cheers. He called for a 21-shout salute for the seniors and was obliged in ear-shattering tones. The players quieted briefly when Jimmy Jerome knelt and led them in a 30-second prayer, then erupted again. Some cried with joy.

Later, Dooley used what was left of his voice to retrace the Tar Heels' winning steps.

"Tech kept taking away the middle," he told reporters. "They did a good job of disguising their defense, lining up in an Oklahoma 52 and shifting into a split six or 7-1. It became a chess game. Vidnovic read them all."

Dooley made the important decision on the crucial fourth and one play at the Tech 27, with Carolina driving for a score and only 1:54 left.

"We decided to go with the option," he said. "We figured Nick would fake the dive and draw them in. He could then option off tackle or pitch to the wingback. He went off tackle and got the first down.

"We punted away (fourth and eight at the Tech 41 with 4:47 left) because we felt we could get good field position on them. No, I didn't have any doubts we'd come back. (Phil) Lamm caught their punt with a guy standing right in front of him. His return (to the Tech 37) put us in good shape. (Dale) Lydecker did a good job. He punted well, especially into the wind. On the last one, he put them on their 10 and he also made the saving tackle on (Lawrence) Williams' punt return (53 yards to the North Carolina 29 late in the game)."

Dooley paused and thought, then jerked his finger toward the players.

"Determination won this one. Determination is the difference between this dressing room and the one across the hall. I said before and I say again, Texas Tech is a fine football team. We just wouldn't let them beat us."

The Best Defense
Is A Good Offense

On the day of the Army game, Bill Dooley was awake by 7:05, footballs spinning in his head. "We play today," was his first thought. He showered and shaved and had a cup of coffee with his wife, Chris, and sons, Billy and Jim. By 8:25 he was walking out the door. Voices called after him, "Good luck" and "Win it."

The North Carolina football coach arrived at his office in the Kenan Stadium fieldhouse in five minutes. There he flipped through a file on Army, a stack of about 100 pages. He closed the file and walked into another room where caretaker Nat Farrington had a pot of coffee brewing. Dooley, still wearing his overcoat, idly leafed through the sports pages of a newspaper. Assistants Pat Wilson and Bobby Collins came in, and the three of them talked about the upcoming game.

"Let's go," Dooley said finally, and the coaches walked over to Ehringhaus Dormitory, where the football team was quartered.

The quarter-mile walk took about 15 minutes, and Dooley and his assistants arrived at Ehringhaus at nine o'clock, walking through the back door, through the kitchen, and into the dining room, cheerily greeting employees. Dooley sat down at a table with his quarterbacks to go over the day's plays, and Collins, defensive coordinator, did the same with the linebackers at another table. Billy Paschall, a reserve quarterback, put aside a crossword puzzle. Chris Kupec, the Tar Heels' starting quarterback, appeared sleepy but never once took his eyes off Dooley.

The conversation was technical. Phrases like "54 rush strong" and "45 draw" predominated.

Soon, the remainder of the team drifted into the dining room and heard the coaches review Army's offense and defense. This brush-up course only took 15 minutes.

"Okay," Dooley said at the end of it, "turn in your scouting reports over here."

The players moved to another area of the dining room and wolfed down a huge breakfast of steak and scrambled eggs.

"I had a funny dream last night," Dean Bolton, dean of student affairs, told Dooley over breakfast. "I dreamed I was the Six Million Dollar Man and I was playing defense against Army. I got kicked out of the game after only four plays because I had already injured six players." Dooley laughed.

At 10 o'clock Dooley walked out of the dormitory and strolled back to his office along a sun-splashed walk. The morning air was crisp and clean.

"What a beautiful day," he sighed. "They made this one for football."

As he crossed a street a car stopped, and the driver motioned him over.

"Hey, coach, this is one I especially want you to win."

Dooley nodded.

In his office once again, Dooley sat down to study a list of football prospects visiting the campus for the weekend. He had to familiarize himself with their names and backgrounds so he could ask intelligent questions when he met them. His desk was cluttered with papers, a carton of cigarettes, a lamp with a Carolina helmet for a base, and a sign that said, "Tar Heel Spoken Here."

At 10:30 Dooley began the walk to Chase Cafeteria to meet with the prospects and their parents. As he left the fieldhouse, he was intercepted by assistant Al Groh, who had four youngsters with him. Dooley greeted them all by name and asked one about a leg injury.

In the parking lot, some youngsters were imitating North Carolina football players.

"Hey, Skip," Dooley said to a youngster wearing a loud red cap with a tassel, "where'd you get that hat?"

"It's my daddy's," the youngster retorted.

"I'm gonna steal that hat," said Dooley, his face breaking into a grin.

The youngster took off like a shot.

"You gonna have to catch me first."

Dooley cackled.

At Chase Cafeteria, Dooley was greeted by recruiter Jim Donnan.

"This is one of the finest-looking groups of prospects I've ever seen," he whispered to Dooley. Then he pointed to one broad-shouldered youngster. "He's a running back. Did the 100 in 9.5 last year. We sent a private plane for him."

Dooley drifted through the crowd, shaking hands with each of the young players, then retired to private conversation with some of them.

"I'm churning on the inside about the game and talking to prospects about something else," Dooley said on his way back to his office.

Dooley stopped for a moment and looked through the majestic pine trees to Kenan Stadium.

"There's no prettier place in the country to play football," he said.

A young boy called out to Dooley, "Is Ronnie Robinson gonna play today?" (Robinson, the team's fine middle guard, had a chipped bone in his ankle.)

"We're gonna see how he runs," Dooley replied. "You want to take his place?"

"Yeah," the boy said, "if I can get in free."

At 11:30 Dooley went downstairs to the coaches' dressing quarters and slipped into powder blue slacks, a white sport shirt, a navy blue sweater, and a light blue jacket. Then he was back in his office, galvanizing his thoughts for the pregame talk.

In the squad meeting room at 12:10, Dooley solemnly went over the game plan, retracing details with clinical ease. He talked about winning and sent his players out onto the field while a rock band sent shivering sounds through the public address system. The stadium filled quickly.

At 1:30 North Carolina took the opening kickoff and smacked in for a touchdown. Dooley was wildly exuberant on the sidelines, cheering, applauding, and slapping his players on the back as they rolled off the field. But the Cadets refused to retreat. They came back and drove for an equalizing touch-down. Dooley, smoking heavily now, flicked his cigarette to the ground in disgust. His defense had hurt him all season, and it looked no better this day.

The game yielded to the overwhelming power of the offenses—each team scoring almost at will. At the end, the North Carolina defense gave up 42 points to a team that had scored no more than 17 against anyone else. But Carolina's Kupec performed gallantly, throwing four touchdown passes and scoring once himself. And runners Mike Voight and James "Boom Boom" Betterson and guard Ken Huff had brilliant games. Carolina simply outscored Army 56-42.

At 4:30 Dooley talked to his players, then went up to a meeting room and told the press what they already knew.

"The offense did a great job," he said, cuddling a bottle of

Ken Huff (68) and Dick Oliver (33) prepare to bounce some North Carolina State players for "Boom Boom" Betterson (34).

soda, "but the defense is going to have to do better if we want to beat Duke next week."

Dooley did a radio interview at 5:30, then walked gingerly to the coaches' dressing room for a shower. After a long, luxurious time under hot water, Dooley came out to towel off.

"I'm tired," he said, "really tired. You get all tensed up during a game...."

The 1974 North Carolina team was the most efficient point-making machine ever at Chapel Hill. That was the good news. The bad news was the defense. The Tar Heels scored with the casual efficacy of Fielding Yost's legendary "Point A Minute" teams at Michigan, putting 364 points up there against their 12 opponents. But they played dead on defense, giving up a monumental 279 points, matching the school's all-time high record by another defenseless Dooley team in 1970.

It was, indeed, another typical Dooley edition in 1974—gaudy offense, lusterless defense. Only this had more of everything. Historically, Dooley had patterned his recruiting toward high-powered offensive players, particularly brutish blocking guards and tackles who could, in the words of coaches, "move 'em out." He had such a player in guard Ken Huff, who blew open holes and helped clear the trail for 1,000-yard runners Mike Voight and James Betterson and provided Chris Kupec with ample time to reach receivers Jimmy Jerome and Charlie Waddell with his long-distance passes. Huff was described as "an ideal guard" by one pro scout. "He has the ability to stay low when he fires into his man. And he has those extra things going for him like quick feet, good balance, and strength." Huff made almost everybody's All-American team in 1974.

"That was a dynamic offensive team," points out former sports publicist Jack Williams. "They could move the ball almost at will. Kupec gave them a dimension that Dooley's teams had not had before. He could throw the long pass, and he was so accurate. He was the best percentage passer in the nation that year. (Actually 69.3 percent, breaking the national season record once held by Tulsa's Jerry Rhome.) I don't think he had

Charlie Waddell makes a great touchdown catch, and North Carolina beats East Carolina 28-17 in 1973.

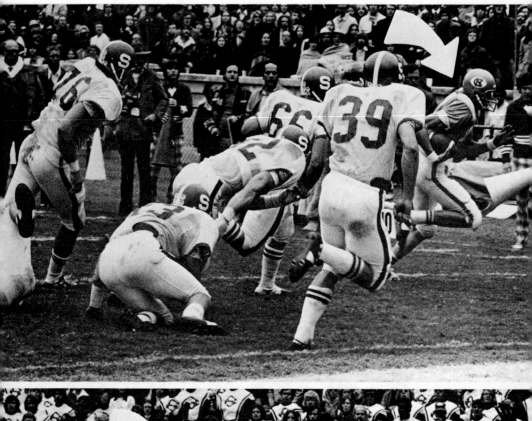

an interception until the next-to-last game of the year. He had thrown almost 100 passes without an interception. And he had great receivers in Jerome and Waddell. See, before this, Dooley had been very successful with the short passing game throwing the short pass to the halfback, fullback, or tailback coming out of the backfield. But as far as having a real long-range passing threat, he had never had one before. But their defense was something else. The only way they won a game, was by out-scoring people. Someone made the comment that this team probably had the greatest offense in the country and a defense that looked like the New York Metropolitan Life Insurance commercial on television."

The aforementioned 56-42 victory over Army was as typi-cal as the Tar Heels could be in 1974. They also scored 45 points against Pittsburgh and gave up 29, but there were times when the exquisite capabilities of the offense simply could not match the self-destructive qualities of the defense. The most forgettable of these games was a 54-32 rout at the hands of Clemson that had Dooley considering a more peaceful occupa-tion.

"The Tar Heel defenders were so bad that day," kidded a sportswriter, "that it took them six minutes to stop Clemson— after they left the field!"

Ridiculed but unbowed, the Tar Heels forged ahead through a bizarre 7-4 season and finally a Sun Bowl meeting with Mississippi State. Here, too, North Carolina surrendered yardage and points but, unlike earlier comic moments, should have beaten the Southeastern Conference team. With Mississippi State holding a 26-24 lead, the Tar Heels seemed intent on pulling it out with a late rally behind Kupec's cool hand. But with 1:23 left and a fourth and one on Mississippi State's 48 yard line, the Tar Heels shot Voight into a rampart of defend-ers. He was stopped a foot or two short of a first down, and Mississippi State ran out the clock. Later, it was revealed that a foulup at the line of scrimmage had cost the Tar Heels their last chance.

Two-part sequence shows North Carolina quarterback Chris Kupec starting and completing a three-yard touchdown run against North Carolina State in 1974. The Tar Heels prevailed, 33-14.

235

Williams recalls: "Mark Griffin, who was an offensive tackle, said when Carolina lined up for that big last play, the Mississippi State players all pointed right to him and said: 'They're coming right over here. They're going to run right here.' And everyone ganged up on that very spot. Kupec didn't call a time out because Dooley had told him, specifically, on this drive to save his time outs until we got into field-goal range. So he was afraid to call time out. He was torn between disobeying his coach and doing what he thought was the right thing."

Kupec had his instructions from the bench to run the Voight off-tackle play, a manuever that had helped the fine back grind out 1,033 yards during the season.

"I called the play," Dooley later confirmed, wishing he had not. "We had been moving the ball well on the ground, so we went with what was working. We would pass if I had to do it again, but I don't."

This singular play provided more ammunition for the headhunters. Dooley, who had long been under attack for his unimaginative offense despite producing high-scoring teams, once again was open season for critics. And they continued to fire at him through the 1975 season. Defense continued to be the bane of North Carolina and this time, there was little offense to counteract its ill effects. Betterson, who had rushed for 1,082 yards in 1974, was hurt and left the primary ball-carrying duties to Voight. Despite being a marked man, Voight performed admirably with another 1,000-yard season and became the Atlantic Coast Conference player of the year in 1975. The Tar Heels had little else than Voight, however, and slumped to 3-7-1. An observer explained the fall from power as a "lack of good senior leadership," tracing back to Dooley's bad recruiting year after the notorious Bill Arnold death in 1971.

"Dooley has always stressed the senior leadership as the key thing," notes sports information director Rick Brewer. "That's what was wrong with the team in 1975. We had five, maybe six seniors. Arnold's death really was the reason for a bad recruiting year in 1971. We couldn't get any good players. They didn't want to come here. A lot of schools used that against us in their recruiting pitches. So of the kids we recruited that year, James Betterson and (quarterback) Billy Paschall were the best. But the other kids...we just didn't get many qual-

North Carolina cheerleaders Jill Coleman and Peaches Hauser and a reticent Rameses.

ity players."

The melancholy of losing tormented the players, particularly Voight. "Losing is so disappointing," he said. "It's a big knot in your stomach that won't go away, an abscess eating away at your gut. Pretty soon, nothing else matters, nothing but winning."

By the spring of 1976, renewed hope blossomed with the season. Dooley does not let his players stay down long. There is a constant reminder of his philosophy at the entrance to the Tar Heel dressing room, a sign that spells "PRIDE." And if they miss seeing it, they cannot miss hearing about it from the man people call "The Alabama Trench Fighter." The winter of discontent had been spent on recruiting missions, speaking tours, and fund-raising efforts, and now the restless Dooley was prepared to climb mountains.

"Winning is great," he said, "and losing is awful. I've been on both sides, and I know. But win or lose, you can never really relax. It's always the same."

Appendix

UNIVERSITY OF NORTH CAROLINA RECORDS

SINGLE GAME—Team

MOST POINTS SCORED—65 vs. Virginia Medical, 1914; vs. Wake Forest, 1928.

MOST POINTS SCORED AGAINST—66 by Virginia, 1912.

LARGEST VICTORY MARGIN—65-0 vs. Virginia Medical, 1914; vs. Wake Forest, 1928.

MOST YARDS RUSHING—482 vs. The Citadel, 1939.

MOST YARDS PASSING—268 vs. Duke, 1966.

MOST TOTAL OFFENSE—675 yards vs. VMI, 1969.

MOST PASSES ATTEMPTED—50 vs. Duke, 1966.

MOST PASSES COMPLETED—22 vs. Duke, 1966.

MOST PASSES INTERCEPTED—6 vs. Maryland, 1963; vs. Duke, 1972.

MOST PASSES HAD INTERCEPTED—5 by Tennessee, 1949; by Notre Dame, 1956; by Duke, 1958.

MOST PUNTS—12 vs. Notre Dame, 1952.

FEWEST FUMBLES—0 vs. N. C. State, 1962; vs. N. C. State, 1963; vs. Miami, 1963; vs. Air Force, 1969; vs. Duke, 1971; vs. N. C. State, 1972.

FEWEST PENALTIES—0 vs. Wake Forest, 1969.

MOST FIRST DOWNS—36 vs. Pittsburgh, 1974.

SINGLE GAME—Individual

MOST POINTS SCORED—30 by Don McCauley vs. Duke, 1970.

MOST TOUCHDOWNS SCORED—5 by Don McCauley vs. Duke, 1970.

MOST TOUCHDOWN PASSES—4 by Chris Kupec vs. Army, 1974.

MOST TD RESPONSIBILITY (RUN AND PASS)—5 by Don McCauley vs. Duke, 1970 (5 rushing) and by Chris Kupec vs. Army, 1974 (4 passing and 1 rushing).

MOST TOUCHDOWN PASSES CAUGHT—3 by Charles Waddell vs. Clemson, 1974.

MOST FIELD GOALS—4 by Ken Craven vs. Clemson, 1971.

MOST YARDS RUSHING—279 by Don McCauley vs. Duke, 1970.

MOST YARDS PASSING—268 by Jeff Beaver vs. Duke, 1966.

MOST TOTAL OFFENSE—416 by Gayle Bomar vs. Wake Forest, 1968.

MOST OFFENSIVE PLAYS—61 by Gayle Bomar vs. Wake Forest, 1968.

MOST TIMES RUSHING—47 by Don McCauley vs. Duke, 1970.

MOST PASSES ATTEMPTED—50 by Jeff Beaver vs. Duke, 1966.

MOST PASSES COMPLETED—22 by Jeff Beaver vs. Duke, 1966.

MOST PASSES CAUGHT—16 by Charlie Carr vs. Air Force, 1966.

MOST PUNTS—12 by Bud Wallace vs. Notre Dame, 1952.

LONGEST RUN FROM SCRIMMAGE—95 yards by S. A. Ashe vs. Trinity, 1891.

LONGEST PASS PLAY—78 yards, Phil Jackson to Yank Spaulding vs. Maryland, 1929.

LONGEST PUNT—85 yards by Tom Burnette vs. N.Y.U., 1937.

LONGEST KICKOFF RETURN—97 yards by Johnny Pecora vs. Richmond, 1941; by Don McCauley vs. Wake Forest, 1969.

LONGEST PUNT RETURN—96 yards by Johnny Branch vs. Maryland, 1930.

LONGEST RUN AFTER INTERCEPTED PASS—100 yards by Bob Gantt vs. Wm. & Mary, 1950.

LONGEST FIELD GOAL—53 yards by Ellis Alexander vs. N. C. State, 1973.

MOST PATs—8 by Ken Craven vs. VMI, 1970 and vs. Duke, 1970; by Ellis Alexander vs. Army, 1974.

MOST INTERCEPTIONS—2 by many players.

MOST YARDS GAINED IN INTERCEPTION RETURNS—100 by Bob Gantt vs. William and Mary, 1950.

SEASON—Team

UNDEFEATED RECORDS—1898 (9-0-0).

MOST WINS—11 in 1972.

MOST DEFEATS—8 in 1951, 1966, 1967.

MOST TIES—3 in 1900, in 1908, in 1931.

MOST POINTS SCORED—359 in 1914 (11 games).

MOST POINTS SCORED BY OPPONENTS—273 in 1968.

LEAST POINTS SCORED—4 in 1888 (2 games), in 1891 (1 game).

LEAST POINTS SCORED BY OPPONENTS—8 in 1898 (9 games).

MOST YARDS RUSHING—3,137 in 1970.

MOST YARDS PASSING—1,766 in 1974.

MOST TOTAL OFFENSE—4,691 in 1974.

MOST PASSES ATTEMPTED—295 in 1966.

MOST FIRST DOWNS—253 in 1974.

MOST PASSES COMPLETED—159 in 1966.

BEST PASSING PERCENTAGE—67.8 in 1974 (122-180).

MOST PASSES INTERCEPTED—21 in 1972.

SEASON—Individual

MOST POINTS SCORED—126 by Don McCauley, 1970.

MOST TOUCHDOWNS SCORED—21 by Don McCauley, 1970.

MOST PAT MADE—41 of 42 by Ken Craven, 1970.

MOST TDs RESPONSIBILITY (RUN AND PASS)—23 by Charlie Justice, 1948 (11 rushing, 12 passing).

MOST TOUCHDOWN PASSES CAUGHT—7 by Art Weiner, 1949.

MOST YARDS RUSHING—1,720 by Don McCauley, 1970.

MOST YARDS PASSING—1,474 by Chris Kupec, 1974.

MOST TOTAL OFFENSE—1,761 by Charlie Justice, 1948.

MOST TIMES RUSHING—324 by Don McCauley, 1970.

MOST PASSES ATTEMPTED—217 by Danny Talbott, 1965.

MOST PASSES COMPLETED—104 by Chris Kupec, 1974.

MOST PASSES CAUGHT—52 by Art Weiner, 1949 and by Charlie Carr, 1966.

MOST YARDS ON PASS RECEPTIONS—837 by Jimmy Jerome, 1974.

MOST TOUCHDOWN PASSES—12 by Charlie Justice, 1948 and by Chris Kupec, 1974.

BEST PASSING PERCENTAGE—69.3 by Chris Kupec, 1974 (104 of 150).

MOST PUNTS—70 by Charlie Justice, 1948.

BEST PUNTING AVERAGE—46.6 (47 punts) by Harry Dunkle, 1939.

MOST FIELD GOALS—11 by Ken Craven, 1971.

MOST PASSES INTERCEPTED—8 by Lou Angelo, 1972.

MOST YARDS GAINED ON INTERCEPTION RETURNS—125 by Bill Maceyko, 1948 (3 interceptions).

CAREER—Team

MOST CONSECUTIVE GAMES WITHOUT DEFEAT—17 (1947-1948)

LONGEST WINNING STREAK—13 (twice—1897-1899 and 1947-1948).

LONGEST LOSING STREAK—12 (1966-1967).

MOST CONSECUTIVE GAMES UNSCORED ON—7 (twice—1901-1902 and 1903-1904).

MOST CONSECUTIVE GAMES WITHOUT SCORING—5 (1906-1907).

MOST CONSECUTIVE GAMES WITHOUT BEING SHUTOUT—42 (1947-1950).

CAREER—Individual

MOST POINTS SCORED—234 by Charlie Justice. 1946-47-48-49.

MOST TOUCHDOWNS SCORED—39 by Charlie Justice, 1946-47-48-49.

MOST PAT MADE—97 of 119 by Bob Cox, 1945-46-47-48.

MOST TDs RESPONSIBILITY (PASS AND RUN)—65 by Charlie Justice, 1946-47-48-49.

MOST TOUCHDOWN PASSES—25 by Charlie Justice, 1946-47-48-49.

MOST TOUCHDOWN PASSES CAUGHT—18 by Art Weiner, 1946-47-48-49.

MOST YARDS RUSHING—3,172 by Don McCauley, 1968-69-70.

MOST YARDS PASSING—2,666 by Jack Cummings, 1957-58-59.

MOST TOTAL OFFENSE—4,883 by Charlie Justice, 1946-47-48-49.

MOST TIMES RUSHING—603 by Don McCauley, 1968-69-70.

HIGHEST RUSHING AVERAGE—6.9 by Ed Sutton, 1954-55-56 (1,334 yards on 193 attempts).

MOST PASSES ATTEMPTED—385 by Danny Talbott, 1964-65-66.

MOST PASSES COMPLETED—196 by Danny Talbott, 1964-65-66.

MOST PASSES CAUGHT—105 by Art Weiner, 1946-47-48-49.

MOST YARDS ON PASS CATCHES—1,720 by Art Weiner, 1946-47-48-49.

BEST PASSING PERCENTAGE (at least 100 completions)—65.7 by Chris Kupec, 1972-73-74 (117-178).

MOST PASSES INTERCEPTED—16 by Lou Angelo, 1970-71-72.

MOST PUNTS—251 by Charlie Justice, 1946-47-48-49.

BEST PUNTING AVERAGE—42.5 by Charlie Justice, 1946-47-48-49.

MOST FIELD GOALS—21 by Don Hartig, 1967-68-69.

ATLANTIC COAST CONFERENCE RECORDS

SINGLE GAME—Individual

MOST POINTS SCORED—30 by Don McCauley vs. Duke, 1970.

MOST TOUCHDOWNS SCORED—5 by Don McCauley vs. Duke, 1970.

MOST FIELD GOALS SCORED—4 by Ken Craven vs. Clemson, 1971.

MOST PATs SCORED—8 by Ken Craven vs. VMI, 1970 and vs. Duke, 1970; by Ellis Alexander vs. Army, 1974.

MOST TD RESPONSIBILITY—5 by Don McCauley vs. Duke, 1970 (5 rushing) and by Chris Kupec vs. Army, 1974 (4 passing and 1 rushing).

MOST NET YARDS GAINED (RUSHING AND PASSING)—416 by Gayle Bomar vs. Wake Forest, 1968.

MOST YARDS GAINED RUSHING (NET)—279 by Don McCauley vs. Duke, 1970.

MOST RUSHES—47 by Don McCauley vs. Duke, 1970.

MOST PASSES ATTEMPTED—50 by Jeff Beaver vs. Duke, 1966.

MOST PASSES CAUGHT—16 by Charlie Carr vs. Air Force, 1966.

BEST PUNTING AVERAGE—54.7 yards by Dick Lackey vs. South Carolina, 1953 (four punts for 219 yards).

MOST KICKOFFS RETURNED—7 by Don McCauley vs. N. C. State, 1967.

SINGLE GAME—Team

MOST TOTAL PLAYS—102 vs. Virginia, 1959.

MOST SAFETIES—1, shared by other teams.

FEWEST FUMBLES—0, shared with other teams.

MOST PASSES ATTEMPTED—50 vs. Duke, 1966.

MOST PATs SCORED—8 vs. VMI, 1970; vs. Duke, 1970; vs. Army, 1974.

MOST FIELD GOALS—4 vs. Clemson, 1971.

FEWEST PENALTIES—0, shared with other teams.

SEASON—Individual

MOST POINTS SCORED—126 by Don McCauley, 1970.

MOST TOUCHDOWNS SCORED—21 by Don McCauley, 1970.

MOST PAT SCORED—41 by Ken Craven, 1970.

MOST NET YARDS RUSHING—1,720 by Don McCauley, 1970.

BEST AVERAGE NET YARDS RUSHING PER GAME—156.4 by Don McCauley, 1970 (1,720 yards in 11 games).

MOST RUSHES—324 by Don McCauley, 1970.

BEST PASSING PERCENTAGE—693 by Chris Kupec, 1974 (104 for 150).

BEST PASSING PERCENTAGE—.678, 1974 (122 for 180).

CAREER—Individual

MOST POINTS SCORED—210 by Don McCauley, 1968-69-70.

MOST TOUCHDOWNS SCORED—35 by Don McCauley, 1968-69-70.

MOST YARDS GAINED RUSHING—3,172 by Don McCauley, 1968-69-70.

MOST RUSHES—603 by Don McCauley, 1968-69-70.

MOST PATs SCORED—94 by Ellis Alexander, 1972-73-74.

MOST TOUCHDOWN CATCHES—12 by Jimmy Jerome, 1972-73-74.

CAROLINA'S ALL-TIME STATISTICAL LEADERS

ALL-TIME LEADING PASSERS
(ranked on completions)

PLAYER, LAST YEAR PLAYED	CMP	ATT	INT	PCT	YDS	TDS
Danny Talbott, 1966	196	385	25	.509	2,018	7
Junior Edge, 1963	193	357	23	.541	2,388	12
Bill Paschall, 1975	176	326	18	.540	2,324	18
Jack Cummings, 1959	170	354	24	.480	2,668	19
Gayle Bomar, 1968	166	347	14	.478	2,102	12
Charlie Justice, 1949	162	321	32	.505	2,249	25
Ray Farris, 1961	158	356	29	.444	2,076	6
Paul Miller, 1971	139	256	13	.543	1,977	17
Gary Black, 1964	132	273	16	.484	1,540	11
Nick Vidnovic, 1973	119	237	11	.502	1,692	17
Chris Kupec, 1974	117	178	5	.657	1,608	13

ALL-TIME TOTAL OFFENSE LEADERS

PLAYER, LAST YEAR PLAYED	TOTAL YARDS
Charlie Justice, 1949	4,883
Don McCauley, 1970	3,182
Gayle Bomar, 1968	3,126
Jack Cummings, 1959	2,777
Junior Edge, 1963	2,699
Danny Talbott, 1966	2,661
Ray Farris, 1961	2,574
Mike Voight (active)	2,564
Bill Paschall, 1975	2,537
Paul Miller, 1971	2,384
Gary Black, 1964	2,061
Ken Willard, 1964	1,949

ALL-TIME LEADING RUSHERS

PLAYER, LAST YEAR PLAYED	YARDS
Don McCauley, 1970	3,172
Charlie Justice, 1949	2,634
Mike Voight (active)	2,564
Ken Willard, 1964	1,949
James Betterson (1975)	1,903
Ike Oglesby, 1972	1,773
Sammy Johnson, 1973	1,490
Ed Sutton, 1956	1,334
Hosea Rodgers, 1948	1,198
Lewis Jolley, 1971	1,137

ALL-TIME LEADING SCORERS

PLAYER, LAST YEAR PLAYED	POINTS
Charlie Justice, 1949	234
Don McCauley, 1970	210
Ellis Alexander, 1974	148
Mike Voight (active)	144
Bob Cox, 1948	133
Ken Craven, 1971	125
Ken Willard, 1964	122
Lewis Jolley, 1971	118
Art Weiner, 1949	114
Don Hartig, 1969	105
Ken Keller, 1955	103

ALL-TIME LEADING PASS RECEIVERS

PLAYER, LAST YEAR PLAYED	CATCHES	YARDS	TDS
Art Weiner, 1949	105	1,720	18
Bob Lacey, 1963	101	1,362	6
Charlie Carr, 1967	94	887	4
Jimmy Jerome, 1974	93	1,472	12
Bob Hume, 1966	62	594	1
Tony Blanchard, 1970	61	896	9
Peter Davis, 1968	53	648	4
Lewis Jolley, 1971	52	868	10
Don McCauley, 1970	52	786	5
Ron Jackson, 1964	52	752	8
John Atherton, 1965	52	698	2

TOP ALL-TIME SINGLE GAME PERFORMANCES

MOST YARDS RUSHING

279 by Don McCauley vs. Duke, 1970.
228 by Mike Voight vs. Clemson, 1975.
209 by Mike Voight vs. East Carolina, 1975.

MOST RUSHES

47 by Don McCauley vs. Duke, 1970.
42 by Mike Voight vs. East Carolina, 1975.
39 by Mike Voight vs. N. C. State, 1975.
39 by Ike Oglesby vs. Illinois, 1971.

MOST YARDS PASSING

268 by Jeff Beaver vs. Duke, 1966.
254 by Bill Paschall vs. Virginia, 1973.
244 by Junior Edge vs. Michigan State, 1962.

MOST PASSES ATTEMPTED

50 by Jeff Beaver vs. Duke, 1966.
32 by Junior Edge vs. Duke, 1963.
31 by Bill Paschall vs. Virginia, 1973

MOST PASSES COMPLETED

22 by Jeff Beaver vs. Duke, 1966.
19 by Bill Paschall vs. Virginia, 1973.
19 by Junior Edge vs. Michigan State, 1962.

MOST PASSES CAUGHT

16 by Charlie Carr vs. Air Force, 1966.
10 by Bob Lacey vs. South Carolina, 1963.
10 by Bob Lacey vs. Michigan State, 1962.

MOST YARDS ON PASS RECEPTIONS

158 by Bob Lacey vs. Michigan State, 1962.
149 by Jimmy Jerome vs. Wake Forest, 1974.
124 by Charlie Carr vs. Air Force, 1966.

MOST YARDS IN TOTAL OFFENSE

416 by Gayle Bomar vs. Wake Forest, 1968.
318 by Danny Talbott vs. Georgia, 1965.
304 by Charlie Justice vs. Georgia, 1948.

LONGEST FIELD GOAL

53 yards by Ellis Alexander vs. N. C. State, 1973.
48 yards by Don Hartig vs. Wake Forest, 1969.
47 yards by Don Hartig vs. Florida, 1968.

ALL-AMERICANS

(Only first teams listed)

GEORGE BARCLAY, Guard

Associated Press (1934)
All-America Board (1934)
Williamson (1934)

ANDY BERSHAK, End

Grantland Rice, Collier's (1937)
NEA (1937)
Williamson (1937)

STEVE MARONIC, Tackle

Central Press (1938)
Liberty (1938)

PAUL SEVERIN, End

Associated Press (1939)
Associated Press (1940)
United Press (1940)
Williamson (1940)

CHARLIE JUSTICE, Halfback

Helm's Hall of Fame
Collier's (1948, 1949)
Associated Press (1948, 1949)
United Press (1948)
All-America Board (1948)
Sport Magazine (1948, 1949)
Williamson (1948, 1949)
Paramount (1948, 1949)
Bill Stern (1948, 1949)
Int. News Service (1948)

ART WEINER, End

Grantland Rice, Look (1948)
N. Y. Daily News (1949)
New York Sun (1949)

KEN POWELL, End

Williamson (1949)
NEA (1949)

IRVIN HOLDASH, Center

NEA (1950)
Williamson (1950)

AL GOLDSTEIN, End

Look, Football Writers (1958)
NEA (1958)

BOB LACEY, End

Look, Football Writers (1963)
Associated Press (1963)

DON McCAULEY, Halfback

Associated Press (1970)
Football Writers of America (1970)
Coaches Association of America (1970)
Walter Camp (1970)
The Football News (1970)

RON RUSNAK, Guard

Associated Press (1972)
United Press (1972)
Football Coaches (1972)
Football Writers (1972)

KEN HUFF, Guard

Associated Press (1974)
Football Coaches (1974)
Time Magazine (1974)
Pop Warner (1974)
Walter Camp (1974)
The Sporting News (1974)
NEA (1974)

CHARLES WADDELL, End

The Sporting News (1974)

ALL-ACC

1953—Second Team: Dick Lackey, fullback.

1954—First Team: Will Frye, end; Second Team: Jack Maultsby, tackle.

1956—First Team: Jimmy Jones, center; Ed Sutton, halfback.

1957—First Team: Buddy Payne, end; Phil Blazer, tackle.

1958—First Team: Al Goldstein, end; Phil Blazer, tackle; Ronnie Koes, center; Jack Cummings, quarterback; Second Team: Wade Smith, halfback; Fred Swearingen, guard.

1959—First Team: Rip Hawkins, center; Second Team: Al Goldstein, end; Jack Cummings, quarterback; Wade Smith, halfback.

1960—First Team: Rip Hawkins, center; Second Team: Bob Elliott, fullback; John Schroeder, end.

1961—First Team: Jim LeCompte, guard; Bob Elliott, fullback; Second Team: Joe Craver, Center; Ray Farris, quarterback.

1962—First Team: Bob Lacey, end; Joe Craver, center; Second Team: Ken Willard, fullback.

1963—First Team: Bob Lacey, end; Ken Willard, halfback; Chris Hanburger, center; Junior Edge, quarterback; Second Team; Jerry Cabe, guard.

1964—First Team: Ken Willard, halfback; Chris Hanburger, center; Second Team: Richy Zarro, guard.

1965—First Team: Danny Talbott, quarterback; Joe Frantangelo, guard; Ed Stringer, center. Player of the Year—Danny Talbott.

1967—First Team: Jack Davenport, defensive back.

1969—First Team: Don McCauley, halfback; Bill Richardson, linebacker; Judge Mattocks, end; Ed Chalupka, guard. Player of the Year—Don McCauley.

1970—First Team: Don McCauley, halfback; Paul Hoolahan, offensive tackle; Flip Ray, defensive tackle. Player of the Year—Don McCauley.

1971—First Team: Lewis Jolley, halfback; Paul Miller, quarterback; Ron Rusnak, offensive guard; Bob Thornton, center; Jerry Sain, offensive tackle; Bill Brafford, defensive end; Bud Grissom, defensive tackle; John Bunting, linebacker; Ken Craven, kicking specialist. Coach of the Year—Bill Dooley.

1972—First Team: Ron Rusnak, offensive guard; Jerry Sain, offensive tackle; Mike Mansfield, linebacker; Jimmy DeRatt, linebacker; Gene Brown, defensive end; Eric Hyman, defensive tackle; Lou Angelo, defensive back.

248

1973—First Team: Robert Pratt, offensive tackle; Charles Waddell, tight end; Jimmy DeRatt, linebacker; Sammy Johnson, halfback.

1974—First Team: Ken Huff, offensive guard; Chris Kupec, quarterback; Jimmy Jerome, wide receiver; James Betterson, halfback; Ronnie Robinson, defensive lineman.

1975—First Team; Mike Voight, halfback. Player of the Year—Mike Voight.

CAROLINA COACHING RECORDS

Name	Years	No. Years	W	L	T
Hector Cowan	1889 (Spring)	1	1	1	0
V. K. Irvine	1894	1	6	3	0
T. C. Trenchard	1895, 1913-1915	4	26	9	2
Gordon Johnston	1896	1	3	4	1
W. A. Reynolds	1897-1900	4	27	7	4
Charles Jenkins	1901	1	7	2	0
H. B. Olcott	1902-1903	2	11	4	3
R. R. Brown	1904	1	5	2	2
William Warner	1905	1	4	3	1
W. S. Keinholz	1906	1	1	4	2
Otis Lamson	1907	1	4	4	1
Edward Green	1908	1	3	3	3
A. E. Brides	1909-1910	2	8	8	0
Branch Bocock	1911	1	6	1	1
W. C. Martin	1912	1	3	4	1
Thomas Campbell	1916, 1919	2	9	7	1
M. E. Fuller	1920	1	2	6	0
Bob Fetzer Bill Fetzer	1921-1925	5	30	12	4
Chuck Collins	1926-1933	8	38	31	9
Carl Snavely	1934-35, 1945-1952	10	59	35	5
Ray Wolf	1936-1941	6	38	17	3
Jim Tatum	1942, 1956-1958	4	19	17	3
Tom Young	1943	1	6	3	0
Gene McEver	1944	1	1	7	1
George Barclay	1953-1955	3	11	18	1
Jim Hickey	1959-1966	8	36	45	0
Bill Dooley	1967-	9	52	47	1

RECORDS AGAINST ALL OPPONENTS

Opponent	Games	UNC W	UNC L	Tied	UNC Pts.	Opp. Pts.
Air Force	5	1	4	0	82	77
Appalachian	1	1	0	0	56	6
Arizona State	1	0	1	0	26	48
Army	2	1	1	0	56	88
Auburn	3	3	0	0	103	0
Bingham's School	4	4	0	0	123	0
Camp Lee	1	1	0	0	6	0
Charlotte YMCA	1	0	1	0	0	8
Cherry Point	2	2	0	0	40	28
Citadel	2	2	0	0	64	7
CLEMSON	24	10	14	0	427	430
Davidson	39	31	4	4	585	97
DUKE	62	29	29	4	812	789
Duquesne	1	1	0	0	13	6
EAST CAROLINA	3	2	1	0	87	84
Florida	9	6	2	1	159	141
Fordham	5	0	3	2	14	55
Furman	2	2	0	0	56	0
Georgetown	13	4	7	2	94	167
Georgia	30	12	16	2	457	466
Georgia Tech	15	3	10	2	173	248
Greensboro A.A.	3	3	0	0	65	0
Guilford	9	9	0	0	241	4
Hampton A.C.	1	0	1	0	0	18
Harvard	2	0	2	0	0	41
Horner's School	1	1	0	0	46	0
Illinois	1	1	0	0	27	0
Kentucky	6	4	2	0	78	66
Kentucky State	1	0	1	0	0	11
Lafayette	1	0	1	0	6	28
Lehigh	2	0	2	0	0	58
Lenoir Rhyne	1	1	0	0	42	7
L.S.U.	3	1	2	0	41	50
MARYLAND	40	22	17	1	746	520
Mercer	1	1	0	0	3	0
Miami	7	4	3	0	121	89
Michigan	2	1	1	0	45	38
Michigan State	3	1	2	0	27	84
Mississippi State	1	0	1	0	24	26
Missouri	1	0	1	0	14	27
Morganton D.D.I.	1	1	0	0	38	0
NATTC	1	1	0	0	23	0
Navy	5	2	3	0	34	111
N. C. STATE	65	43	16	6	1,150	527
Norfolk A. C.	1	1	0	0	41	0
NOTRE DAME	16	1	15	0	147	402
New York University	4	4	0	0	54	26

Opponent	Games	UNC W	UNC L	Tied	UNC Pts.	Opp. Pts.
Oak Ridge	6	6	0	0	167	0
OHIO STATE	4	1	3	0	42	105
Ohio University	1	1	0	0	42	7
Oklahoma	3	0	3	0	12	63
Penn	6	2	4	0	39	126
Penn State	1	1	0	0	19	0
Pittsburgh	1	1	0	0	45	29
Princeton	2	0	2	0	0	59
Rice	1	0	1	0	13	27
Richmond	12	11	1	0	303	55
Riverside	1	1	0	0	40	0
Rutgers	2	0	2	0	0	24
Sewanee	5	2	1	2	48	15
South Carolina	45	29	12	4	713	389
Southern California	1	1	0	0	8	7
Texas	4	1	3	0	61	114
T.C.U.	1	1	0	0	21	14
Texas Tech	1	1	0	0	32	28
Tennessee	31	10	20	1	345	556
TULANE	14	3	9	2	181	289
U.S.S. Franklin	1	1	0	0	12	0
Vanderbilt	12	7	5	0	177	169
VIRGINIA	80	44	33	3	1,397	1,137
Virginia Medical	2	2	0	0	80	0
VMI	21	14	6	1	412	169
VPI	25	8	11	6	231	260
WAKE FOREST	72	46	24	2	1,300	513
Washington & Lee	10	5	3	2	109	50
WILLIAM & MARY	11	9	0	2	224	111
Yale	7	0	7	0	13	200
TOTALS	787	424	314	49	12,471	9,418

1888

UNC	4	Wake Forest 6
UNC	0	Trinity 16

1889

UNC	33	Wake Forest 0
UNC	17	Trinity 25
UNC	8	Wake Forest 18
UNC	1	Trinity 0

1891

UNC	4	Trinity 6
UNC	0	Wake Forest 1

1892

UNC	40	Richmond 0
UNC	18	Virginia 30
UNC	24	Trinity 0
UNC	64	Auburn 0
UNC	24	Vanderbilt 0
UNC	26	Virginia 0

1893

UNC	44	Washington & Lee 0
UNC	4	VMI 10
UNC	4	Trinity 6
UNC	60	Tennessee 0
UNC	40	Wake Forest 0
UNC	0	Lehigh 34
UNC	0	Virginia 16

1894

UNC	44	N. C. A&M 0
UNC	16	N. C. A&M 0
UNC	28	Trinity 0
UNC	36	Sewanee 4
UNC	6	Lehigh 24
UNC	0	Rutgers 5
UNC	20	Georgetown 4
UNC	28	Richmond 0
UNC	0	Virginia 34

1895

UNC	36	N. C. A&M 0
UNC	34	Richmond 0
UNC	6	Georgia 0
UNC	12	Vanderbilt 0
UNC	0	Sewanee 0
UNC	10	Georgia 6

UNC	16	Wash. & Lee 0
UNC	32	VPI 5
UNC	0	Virginia 6

1896

UNC	26	Guilford 4
UNC	34	Guilford 0
UNC	0	VPI 0
UNC	16	Georgia 24
UNC	0	Charlotte AC 8
UNC	0	Hampton 18
UNC	30	Greensboro AC 0
UNC	0	Virginia 46

1897

UNC	40	N. C. A&M 0
UNC	16	Guilford 0
UNC	24	Greensboro AA 0
UNC	28	Clemson 0
UNC	0	VPI 4
UNC	12	Sewanee 6
UNC	0	Vanderbilt 31
UNC	16	Tennessee 0
UNC	14	Bingham's Sch. 0
UNC	0	Virginia 12

1898

UNC	18	Guilford 0
UNC	34	N. C. A&M 0
UNC	11	Greensboro AA 0
UNC	11	Oak Ridge 0
UNC	28	VPI 6
UNC	11	Davidson 0
UNC	53	Georgia 0
UNC	29	Auburn 0
UNC	6	Virginia 2

1899

UNC	34	N. C. A&M 0
UNC	16	Oak Ridge 0
UNC	45	Guilford 0
UNC	10	Davidson 0
UNC	46	Horner's Sch. 0
UNC	11	N. C. A&M 11
UNC	6	Maryland 0
UNC	0	Navy 12
UNC	0	Princeton 30
UNC	5	Georgia 0
UNC	0	Sewanee 5

1900

UNC	38	DDI 0
UNC	0	VPI 0

UNC 22   Tennessee 5
UNC 48   Vanderbilt 0
UNC 0   Sewanee.............. 0
UNC 55   Georgia 0
UNC 0   Virginia 17
UNC 0   Georgetown 0

1901

UNC 28   Oak Ridge 0
UNC 39   N. C. A&M............. 0
UNC 42   Guilford 0
UNC 6   Davidson 0
UNC 27   Georgia............... 0
UNC 10   Auburn 0
UNC 30   N. C. A&M............. 0
UNC 6   Virginia 23
UNC 10   Clemson 22

1902

UNC 16   Guilford 0
UNC 35   Oak Ridge 0
UNC 10   Furman............... 0
UNC 27   Davidson 0
UNC 0   VPI 0
UNC 17   VMI 10
UNC 0   N.C. A&M 0
UNC 5   Georgetown 12
UNC 12   Virginia 12

1903

UNC 15   Guilford 0
UNC 45   Oak Ridge 0
UNC 17   U. of S. C. 0
UNC 28   VMI 6
UNC 0   Georgetown 33
UNC 5   Kentucky 6
UNC 0   VPI 21
UNC 11   Clemson 6
UNC 16   Virginia 0

1904

UNC 29   Guilford 0
UNC 0   Davidson 0
UNC 50   Bingham 0
UNC 27   U. of S. C. 0
UNC 41   Norfolk A.C. 0
UNC 6   VPI 0
UNC 0   Georgetown 16
UNC 6   N. C. A&M............. 6
UNC 11   Virginia 12

1905

UNC 6   Davidson 0

UNC 6   Pennsylvania 17
UNC 0   Naval Academy 38
UNC 6   VPI 35
UNC 36   Georgetown 0
UNC 0   N.C. A&M 0
UNC 17   VMI 0
UNC 17   Virginia 0

1906

UNC 0   Davidson 0
UNC 0   Pennsylvania 11
UNC 12   Richmond Col. 0
UNC 6   Lafayette 28
UNC 0   VPI 0
UNC 0   Georgetown 4
UNC 0   Naval Academy 40

1907

UNC 0   Pennsylvania 37
UNC 0   W&L 0
UNC 38   Oak Ridge 0
UNC 14   William & Mary 0
UNC 4   Virginia 9
UNC 6   Clemson 15
UNC 12   Georgetown 5
UNC 13   Richmond Col. 11
UNC 6   VPI 20

1908

UNC 17   Wake Forest............ 0
UNC 0   Tennessee 12
UNC 0   W&L................. 0
UNC 0   Davidson 0
UNC 6   Georgetown 6
UNC 17   Richmond Col. 12
UNC 0   VPI 10
UNC 22   U. of S. C. 0
UNC 0   Virginia 31

1909

UNC 18   Wake Forest............ 0
UNC 3   Tennessee 0
UNC 0   VMI 3
UNC 5   Georgetown 0
UNC 22   Richmond Col. 0
UNC 0   VPI 15
UNC 6   W&L.................. 0
**Virginia vs. UNC (cancelled,
account of death of player)**

1910

UNC 6   VMI 0

UNC 0   Kentucky 11
UNC 0   Davidson 6
UNC 37   Wake Forest 0
UNC 0   Georgetown 12
UNC 0   VPI 20
UNC 0   W&L 5
UNC 27   U. of S.C. 6
UNC 0   Virginia 7

1911

UNC 12   Wake Forest 3
UNC 12   Bingham 0
UNC 5   Davidson 0
UNC 12   USS Franklin 0
UNC 0   VPI 0
UNC 21   U. of S. C. 0
UNC 4   W&L 0
UNC 0   Virginia 28

1912

UNC 13   Davidson 0
UNC 9   Wake Forest 2
UNC 47   Bingham 0
UNC 0   VPI 26
UNC 10   Georgetown 37
UNC 6   U. of S. C. 6
UNC 0   W&L 31
UNC 0   Virginia 66

1913

UNC 7   Wake Forest 0
UNC 15   Va. Med. Col 0
UNC 7   Davidson 0
UNC 13   U. of S. C. 3
UNC 7   VPI 14
UNC 6   Georgia 19
UNC 0   W&L 14
UNC 29   Wake Forest 0
UNC 7   Virginia 26

1914

UNC 41   Richmond 0
UNC 65   Va. Medical 0
UNC 53   Wake Forest 0
UNC 48   South Carolina 0
UNC 41   Georgia 6
UNC 40   Riverside 0
UNC 10   Vanderbilt 9
UNC 16   Davidson 3
UNC 30   VMI 7
UNC 12   Wake Forest 7
UNC 3   Virginia 20

1915

UNC 14   Citadel 7
UNC 35   Wake Forest 0
UNC 0   Georgetown 38
UNC 3   VMI 3
UNC 3   Georgia Tech 23
UNC 9   Clemson 7
UNC 41   Davidson 6
UNC 0   Virginia 14

1916

UNC 20   Wake Forest 0
UNC 0   Princeton 29
UNC 0   Harvard 21
UNC 6   Georgia Tech 10
UNC 38   VMI 13
UNC 7   VPI 14
UNC 10   Davidson 6
UNC 46   Furman 0
UNC 7   Virginia 0

1917

(No football team this year on account of
the War)

1918

(No football team this year on account of
the War)

1919

UNC 9   Rutgers 19
UNC 7   Yale 34
UNC 6   Wake Forest 0
UNC 13   N. C. State 12
UNC 0   Tennessee 0
UNC 7   VMI 29
UNC 10   Davidson 0
UNC 6   Virginia 0

1920

UNC 6   Wake Forest 0
UNC 0   Yale 21
UNC 7   South Carolina 0
UNC 3   N. C. State 13
UNC 0   Maryland 13
UNC 0   VMI 23
UNC 0   Davidson 7
UNC 0   Virginia 14

254

1921

UNC 21	Wake Forest	0
UNC 0	Yale	34
UNC 7	U. of S. C.	7
UNC 0	N. C. State	7
UNC 16	Maryland	7
UNC 20	VMI	7
UNC 0	Davidson	0
UNC 7	Virginia	3
UNC 14	Florida	10

1922

UNC 62	Wake Forest	3
UNC 0	Yale	18
UNC 20	Trinity	0
UNC 10	U. of S. C.	7
UNC 14	N. C. State	9
UNC 27	Maryland	3
UNC 19	Tulane	12
UNC 9	VMI	7
UNC 20	Davidson	6
UNC 10	Virginia	7

1923

UNC 22	Wake Forest	0
UNC 0	Yale	53
UNC 14	Trinity	6
UNC 14	N. C. State	0
UNC 0	Maryland	14
UNC 14	South Carolina	0
UNC 0	VMI	9
UNC 14	Davidson	3
UNC 0	Virginia	0

1924

UNC 6	Wake Forest	7
UNC 0	Yale	27
UNC 6	Trinity	0
UNC 10	N. C. State	0
UNC 0	Maryland	6
UNC 7	U. of S. C.	10
UNC 3	VMI	0
UNC 6	Davidson	0
UNC 0	Virginia	7

1925

UNC 0	Wake Forest	6
UNC 7	U. of S. C.	0
UNC 41	Duke	0
UNC 17	N. C. State	0
UNC 3	Mercer	0
UNC 16	Maryland	0
UNC 23	VMI	11
UNC 13	Davidson	0
UNC 3	Virginia	3

1926

UNC 0	Wake Forest	13
UNC 0	Tennessee	34
UNC 7	U. of S. C.	0
UNC 6	Duke	0
UNC 6	Maryland	14
UNC 12	N. C. State	0
UNC 28	VMI	0
UNC 0	Davidson	10
UNC 0	Virginia	3

1927

UNC 8	Wake Forest	9
UNC 0	Tennessee	26
UNC 7	Maryland	6
UNC 6	U. of S. C.	14
UNC 0	Georgia Tech	13
UNC 6	N. C. State	19
UNC 0	VMI	7
UNC 27	Davidson	0
UNC 18	Duke	0
UNC 14	Virginia	13

1928

UNC 65	Wake Forest	0
UNC 26	Maryland	19
UNC 0	Harvard	20
UNC 14	VPI	16
UNC 7	Georgia Tech	20
UNC 6	N. C. State	6
UNC 0	U. of S. C.	0
UNC 30	Davidson	7
UNC 24	Virginia	20
UNC 14	Duke	7

1929

UNC 48	Wake Forest	0
UNC 43	Maryland	0
UNC 18	Georgia Tech	7
UNC 12	Georgia	19
UNC 38	VPI	13
UNC 32	N. C. State	0
UNC 40	U. of S. C.	0
UNC 26	Davidson	7
UNC 41	Virginia	7
UNC 48	Duke	7

1930

UNC 13	Wake Forest	7
UNC 39	VPI	21
UNC 28	Maryland	21
UNC 0	Georgia	26
UNC 7	Tennessee	9
UNC 6	Georgia Tech	6
UNC 13	N. C. State	6
UNC 6	Davidson	7

UNC 41	Virginia	0
UNC 0	Duke	0

1931

UNC 37	Wake Forest	0
UNC 0	Vanderbilt	13
UNC 0	Florida	0
UNC 7	Georgia	32
UNC 0	Tennessee	7
UNC 18	N. C. State	15
UNC 19	Georgia Tech	19
UNC 20	Davidson	0
UNC 0	Duke	0
UNC 13	Virginia	6

1932

UNC 0	Wake Forest	0
UNC 7	Vanderbilt	39
UNC 7	Tennessee	20
UNC 6	Georgia	6
UNC 14	Georgia Tech	43
UNC 13	N. C. State	0
UNC 18	Florida	13
UNC 12	Davidson	0
UNC 0	Duke	7
UNC 7	Virginia	14

1933

UNC 6	Davidson	0
UNC 13	Vanderbilt	20
UNC 0	Georgia	30
UNC 0	Florida	9
UNC 6	Georgia Tech	10
UNC 6	N. C. State	0
UNC 26	Wake Forest	0
UNC 0	Duke	21
UNC 14	Virginia	0

1934

UNC 21	Wake Forest	0
UNC 7	Tennessee	19
UNC 14	Georgia	0
UNC 6	Kentucky	0
UNC 7	N. C. State	7
UNC 26	Georgia Tech	0
UNC 12	Davidson	2
UNC 7	Duke	0
UNC 25	Virginia	6

1935

UNC 14	Wake Forest	0
UNC 38	Tennessee	13
UNC 33	Maryland	0
UNC 14	Davidson	0
UNC 19	Georgia Tech	0
UNC 35	N. C. State	6
UNC 56	VMI	0

UNC 0	Duke	25
UNC 61	Virginia	0

1936

UNC 14	Wake Forest	7
UNC 14	Tennessee	6
UNC 14	Maryland	0
UNC 14	NYU	13
UNC 7	Tulane	21
UNC 21	N. C. State	6
UNC 26	Davidson	6
UNC 7	Duke	27
UNC 14	South Carolina	0
UNC 59	Virginia	14

1937

UNC 13	South Carolina	13
UNC 20	N. C. State	0
UNC 19	NYU	6
UNC 28	Wake Forest	0
UNC 13	Tulane	0
UNC 0	Fordham	14
UNC 26	Davidson	0
UNC 14	Duke	6
UNC 40	Virginia	0

1938

UNC 14	Wake Forest	6
UNC 21	N. C. State	0
UNC 14	Tulane	17
UNC 7	NYU	0
UNC 34	Davidson	0
UNC 0	Duke	14
UNC 7	Virginia Tech	0
UNC 0	Fordham	0
UNC 20	Virginia	0

1939

UNC 50	Citadel	0
UNC 36	Wake Forest	6
UNC 13	VPI	6
UNC 14	N.Y.U.	7
UNC 14	Tulane	14
UNC 30	Pennsylvania	6
UNC 17	N. C. State	0
UNC 32	Davidson	0
UNC 3	Duke	13
UNC 19	Virginia	0

1940

UNC 56	Appalachian	6
UNC 0	Wake Forest	12
UNC 27	Davidson	7
UNC 21	T.C.U.	14
UNC 13	N. C. State	7
UNC 13	Tulane	14
UNC 0	Fordham	14

UNC 13   Richmond Col. 14
UNC 6   Duke 3
UNC 10   Virginia 7

1941

UNC 42   Lenoir-Rhyne 6
UNC 7   U. of S. C. 13
UNC 20   Davidson 0
UNC 14   Fordham 27
UNC 6   Tulane 52
UNC 0   Wake Forest 13
UNC 7   N. C. State 13
UNC 27   Richmond Col. 0
UNC 0   Duke 20
UNC 7   Virginia 28

1942

UNC 6   Wake Forest 0
UNC 18   U. of S. C. 6
UNC 0   Fordham 0
UNC 13   Duquesne 6
UNC 14   Tulane 29
UNC 14   N. C. State 21
UNC 43   Davidson 14
UNC 13   Duke 13
UNC 28   Virginia 13

1943

UNC 7   Georgia Tech 20
UNC 19   Penn State 0
UNC 23   NATTC................ 0
UNC 7   Duke 14
UNC 27   N. C. State 13
UNC 21   U. of S. C. 6
UNC 9   Pennsylvania 6
UNC 6   Duke 27
UNC 54   Virginia 7

1944

UNC 0   Wake Forest 7
UNC 0   Army 46
UNC 0   Georgia Tech 28
UNC 20   Cherry Pt. M. 14
UNC 0   U. of S. C. 6
UNC 0   William & Mary 0
UNC 6   Yale 13
UNC 0   Duke 33
UNC 7   Virginia 26

1945

UNC 6   Camp Lee 0
UNC 14   Georgia Tech 20
UNC 14   VPI 0
UNC 0   Penn 49
UNC 20   Cherry Pt. M. 14
UNC 6   Tennessee 20
UNC 6   W&M 0
UNC 13   Wake Forest 14
UNC 7   Duke 14
UNC 27   Virginia 18

1946

UNC 14   VPI 14
UNC 21   Miami 0
UNC 33   Maryland 0
UNC 21   Navy 14
UNC 40   Florida 19
UNC 14   Tennessee 20
UNC 21   W&M 7
UNC 26   Wake Forest 14
UNC 22   Duke 7
UNC 49   Virginia 14
UNC 10   Georgia 20
  (Sugar Bowl Game)

1947

UNC 14   Georgia 7
UNC 0   Texas 34
UNC 7   Wake Forest 19
UNC 13   W&M 7
UNC 35   Florida 7
UNC 20   Tennessee 6
UNC 41   N. C. State 6
UNC 19   Maryland 0
UNC 21   Duke 0
UNC 40   Virginia 7

1948

UNC 34   Texas 7
UNC 21   Georgia 14
UNC 28   Wake Forest 6
UNC 14   N. C. State 0
UNC 34   L.S.U. 7
UNC 14   Tennessee 7
UNC 7   W&M 7
UNC 49   Maryland 20
UNC 20   Duke 0
UNC 34   Virginia 12
UNC 6   Oklahoma 14
  (Sugar Bowl Game)

1949

UNC 26   N. C. State 6
UNC 21   Georgia 14
UNC 28   U. of S. C. 13
UNC 28   Wake Forest 14
UNC 7   LSU 13
UNC 6   Tennessee 35
UNC 20   W&M 14
UNC 6   Notre Dame 42
UNC 21   Duke 20
UNC 14   Virginia 7
UNC 13   Rice 27
  (Cotton Bowl Game)

1950

UNC 13   N. C. State 7
UNC 7   Notre Dame 14
UNC 0   Georgia 0
UNC 7   Wake Forest 13
UNC 40   W&M 7
UNC 0   Tennessee 16

UNC 7	Maryland	7
UNC 14	U. of S. C.	7
UNC 0	Duke	7
UNC 13	Virginia	44

1951

UNC 21	N. C. State	0
UNC 16	Georgia	28
UNC 20	Texas	45
UNC 21	U. of S. C.	6
UNC 7	Maryland	14
UNC 7	Wake Forest	39
UNC 0	Tennessee	27
UNC 14	Virginia	34
UNC 7	Notre Dame	12
UNC 7	Duke	19

1952

UNC 7	Texas	28
UNC 7	Wake Forest	9
UNC 14	Notre Dame	34
UNC 14	Tennessee	41
UNC 7	Virginia	34
UNC 27	U. of S. C.	19
UNC 0	Duke	34
UNC 34	Miami	7

1953

UNC 29	N. C. State	7
UNC 39	W&L	0
UNC 18	Wake Forest	13
UNC 0	Maryland	26
UNC 14	Georgia	27
UNC 6	Tennessee	20
UNC 0	U. of S. C.	18
UNC 14	Notre Dame	34
UNC 33	Virginia	7
UNC 20	Duke	35

1954

UNC 20	N. C. State	6
UNC 7	Tulane	7
UNC 7	Georgia	21
UNC 0	Maryland	33
UNC 14	Wake Forest	7
UNC 20	Tennessee	26
UNC 21	U. of S. C.	19
UNC 13	Notre Dame	42
UNC 26	Virginia	14
UNC 12	Duke	47

1955

UNC 6	Oklahoma	13
UNC 25	N. C. State	18
UNC 7	Georgia	28
UNC 7	Maryland	25
UNC 0	Wake Forest	25
UNC 7	Tennessee	48
UNC 32	South Carolina	14

UNC 7	Notre Dame	27
UNC 26	Virginia	14
UNC 0	Duke	6

1956

UNC 6	N. C. State	26
UNC 0	Oklahoma	36
UNC 0	South Carolina	14
UNC 12	Georgia	26
UNC 34	Maryland	6
UNC 6	Wake Forest	6
UNC 0	Tennessee	20
UNC 21	Virginia	7
UNC 14	Notre Dame	21
UNC 6	Duke	21

1957

UNC 0	N. C. State	7
UNC 26	Clemson	0
UNC 13	Navy	7
UNC 20	Miami	13
UNC 7	Maryland	21
UNC 14	Wake Forest	7
UNC 0	Tennessee	35
UNC 28	South Carolina	6
UNC 21	Duke	13
UNC 13	Virginia	20

1958

UNC 14	N. C. State	21
UNC 21	Clemson	26
UNC 8	Southern Cal	7
UNC 6	South Carolina	0
UNC 27	Maryland	0
UNC 26	Wake Forest	7
UNC 21	Tennessee	7
UNC 42	Virginia	0
UNC 24	Notre Dame	34
UNC 6	Duke	7

1959

UNC 18	Clemson	20
UNC 8	Notre Dame	28
UNC 20	N. C. State	12
UNC 19	South Carolina	6
UNC 7	Maryland	14
UNC 21	Wake Forest	19
UNC 7	Tennessee	29
UNC 7	Miami	14
UNC 41	Virginia	0
UNC 50	Duke	0

1960

UNC 0	N. C. State	3
UNC 12	Miami	29
UNC 12	Notre Dame	7
UNC 12	Wake Forest	13
UNC 6	South Carolina	22
UNC 14	Tennessee	27

UNC 0	Clemson	24
UNC 19	Maryland	22
UNC 7	Duke	6
UNC 35	Virginia	8

1961

UNC 27	N. C. State	22
UNC 0	Clemson	27
UNC 14	Maryland	8
UNC 17	South Carolina	0
UNC 0	Miami	10
UNC 22	Tennessee	21
UNC 0	L.S.U.	30
UNC 3	Duke	6
UNC 14	Wake Forest	17
UNC 24	Virginia	0

1962

UNC 6	N. C. State	7
UNC 7	Ohio State	41
UNC 6	Michigan State	38
UNC 13	Maryland	31
UNC 19	South Carolina	14
UNC 23	Wake Forest	14
UNC 6	Clemson	17
UNC 11	Virginia	7
UNC 7	Notre Dame	21
UNC 14	Duke	16

1963

UNC 11	Virginia	7
UNC 0	Michigan State U.	31
UNC 21	Wake Forest	0
UNC 14	Maryland	7
UNC 31	N. C. State	10
UNC 7	South Carolina	0
UNC 28	Georgia	7
UNC 7	Clemson	11
UNC 27	Miami	16
UNC 16	Duke	14
UNC 35	Air Force	0
	(Gator Bowl Game)	

1964

UNC 13	N. C. State	14
UNC 21	Michigan State	15
UNC 23	Wake Forest	0
UNC 3	LSU	20
UNC 9	Maryland	10
UNC 24	S. Carolina	6
UNC 8	Georgia	24
UNC 29	Clemson	0
UNC 27	Virginia	31
UNC 21	Duke	15

1965

UNC 24	Michigan	31
UNC 14	Ohio State	3
UNC 17	Virginia	21

UNC 10	N. C. State	7
UNC 12	Maryland	10
UNC 10	Wake Forest	12
UNC 35	Georgia	47
UNC 17	Clemson	13
UNC 0	Notre Dame	17
UNC 7	Duke	34

1966

UNC 0	Kentucky	10
UNC 10	N. C. State	7
UNC 21	Michigan	7
UNC 0	Notre Dame	32
UNC 0	Wake Forest	3
UNC 3	Georgia	28
UNC 3	Clemson	27
UNC 14	Air Force	20
UNC 25	Duke	41
UNC 14	Virginia	21

1967

UNC 7	N. C. State	13
UNC 10	South Carolina	16
UNC 11	Tulane	36
UNC 7	Vanderbilt	21
UNC 8	Air Force	10
UNC 14	Maryland	0
UNC 10	Wake Forest	20
UNC 0	Clemson	17
UNC 17	Virginia	40
UNC 20	Duke	9

1968

UNC 6	N. C. State	38
UNC 27	South Carolina	32
UNC 8	Vanderbilt	7
UNC 24	Maryland	33
UNC 22	Florida	7
UNC 31	Wake Forest	48
UNC 15	Air Force	28
UNC 6	Virginia	41
UNC 14	Clemson	24
UNC 25	Duke	14

1969

UNC 3	N. C. State	10
UNC 6	South Carolina	14
UNC 38	Vanderbilt	22
UNC 10	Air Force	20
UNC 2	Florida	52
UNC 23	Wake Forest	3
UNC 12	Virginia	0
UNC 61	VMI	11
UNC 32	Clemson	15
UNC 13	Duke	17

1970

UNC 20	Kentucky	10
UNC 19	N. C. State	0
UNC 53	Maryland	20
UNC 10	Vanderbilt	7

UNC 21	South Carolina	.35
UNC 17	Tulane	.24
UNC 13	Wake Forest	.14
UNC 30	Virginia	.15
UNC 62	VMI	.13
UNC 42	Clemson	7
UNC 59	Duke	.34
UNC 26	Arizona State	.48
	(Peach Bowl Game)	

1971

UNC 28	Richmond	0
UNC 27	Illinois	0
UNC 35	Maryland	.14
UNC 27	N. C. State	7
UNC 29	Tulane	.37
UNC 0	Notre Dame	.16
UNC 7	Wake Forest	3
UNC 36	Wm. & Mary	.35
UNC 26	Clemson	.13
UNC 32	Virginia	.20
UNC 38	Duke	0
UNC 3	Georgia	7
	(Gator Bowl Game)	

1972

UNC 28	Richmond	.18
UNC 31	Maryland	.26
UNC 34	N. C. State	.33
UNC 14	Ohio State	.29
UNC 31	Kentucky	.20
UNC 21	Wake Forest	0
UNC 26	Clemson	.10
UNC 23	Virginia	3
UNC 14	Duke	0
UNC 42	E.C.U.	.19
UNC 28	Florida	.24
UNC 32	Texas Tech	.28
	(Sun Bowl Game)	

1973

UNC 34	Wm. & Mary	.27
UNC 3	Maryland	.23
UNC 14	Missouri	.27
UNC 26	N. C. State	.28
UNC 16	Kentucky	.10
UNC 0	Tulane	.16
UNC 28	East Carolina	.27
UNC 40	Virginia	.44
UNC 29	Clemson	.37
UNC 42	Wake Forest	0
UNC 10	Duke	.27

1974

UNC 42	Ohio U.	7
UNC 31	Wake Forest	0
UNC 12	Maryland	.24
UNC 45	Pittsburgh	.29
UNC 28	Georgia Tech	.29
UNC 33	N. C. State	.14
UNC 23	South Carolina	.31
UNC 24	Virginia	.10
UNC 32	Clemson	.54
UNC 56	Army	.42
UNC 14	Duke	.13
UNC 24	Mississippi State	.26
	(Sun Bowl Game)	

1975

UNC 33	William & Mary	7
UNC 7	Maryland	.34
UNC 7	Ohio State	.32
UNC 31	Virginia	.28
UNC 14	Notre Dame	.21
UNC 20	N. C. State	.21
UNC 17	East Carolina	.38
UNC 9	Wake Forest	.21
UNC 35	Clemson	.38
UNC 17	Tulane	.15
UNC 17	Duke	.17

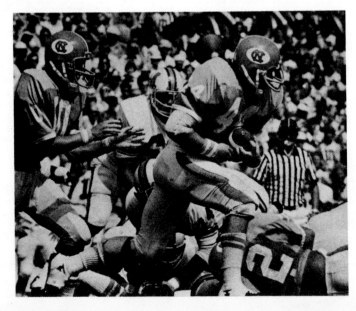

THE STORY SINCE 1888

Year	W	L	T	Pts.	Opp. Pts.	Coach	Captain
1888	0	2	0	4	22		Bob Bingham-Steve Bragaw
1889	2	2	0	58	43	Hector Cowan	Lacy Little-Steve Bragaw
1891	0	2	0	4	7	W. P. Graves	Mike Hoke-George Graham
1892	5	1	0	196	30		Mike Hoke
1893	3	4	0	152	66		A. S. Barnard
1894	6	3	0	178	71	V. K. Irvine	Charles Baskerville
1895	7	1	1	146	17	T. C. Trenchard	Edwin Gregory
1896	3	4	1	106	100	Gordon Johnston	Robert Wright
1897	7	3	0	150	53	W. A. Reynolds	Arthur Belden
1898	9	0	0	201	8	W. A. Reynolds	Frank Rogers
1899	7	3	1	173	58	W. A. Reynolds	Samuel Shull
1900	4	1	3	163	22	W. A. Reynolds	Frank Osborne
1901	7	2	0	198	45	Charles Jenkins	Albert M. Carr
1902	5	1	3	122	34	H. B. Olcott	Frank Foust
1903	6	3	0	137	72	H. B. Olcott	G. Lyle Jones
1904	5	2	2	170	34	Robert R. Brown	R. S. Stewart
1905	4	3	1	82	90	William Warner	Foy Roberson
1906	1	4	2	18	83	W. S. Keinholz	Romy Story
1907	4	4	1	93	97	Dr. Otis Lamson	Joseph S. Mann
1908	3	3	3	62	71	Edward Green	George Thomas
1909	5	2	0	54	18	A. E. Brides	C. C. Garrett
1910	3	6	0	70	67	A. E. Brides	Earl Thompson
1911	6	1	1	66	31	Branch Bocock	Bob Winston
1912	3	4	1	85	168	William C. Martin	William Tillett
1913	5	4	0	91	76	T. C. Trenchard	L. L. Abernethy
1914	10	1	0	359	52	T. C. Trenchard	Dave Tayloe
1915	4	3	1	105	98	T. C. Trenchard	Dave Tayloe
1916	5	4	0	134	93	Thomas J. Campbell	George Tandy
1919	4	3	1	49	94	Thomas J. Campbell	J. M. Coleman
1920	2	6	0	16	91	Myron E. Fuller	Beemer Harrell
1921	5	2	2	85	75	R. A. and W. M. Fetzer	Robbins Lowe
1922	9	1	0	200	72	R. A. and W. M. Fetzer	Grady Pritchard
1923	5	3	1	77	85	R. A. and W. M. Fetzer	Roy Morris
1924	4	5	0	38	57	R. A. and W. M. Fetzer	Pierce Matthews
1925	7	1	1	123	20	R. A. and W. M. Fetzer	Herman McIver
1926	4	5	0	59	74	Chuck Collins	Manly Whisnant
1927	4	6	0	86	107	Chuck Collins	Garrett Morehead
1928	5	3	2	186	115	Chuck Collins	Harry Schwartz
1929	9	1	0	346	60	Chuck Collins	Ray Farris, Sr.
1930	5	3	2	153	103	Chuck Collins	Strud Nash
1931	4	3	3	114	92	Chuck Collins	(Game Captains)
1932	3	5	2	84	142	Chuck Collins	(Game Captains)
1933	4	5	0	71	90	Chuck Collins	Bill Croom
1934	7	1	1	125	34	Carl Snavely	George Barclay
1935	8	1	0	270	44	Carl Snavely	H. Snyder-H. Montgomery
1936	8	2	0	190	100	Ray Wolf	Dick Buck
1937	7	1	1	173	39	Ray Wolf	Andy Bershak-Crowell Little
1938	6	2	1	117	37	Ray Wolf	Steve Maronic-G. Watson
1939	8	1	1	228	52	Ray Wolf	G. Stirnweiss-J. Woodson
1940	6	4	0	159	98	Ray Wolf	P. Severin-G. Kimball
1941	3	7	0	130	172	Ray Wolf	H. Dunkle-C. Suntheimer
1942	5	2	2	149	102	Jim Tatum	J. Austin-F. Marshall
1943	6	3	0	173	93	Tom Young	Craven Turner
1944	1	7	1	33	173	Gene McEver	Bobby Weant
1945	5	5	0	113	149	Carl Snavely	Bill Walker-Bill Voris
1946	8	2	1	261	129	Carl Snavely	C. Highsmith-R. Strayhorn
1947	8	2	0	210	93	Carl Snavely	J. Wright-G. Sparger
1948	9	1	1	261	94	Carl Snavely	H. Rodgers-D. Stiegman
1949	7	4	0	190	205	Carl Snavely	Charlie Justice
1950	3	5	2	101	122	Carl Snavely	I. Holdash-D. Bunting

Year	W	L	T	Pts.	Opp. Pts.	Coach	Captain
1951	2	8	0	120	224	Carl Snavely	J. Dudeck-Bob Gantt
1952	2	6	0	110	206	Carl Snavely	G. Norris-B. Wallace
1953	4	6	0	173	187	George Barclay	Ken Yarborough
1954	4	5	1	140	222	George Barclay	(Game Captains)
1955	3	7	0	117	218	George Barlcay	R. Perdue-Will Frye
1956	2	7	1	99	183	Jim Tatum	Ed Sutton-G. Stavnitski
1957	6	4	0	142	129	Jim Tatum	Dave Reed-Buddy Payne
1958	6	4	0	195	109	Jim Tatum	Phil Blazer-G. Hathaway
1959	5	5	0	198	142	Jim Hickey	Jack Cummings-W. Smith
1960	3	7	0	117	161	Jim Hickey	Rip Hawkins-Frank Riggs
1961	5	5	0	121	141	Jim Hickey	Bob Elliott-Jim LeCompte
1962	3	7	0	112	206	Jim Hickey	Joe Carver-W. Marslender
1963	9	2	0	197	103	Jim Hickey	Gene Sigmon-Roger Smith
1964	5	5	0	178	135	Jim Hickey	C. Hanburger-Ron Tuthill
1965	4	6	0	146	195	Jim Hickey	Hank Barden-Ed Stringer
1966	2	8	0	90	196	Jim Hickey	D. Talbott, B. Hume, H. Sadler
1967	2	8	0	104	182	Bill Dooley	David Riggs-Jack Davenport
1968	3	7	0	178	270	Bill Dooley	Gayle Bomar-Mike Smith
1969	5	5	0	200	164	Bill Dooley	Seven Seniors
1970	8	4	0	346	279	Bill Dooley	McCauley, Ray, Richardson
1971	9	3	0	288	152	Bill Dooley	Paul Miller-John Bunting
1972	11	1	0	324	210	Bill Dooley	Gene Brown-Ron Rusnak
1973	4	7	0	242	265	Bill Dooley	Terry Taylor-Sammy Johnson
1974	7	5	0	364	279	Bill Dooley	Chris Kupec-Ken Huff
1975	3	7	1	207	272	Bill Dooley	Six Seniors
	424	314	49	12,471	9,418		

MONOGRAM CLUB MEMBERS-ALL SPORTS

(Lettermen in all sports from the first awarding of "NC's" through the spring of 1936. The monogram list compiled by F. Carlyle Shepard in the spring of 1925 was used. "NC" winners since then have been taken from records in the Athletic Office.)

Abbot, Peyton Bryant
Abels, Byron Clifford
Abels, Lucas Clarence
Abernethy, Franklin Pierce, Jr.
Abernethy, LeRoy Franklin
Abernethy, Lonnie Lee
Abernethy, Oscar Marvin
Abernethy, Richard Blythe, Jr.
Adam, Robert Leonard
Adams, Joel Barker
Aderholt, Marcus Lafayette, Jr.
Adkins, Fenton Andrew
Aitken, Stuart Cruickshank
Albright, Charles Alexander
Albright, Robert Mayne, Jr.
Alderman, Herbert Edward
Alexander, Roy Whitney
Alexander, Thomas Willis, Jr.
Allen, Archie Turner, Jr.
Allen, Ernest Marvin, Jr.
Allen, Reynold Tatum
Allison, James Richard
Allison, Thomas Tillett
Alston, Charles Skinner
Ambrose, Raymond Gordon
Anderson, Arthur Ernest
Andrews, Ezra Preston
Andrews, Nathan Hardy, Jr.
Applewhite, Blake Deans
Armfield, Walter Frank
Armstrong, Charles Wallace
Arnold, Broddie Duke
Ashby, Clarence Garnett
Ashe, Samuel Acourt, Jr.
Atkinson, Alexander Morse
Auman, Jason MacGregor
Austin, James Wilson
Austin, Rufus Eugene
Avery, Isaac Thomas, Jr.
Axley, Lowry
Aycock, Benjamin Franklin

Baden, James
Bagby, George Lewis
Baggs, Henry McKean
Bagwell, Raleigh Mays
Bailey, Fletcher Hamilton
Bailey, Karl Braswell
Bailey, Kenneth Hubert
Baird, James Andrew
Ball, James Weeks
Bannon, Barney Dervin
Barber, Howard Windfield
Barclay, George Thomas
Barden, Graham Arthur
Bardin, Benjamin Hume
Barham, Reuben Dennis
Barker, Frank Pendleton

Barkley, Minor
Barnard, Alfred Smith
Barnes, Rudolph
Barnhardt, James Leonard
Barrett, Elmer Gordon, Jr.
Barry, James Edward
Bartos, Henry
Barwick, Eugene Thomas
Baskerville, Charles
Bass, Thomas Edward
Battle, William Kemp
Baucom, Clifford Randall
Beale, William Earle
Bear, Charles Edgar
Bear, Richard D.
Belden, Arthur Williams
Belden, Louis DeKeyser
Belk, William Parks
Bell, James Andrew
Bell, Malcolm, Jr.
Bellamy, Hargrove
Bellamy, Robert Harllee
Bennett, Frank, Jr.
Bennett, Paul
Berkeley, Greenville Ramsey
Bershak, Andrew A.
Biggs, James Crawford
Bissett, Harold Edwin
Bingham, Robert Worth
Bivins, Edward Chatham
Black, Hugh Clifton
Blackwood, Cosby Glenn
Blalock, Merritt Edward, Jr.
Blankenship, Stephen Pettus
Blanton, William Hackett
Blaylock, Spencer Lorraine
Block, Norman
Blood, Ernest Benjamin
Blount, John Gray
Blount, Samuel Masters
Blount, William Augustus, Jr.
Blue, Luther Avon, Jr.
Blythe, Charles Edgar
Bonner, Allan Baker
Bonner, Merle Dumont
Boren, Norman Addison
Borland, Richard Seaton
Boshamer, Cary Carlisle
Bower, Jack Calhoun
Branch, John Dunn
Brandt, George Frederick
Bragaw, Stephen Cambreleng
Braswell, Robert Russell
Brem, Tod Robinson
Brem, Walter Vernon, Jr.
Bridges, LeRoy Clifford
Bridgers, Henry Clark, Jr.
Bridgers, Robert Rufus

263

Brown, Alexander MacLeod
Brown, Charles, Jr.
Brown, Clement Cook, Jr.
Brown, David Robert
Brown, Henry Nicholas, III
Brown, Herbert Thompson
Brown, L. Ames
Brown, Peyton Randolph
Brown, Sanford Wiley
Brown, Theron Renfry
Brown, Verney Edd
Brown, William Howard
Bruce, Paul Ernest
Bruner, Weston, Jr.
Bruton, Gaston Swindell
Bryant, Victor Silas
Bryson, Herman Jennings
Buchanan, George Hampton, Jr.
Buck, Richard Dale
Buie, Dugal McRea
Bullard, Edgar William
Bullitt, James Bell
Burnett, Joseph Henry, Jr.
Burnett, Robert Shepard
Burnette, Thomas D.
Burroughs, John William
Burt, Edward Ramsey, Jr.
Busbee, Perrin
Busbee, Richard Smith
Butler, George Phineas
Butler, James Edward
Butt, Israel Harding
Butt, William Horace
Buxton, Cameron Belo
Bynum, Carnie Washington

Calder, Robert Edward
Calmes, James Drayton
Capehart, William Jonathan
Carmichael, Richard Cartwright
Carmichael, William Donald, Jr.
Carpenter, Caius Hunter
Carpenter, Ernest Willoughby
Carr, Albert Marvin
Carr, John Robert
Carr, William Frederick
Carrington, George Lunsford
Carruth, James Robert
Carter, Kenneth William
Carter, Walter
Carson, James McIntyre
Case, Wallace Talmadge
Cash, Thomas Hamilton
Cathey, George
Chambers, Lenoir, Jr.
Chandler, Stuart McVeigh
Chatham, Charles Gwyn
Cheatham, G. C.
Cheshire, John
Childers, William Odell
Choate, Page
Clarkson, Francis Osborne
Cleland, Thomas Montgomery
Clemmons, Thomas Elbert
Cobb, Collier, Jr.
Cobb, John Blackwell
Cobb, William Battle
Cochran, Frederick Cline
Cocke, Jerre Ellis

Coffey, Carl Sylvester
Coffey, John Nelson
Coffin, William Edwin, Jr.
Coffin, Wilson
Cohen, Gabriel Murrell
Cohen, Jerome Jacob
Colburn, Burnham Standish, Jr.
Cole, Otis Oscar
Coleman, James Millar
Collier, Harris Taylor
Collins, Cyril William
Collins, Paul Cameron
Coltrane, William Homer
Combs, Alvah Haff
Condon, Martin Joseph, Jr.
Cone, Caesar
Conklin, Donald Rouse
Connell, Earl Beardsley
Conte, Louis Benedict, Jr.
Cook, John H.
Cooner, Bunyon Randolph
Cooper, John Henry
Copeland, James Watson, Jr.
Corbett, Harlan Davis
Cordle, Thomas Llewellyn
Cordon, Edward Broad
Corpening, Linwood Elisha
Corpening, William M.
Council, Walter Wooten
Covington, Richard Olive, Jr.
Cowell, Horace Baxter
Cowper, George Vernon, Jr.
Cowper, Marion Rountree
Cox, Albert Lyman
Cox, Frank Calvin
Cox, Howard Enoch
Coxe, Fred Jackson
Coxe, Thomas Chatterton, Jr.
Coxe, Tench Charles
Coxe, William P. T.
Cozart, Sydnor Moye
Cramer, Carl Delbert
Crawford, Frederick M.
Crawford, Carl Brooks
Crew, Stanley Ellis
Cromartie, Robert Samuel
Croom, William David, Jr.
Crosswell, James Earl
Crouch, Fred Pfohl
Crowell, Rupert Johnson
Crutchfield, William Jesse
Crystal, Robert Garrison
Cummings, Carey Van
Cunningham, George Lumpkin
Cunningham Herbert Banatine
Curlee, Arle Theodore
Curlee, Thomas Haywood
Currie, Ralph Plubius
Currie, Wilbur H.
Currie, William Pinckney Martin
Curtis, Nathaniel Cortlandt
Cuthberson, William Reynolds
Cuthrell, Hugh Hamlin

Dalrymple, Temple Epps
Dameron, Emerson Penn
Daniel, David Allen
Daniel, John Wallace
Daniel, William Warren
Daniels, Arthur Francis

Darden, Douglas Beaman
Dashiell, Frederick Knowles
Davis (given name unknown)
Davis, Archibald Kimbrough
Davis, James Blaine
Davis, Charlie Walker
Davis, Gus Obie
Davis, Robert Cowan
Davis, Paul Plato
Deans, Archibald Battle
DeGray, Edward John
Denson, Eugene Grisson
Dermid, Jefferson Davis
DeRose, Anthony John
Devereaux, Robert Eddins
Devin, William Augustus
Devin, William Augustus, Jr.
Diehl, Frank Marion
Dill, Green Redmond
Dillard, John Richardson
Ditt, Arthur Harvey
Dixon, James Glenn
Dodderer, William Andrew
Donnahoe, Mark Earle
Donnell, George Stratford
Donelly, John
Dortch, Gaston Lewis
Dortch, Gavin Hoge, Jr.
Dortch, Hugh
Dowd, William Cary, Jr.
Doyle, Aloysius Thomas
Drake, John Oliver
Drane, Frederick Blount
Drane, Robert Wesley, Jr.
Dry, William Henry
Dudley, Leighton Wesley
Dula, Frederick Mast
Duls, John Ferdinand
Duncan, Vernon VanDuke
Dunham, Wallace G.
Dunlap, Joseph Paul
Dunlap, Lucius Victor

Eames, Richard Davis
Eby, Clyde, Jr.
Edgerton, Earl Dock
Edwards, Jesse Paul
Edwards, John Reid
Edwards, Thomas Jones
Edwards, Wiley Burr
Efland, Simpson L.
Elgin, Duncan Vogely
Elliott, Galen Omer
Elliott, Madison Lee
Ellis, Alexander Caswell
Ellisberg, Mortimer
Ellison, Charles Frank, Jr.
Emerson, Horace Mann
Endicott, Thomas Pennington
Engle, Ralph Barnwell
Epstein, Joseph Niles
Erickson, Charles Perry
Ervin, Carl Edgar
Erwin, Jesse Harper, Jr.
Erwin, Roy Vance
Eskew, Walter Eugene
Eutsler, Eugene Ernest
Evans, Emanuel Joshua
Everett, James Alphonse
Evins, Thomas Moore

Farlow, Newton Fernando
Farmer, Charles Martin
Farmer, John Deaver
Farrall, Frank Morgan
Farrell, Henry Darrow
Farris, Jack Brodie
Farris, Ray Simpson
Farthing, Fred Robert
Faulkner, Nolan Bradford
Fearrington, Frederick
Feimster, Walter Connor, Jr.
Fenner, Julian Baker
Ferebee, Emmett Crews
Ferebee, Willoughby Dozier
Ferguson, Fred Jaynes
Ferguson, Herbert Reeves
Ferrell, James William, Jr.
Finlay, James Ferguson
Fischel, Louis William
Fisher, Joseph Jerome
Fisher, Junius Virgile
Fisher, William, Jr.
Fitzsimmons, Edward Owen
Fleming, Frank Reaves
Floyd, John Buckner
Foard, Edison Glenn
Folger, Augustine William
Fordham, Christopher Columbus, Jr.
Fordham, Jefferson Barnes
Foreman, John Born
Fort, John
Fountain, George Marion
Foust, Frank Lee
Foust, Henry Price
Fox, Dennis Bryan
Frankel, Julian Carter
Fulcher, Edgar Lytel
Fulenwider, Lane
Fullenwider, Phifer
Fuller, Edward James
Fuller, Paul Johnson
Fuller, Walter Pliny
Furches, Stephen Lewis
Fysal, Ellis Daher

Gabori, Richard Frederick
Gaither, James Frierson
Gallagher, Phillip Hiss
Gammon, Edgar Graham, Jr.
Gant, Allen Erwin
Gardiner, Robert Morris
Gardner, Oliver Max
Gardner, Ralph Webb
Gardner, Wade Anderson
Gardner, Voige McDuffie
Garland, Robert Franklin
Garrett, Cecil Clark
Garrett, Howard Richard
Gay, Archibald Cree
Gay, Kenneth Alexander
Geddie, Rowland Hill
Gewolb, Marvin Herbert
Gholson, Thornton Patton
Gholson, Wilbur Lytle
Gibbs, Norfleet Mann
Gibson, Porter Clyde
Giddens, Samuel G.
Giersch, Maurice Sandrock
Giersch, Otto Lumley
Gilbreath, John Ulpin

Giles, Denison
Gilliam, Henry Augustus
Gillon, Baxter Moor
Glace, Ivan Maxwell. Jr.
Glover, Clifford Clarke
Goldman, Gerson Mandel
Goodes, Benjamin Lawrence
Goodridge, Noah
Goodwin, Benjamin Harvey
Graham, Archibald
Graham, Edward Kidder
Graham, Eugene Barrien
Graham, George Mordecai
Graham, George Washington, Jr.
Graham, Reuben Holmes
Graham, Theodore Alexander
Graham, Thomas Pegram
Graham, William Alexander
Grandin, Elliott Culver
Grant, Bryan Morel, Jr.
Graves, Ernest
Graves, Henry Louis
Graves, Louis
Gray, James Cornelius
Gray, Robert McDonald
Green, Deleon Fillyaw
Green, George Chancellor
Green, John Robert
Green, Thomas Mears
Green, Winton Wallace
Greene, Eugene Alston
Gregory, Edwin Clarke
Gresham, John Thomas, Jr.
Griffith, James Thomas, Jr.
Griffith, Robert Henry
Grimes, William
Groome, Cicero Hunt
Groover, Walter Rufus
Grossman, Phillip D.
Grubb, Foy Eugene
Gudger (given name unknown)
Gudger, Vonno Lamar
Guion, Louis Isaac
Gulick, James Wharton
Gunter, John Wadsworth
Gwalthney, Robert Howell
Gwynn, Harvey William
Gwynn, John Minor

Hackney, Bunn Washington, Jr.
Hackney, James Acra
Hackney, Rufus Rastus
Hagan, James Guy
Hairston, Nelson George
Hall, James H.
Hamer, George Winston
Hamilton, Oscar Alexander
Hamlen, Hubert Chesley
Hamlet, Christopher Columbus, Jr.
Hampton, Kenneth Dunlap
Hanby, Howard Alexander
Hanes, James Gordon
Hanes, John Wesley
Harden, Boyd
Harden, James Turner
Harden, Robert Norman
Hardison, James Archibald, Jr.
Harper, William Lacy
Harrell, Beamer Clifford
Harris, John Edgar

Harris, Harvey William
Harris, Richard Alexander, Jr.
Harris, William Clinton
Harris, William Cliff
Harriss, Charles Johnson
Harrison, John Baugham
Harrison, William Burwell
Hart, Bythial Mabry
Hart, Julian Gilliam
Harvell, William Espy
Hasty, Claude Herndon
Hatley, James Boyd
Havner, Alfred Sidney
Hawfield, Clayton
Hawkins, Thomas William, Jr.
Hawthorne, Thomas Joseph
Hayes, Jack
Haywood, Fabius Julius
Haywood, Fabius Julius, Jr.
Heafner, Samuel Byron
Hearn, Bunn, Jr.
Hearn, Williamson Edward
Hedgepeth, Harry Malcomb
Henderson, Archibald, Jr.
Henderson, John Middleton
Hendlin, Harry Howell
Hendren, William Mayhew
Hendrix, William Houston, Jr.
Henley, James Everett
Henry, David Probasco
Henson, Thomas Albert
Herty, Charles Holmes, Jr.
Hester, Addison Reed
Hicks, Richard Hilton
Higby, Floyd Dorian, Jr.
Hill, Stuart Hall
Hiller, Morton Paul
Hilton, Joseph Truman
Hines, Samuel Philip
Hines, Wilmer Moore
Hinton, George Roy
Hobbs, Lewis Lyndon
Hobgood, James Edward
Hodges, Harry Meade, Jr.
Hodges, Henry
Hoffman, Joseph Filson, Jr.
Hogan, Henry Sanders
Hoke, Michael
Holderness, Haywood Dail
Holmes, Thomas Hall, Jr.
Holshouser, Herman Alexander
Holt, Don Shaw
Holt, Earl Pendleton
Homewood, Roy McRae
Honeycutt, Samuel Tilden
Honig, John
Hornaday, Flavius Durante
Horney, William Johnston, Jr.
Houghton, Mathews Amos
House, Henry Charles, Jr.
Houston, Henry Clay
Howard, Nelson Ferebee
Howell, Edward Vernon
Howell, Logan Douglas
Howell, Robert Vance
Hubbard, Charles Spence
Hubbard, Robert Bronson
Hudgins, Daniel Edward
Hudson, James Spearman
Huggins, William Cantwell

266

Huggins, William Sloan
Hughes, Samuel Edwin, Jr.
Hughes, Thomas Spurgeon
Hume, James
Humphries, John William
Hunter, James Scott, Jr.
Huske, William Oliver
Hussey, William Thaddeus
Hutchins, James Alexander, Jr.
Hutchins, John Manning
Hutchinson, Joel Jenkins, Jr.
Hyman, Orren Williams

Idol, Percy Cornelius
Irby, Gray Pope
Irwin, James Preston
Irwin, Thomas Andrew
Isley, Christian Leonard, Jr.

Jackson, Don Fletcher
Jackson, Phillip
Jackson, Rudolph Hoyt
Jacobi, David Beuthner
Jacocks, William Picard
James, James Burton
Jarrell, William Walker
Jeanes, Isaac Warner, II
Jennette, William Carl
Jennings, Olin Henry
Jensen, Clarence Arthur
Jernigan, Ernest Casper
Jessup, Robert Moore
Johnson, Bayard Cleveland
Johnson, Earl
Johnson, Ferdie Badger
Johnson, John Gray
Johnson, Lawrence Branch
Johnson, Woodrow Wilson
Johnston, Henry
Johnston, Robert Alexander
Johnston, Richard Hall
Johnston, Robert Pulliam
Johnston, Samuel Nash
Johnston, Troy Ausborne
Johnston, Wilfred Ivey
Jonas, Charles Raper
Jonas, Donald Roosevelt
Jones, Andrew Jeatus
Jones, Charles McDaniel
Jones, Frank Carlton
Jones, George Lyle
Jones, Harry Murray
Jones, John Lawrence
Jones, Kenneth Anderson
Jones, Lawrence O'Brien Branch
Jones, Mark Manard
Jones, P. Sentelle
Jones, Zebulon Baird Vance
Joyce, Emmett Bernard
Joyner, Claudius Cameron
Joyner, Claude Reuben
Juliber, Edward Browne

Kahn, Edwin Bernard
Kaluk, Nick
Kanner, Murray
Kaveny, Paul Felix
Keeney, Barnaby Conrad
Kellam, Claude Doby
Kenan, William Rand, Jr.
Kephart, William Perry

Kernodle, James Loftin
Kernodle, Lovick Harden
Kerr, Langdon Chevis
Kimrey, Donald S.
Kind, Phillip, Jr.
King, Franklin Bernard
Kinlaw, William Bernard
Kirkman, William Robert
Kirkpatrick, David Alexander
Kirven, James Dupont
Kluttz, Warren Lawson
Koenig, William Smith
Koehler, Herman Jules
Kornegay, William Emmett

Lambeth, Harvey Allen
Lambeth, Mark Thomas
Lambeth, Walter Moore
Landis, Platt Walker
Lanier, James Conrad
Lanier, Thornwell
Lashley, Walter
Lassiter, James Harry
Lassiter, John Hanes
Latham, Joseph Roscoe
Lawson, Charles Franklin
Lawson, Robert Baker
Laxton, Erwin LeVendre
Leak, James Augustus, Jr.
Leary, Elwyn Preston
Lee, Joseph Raymond
Leggett, Clifton Lanier
LeGore, Floyd Ralston
LeGrand, Harry Elwood
Leonard, Frank Alfred
Lester, William Evans
Levinson, Martin
Levitan, Walter Morris
Lewis, McDaniel
Lewis, William Figures
Liipfert, Benjamin Bailey
Lilly, Edmund Jones
Lilly, Joel Alexander
Lindsay, Raleigh Cabell
Lineberger, Henry Abel
Linville, William Clinton
Litchfield, Charles Aycock
Little, Chester Crowell
Little, George Roscoe
Little, Lacy LeGrand
Lipscomb, Charles Thomas, Jr.
Lipscomb, Edward Russell
Liskin, Phillip
Llewellyn, Clement Manly
Llorens, Thomas Vicante
Long, Albert Anderson
Long, Giles Mebane
Long, Henry Cyrus, Jr.
Long, Morris Henry
Longest, Edward Cecil
Love, James Franklin
Lowder, Wilbur Dodson
Lowe, Frank Robbins
Lowry, Walter Gwynn
Lufty, Napoleon Bonaparte
Lumpkin, Nathaniel Wilson, Jr.
Lyle, Samuel Harley, Jr.
Lynch, Peter Francisco
Lynch, Percy Philip, Jr.
Lyon, Henry Wise

267

Lyons. Olen
Lytle, Samuel

McAlister, John Worth
McCachren. David Downs
McCachren. James Roland
McCachren. William Henry
McCarn. Lester Wahava
McCaskill. James Norman
McDade. Roy Arnold, Jr.
McDaniel. George Dawson
McDonald, Alan Cameron, Jr.
McDonald. Alfred
McDonald. Alexander Milton
McDonald. Angus Morris
McDonald. Samuel Howard
McDuffie. Lewis Robert
McFadyn. A. P.
McGee. Allen Marshall
McGlinn, John Alexander, Jr.
McGougan, James Vance
McIntosh. Frank Jenkins
McIver. Charlie
McIver. Evan Gordon
McIver. Henry Staton
McIver, Herman Martin
McKee. John Sasser
McKeithan. Ernest Harlan
McLean, Joseph Altira
McLean, Robert Clay
McMurry. Jesse Jenkins, Jr.
McNeill. Thomas Alexander, Jr.
McPherson. Rufus Alexander
McRae. Edwin Earl
McRae, Duncan
MacRae, Cameron
MacRae, James C.
MacRae. Lawrence
Mackie. Edgar Berry
Magner. James Edward
Mahler. Carl Kampen
Makeley. Metrah. Jr.
Maness. John Moses
Mangum. Adolphus Williamson
Mangum, Charles Staples
Manly, Leo Henry
Mann. James Emory
Mann, Joseph Spencer
Manning. John Hall
Manter. W. J.
Mark. Alexander
Markham, William Sater, Jr.
Marland. Kenneth Milton
Marpet, Arthur Robert
Marsh. Frank Baker
Marshburn. Robert Franklin
Martin. Edward Watts
Martin, Joseph Bonaparte
Mason. George Bason
Mason. Solomon Pool
Mason, William Beverly. Jr.
Massey, Moulton Baxton
Matheson, Frank Mitchell
Matheson, Robert Arthur. Jr.
Matthews, Pierce Yarrell
Mathewson. Clarke
Maus, James Reginald
Medford. William Clinton
Medwin. Julius Alfred

Melchor, Lawson E.
Meroney, David Welch
Merritt, Chancie Lee
Merritt, William Daniels
Merritt. William Edgar
Michaels. Edward Griffin
Miller, J. I.
Milstead, Andrew Dallam
Milstead. John Woodson
Milton. Leon Vincent
Minor. William Thomas, Jr.
Montgomery. Harry Howard
Montgomery, James C.
Montgomery, Wade Anderson
Moore, Charles Joyce
Moore, Claude
Moore, Davis Lee
Moore, George Albert
Moore, James Edwin
Moore, John Allen
Moore, Leonidas Holt
Moore, Louis Toomer
Moore, Lloyd Tolson
Moore, Richard Henry
Moore, William Julius
Moore, William Percy
Morehead. Garrett
Morgan, David Bradley, Jr.
Morris, Fred Detwiley
Morris, John De
Morris, Roy Wilson
Morris, William Worth
Morrison, Fred Wilson
Morrow, Earl
Morrow, James Holland
Motsinger. John Fairbanks
Moye, Elbert Alfred. Jr.
Mullis, Clyde Edward
Mullis, Oscar Lee
Murnick, Joseph H.
Murphy, Walter
Myers, Marvin Phillips

Nash, Edmund Strudwick, Jr.
Nash, Samuel Simpson, Jr.
Nash, Thomas Palmer
Neiman, Abe Bernard
Neiman, David
Nelson, Herbert Andrews
Nelson, Melvin
Nethercutt, George Earl
Neville, Ernest Long
Newcombe. Arthur Rowell
Newcombe, Elliott Hill
Newton. James Sprunt
Nichols, William James
Nicklin, Samuel Strang
Nixmos, Horace
Nims, David Anderson
Noble, Albert Morris. Jr.
Noble, Robert Primrose
Noble, Stewart Grayson
Norfleet, Ashley Curtis
Norris, John Ernest
Norwood. Eston Gibbons
Norwood. John Wilkins, Jr.
Novich, Max Mordecai

Oates, Malcolm Norval

O'Brien, William Joseph, Jr.
Oldham, George Willis
Oldham, Jesse Morrow
Oldham, Wade Hampton
Orr, Joseph Lee
Orr, Manlius
Osborne, Francis Moore
Osborne, Virgil Waite
Owen, Frank Redding

Page, Thaddeus Shaw
Palmer, Edward John
Palmore, Julian Ivanhoe
Parker, Benjamin Carl
Parker, Carl Putnam
Parker, David Henry
Parker, Fred Pope, Jr.
Parker, Jesse Coe, Jr.
Parker, John Archibald
Parker, John Merrel
Parker, Raymond Gay
Parker, Talbot Fort
Parker, Walter Rea
Parsley, Robert Aubrey
Parsley, William Murdock
Parsons, Thomas Leake, Jr.
Patterson, Andrew Henry
Patterson, Earl Victor
Patterson, Fred Marion
Patterson, John Durant
Patterson, William Hazel
Pattisall, Richard Odell
Paxton, Branch Edwards
Peacock, John Gaston
Pearsall, Frederick Leonidas
Pearson, George Dowell
Pember, Howard S.
Pendergraft, Paul D.
Perkins, Aubrey Alphonse
Perry, Bennett Hester
Perry, Sidney Curtis
Perry, William Alva
Pharr, Frederick C.
Phifer, Isaac Avery
Phillips, Drury McNeill
Philpott, Benjamin Cabell, Jr.
Phipps, Harry Lee
Phipps, John Moore
Phoenix, Clarence Beall
Pierce, George Norman
Pijanowski, Walter Joseph
Pippin, Norman Ralph
Pittman, Wiley Hassell Marion
Poole, James Wyche
Pope, William Crawford
Porter, Andrew Lindsay
Potter, William Hallister
Potts, Ramsay Douglas
Powell, John William Gordon
Powell, William Curtis
Poindexter, Charles Crawford
Poyner, William Griggs
Pratt, Joseph Hyde, Jr.
Presson, Samuel Lee, Jr.
Price, James Curtis
Price, Thomas Moore
Prince, Hugh Williamson
Pritchard, William Grady
Pritchett, Hoyt Baker

Proctor, Edward Knox
Prouitt, Roy Alden
Pugh, James Thomas
Purrington, Alfred Luther, Jr.
Purser, Carr Robinson
Purser, John Raymond, Jr.

Quarles, James Norment

Rainey, John Marion
Ramsey, James Graham
Ramsey, Joseph Bunn
Rand, Herbert Hinton
Rand, Marshall Dunstin
Rand, Oliver Gray
Randolph, Philip Sprague
Raney, George Hall
Rankin, Frank Bisaner
Rankin, James Guy
Ranson, Jack
Ranson, John Oliver
Ranson, Lucius Henry
Ranson, Murphy Dale
Ranson, Paul Jones
Ranson, Paul Lacy
Ravenel, Samuel Fitzsimmons
Ray, Marvin
Raymer, Furches Barker
Redfern, Charles Maurice, Jr.
Redmon, Herman Leslie
Reid, Edward Solomon
Reid, James William
Reid, Robert Alexander
Reid, William Gordon
Rendleman, David Atwell
Reynolds (given name unknown)
Reynolds, Robert Rice
Rhem, Joseph Franklin
Rhinehart, Herman Allen
Rhodes, Leland Brown
Richards, Powell
Richardson, Pinckney Watt
Riley, Thomas Hurley
Ritch, Marvin Lee
Robbins, Jesse Manly
Robbins, Roswell Brackin
Roberts, Oren Ernest
Roberson, Fcy
Robertson, Thomas Ross
Robertson, William Ross
Robinson, Gordon Charles
Robinson, George Fleming
Rodgers, Herbert Blair
Rogers, Francis Ovington
Rogers, George Oroon
Rood, Carlton Alexander
Rood, Wilson Andrew
Rose, Thomas Duncan
Rosser, Roy Pleasant
Rourk, William Asbury
Rousseau, James Park
Royall, William Allen
Ruble, Raymond John
Ruffin, Colin Bradley
Russ, Walter Scott
Russell, Joseph Brent
Ruth, Earl Baker
Rutzler, George Frederick
Rutzler, Robert Lee

269

Sams, John Robert
Sanders, George Waterhouse
Sandlin, Henry Howard
Sapp, Clarence Odell
Satterfield, Henry Clement, Jr.
Saunders, William P. T.
Scarborough, Albert Moses
Schmukler, Milton
Schwartz, Benjamin
Schwartz, Harry Lewis
Scott, James Graham
Scott, William Lafayette
Seagle, Perry Edgar
Sears, Benjamin Belvin
Seyffert, George Francis
Shaffer, Charles Milton
Shamberger, Lacy Lee
Shapiro, Edward
Shapiro, Moses Minz
Sharpe, Thomas Allen
Sharpe, William David Pope, Jr.
Shaw, Howard Burton
Shaw, William Alger
Sheffield, James Harold
Shepard, Frederick Carlyle
Shepard, Thomas Harrison, Jr.
Sher, Phillip
Shields, James Duncan
Shields, Leon Grady
Shirley, Ernest Raeford
Shore, Frank Marion, Jr.
Shores, William Irving
Shuford, Emmett Graydon
Shuford, Harney Ferguson
Shuler, James Ernest
Shull, Samuel Eakin
Siddall, Roger Shore
Sides, Robert Lee
Sifford, Ernest Jerrod
Sinclair, David Cunningham
Singletary, Snowdon, Jr.
Singletary, William Curry
Sitton, Charles Vedder
Sloan, David Bryan
Slocumb, Paul
Slusser, Frank Willard
Small, Walter Lowry
Smathers, William Frank
Smiley, Thomas Bryan
Smith, Alan Alexander
Smith, Claibone Thweatt
Smith, Edwin Bretney
Smith, Henry Clark
Smith, James Kenneth
Smith, John Franklin
Smith, Junius McRae
Smith, Oswald Patton
Smith, Peyton McGuire
Smith, Robert Bruce
Smith, Thomas Clark
Smith, William Edward, Jr.
Smith, William
Smith, Winslow Willkings
Snipes, Edgar Thomas
Snipes, Eugene Malcolm
Snipes, Harvey Grant
Snipes, William Seaton
Snyder, Daniel Marshall
Snyder, Herman Pressley
Solomon, Abram Shrier
Solomon, Harry Meyer
Spainhour, Carl Michael

Sparrow, George Antrim
Spaugh, Rufus Arthur
Spaulding, Leon Adelbert
Spell, James Bryan
Spence, Ralph Case
Spencer, Charles Edward
Spencer, Earl Montgomery
Spruill, Corydon Perry, Jr.
Spruill, Frank Shepard
Stafford, Crook Graham
Stafford, John Springs
Stallings, Luby Frederick
Stanly, Benjamin Edward
Stanton, George Washington
Starling, Homer Cortez
Steele, Robert Thomas Stephen
Stem, Frederick Booth
Stephens, George
Stephens, James Linley
Stevens, Ralph Edwin
Steward, Luther Corwin, Jr.
Stewart, Barney Cleveland
Stewart, Roach Sidney
Stewart, Robert M.
Stewart, Oliver Conrad
Stone, Joseph Shepard
Story, Romy
Strayhorn, R. Hammond
Strange, Robert, Jr.
Strickland, Matthew Emmett
Strong, George Vaughan
Struthers, James Arthur
Sullivan, Henry Shumate
Sullivan, Louis Gray
Supple, Adrian Dwight
Sutton, Frederick Isler
Sweeney, Norcom
Sweetman, Edward Martin, **Jr.**
Swift, Vance Everett
Swink, Jonas Herman

Tabb, William Shields
Tandy, George Wendell
Tankersly, Edward William
Tate, John Austin
Tatum, James Moore
Tayloe, David Thomas, **Jr.**
Tayloe, John Cotton
Taylor, Carl Duffy
Taylor, Edmon Rhett
Taylor, Richard Moore
Teague, Samuel Farris
Teague, Sherrill Burette
Tennent, Charles Gailiard
Tennent, George Raby
Tenney, Edwin Wright
Tenny, John Brooks
Thatch, Harry Smith
Thomas, Charley Walter
Thomas, William George
Thompson, Earl Asbury
Thompson, Eugene Graham
Thompson, George Dewey
Thompson, Holland **McTyeire**
Thompson, James Alfred
Thompson, John Melvin
Thompson, Kern Lee, Jr.
Thompson, Seymour Columbus
Thorpe, James Battle
Thorpe, Richard Young
Tillett, John
Tillett, William Smith, **Jr.**

270

Tilley, Reginald Robert
Topkins, Matthew
Townsend, Newman Alexander
Travis, Louis Grady
Trimpey, John Surrey
Tsuman, Harry Peter
Tull, Edward Rountree
Turner, Willie Person Mangum
Twiford, Clement Wake

Ullman, Fred E.
Umstead, Alexander Bruce
Umstead, Frank Graham
Underwood, Neal Alexander
Underwood, William Emmett Kyle
Upchurch, Lonnie Milton
Usher, Peter Clyde
Uzzell, William Edward

VanLandingham, Ralph, Jr.
Vanstory, William Alfred
Vaughan, Evan James
Venable, Charles Scott
Venable, John Manning
Vick, Thurman
Voliva, Edward Lemuel

Waddell, Charles Edward, Jr.
Wadsworth, Harvey Bryan
Wadsworth, James Edgar
Wakeley, Frank Hart
Wakeley, William Easton
Wakeley, William Easton, Jr.
Waldrop, Joseph Edmund
Walker, Erwin Goode
Ward, Melvin Churchill
Wardlaw, Charles Digby
Warren, Addison Exum
Warren, John McCullen
Waters, Jay Shirley
Waters, Zack James
Watkins, Robert Young
Watkins, Thomas Henry
Watson, George David
Watt, Lawrence Eugene
Watts, Clifford Glenn
Weathers, Virgil Stowe
Webb, Bruce
Webb, Leon Douglas
Webb, Robert Hoke
Webb, Van Wyck Hoke
Webber, William Slade
Webster, Bernie Latcher
Weeks, Hassell Howard
Weil, Lionel Solomon
Westmoreland, Joseph Robert
Whedbee, Harry West
Whisnant, Albert Miller, Jr.
Whisnant, Manly Dowell
Whitaker, Ferdinand Cary
Whitaker, Frank Ogburn
Whitaker, Harry Foote
Whitaker, Joel D., Jr.
Whitaker, William Pell, Jr
White, Joseph Harvey
White, Rufus
White, Thomas Skinner, Jr.
White, William Dabney
White, William Elliott
Whitehead, Burgess Urquhart
Whitener, Abel Gross
Whiting, Seymour Webster

Wiggins, James Middleton
Wiley, John Fleming
Willard, Edward Payson
Willcox, John
Williams, Daniel McGregor
Williams, Isham Roland
Williams, James Leonard
Williams, John Roy
Williams, Macon McCorkle
Williams, Marion Murphy
Williams, Marshall McDairmid, Jr.
Williams, Robert Ecker
Williams, Robert Fleet
Williams, Woodward White
Williams, Zack Maroney
Williamson, Harry Webb
Willis, Meade Homer, Jr.
Willis, Richard Troth
Wilson, Henry Van Peters, Jr.
Wilson, Hugh McLean
Wilson, Lawrence Girard
Wilson, S. L.
Wilson, William Gilliam, Jr.
Wilson, William Miller
Wimberley, Benjamin
Winborne, John Wallace
Winborne, Stanley
Winborne, Vaughn Sharp
Winn, John Harvey
Winstead, Lamar Herbert
Winston, Robert Alonzo
Winston, Robert Watson, Jr.
Witherington, Isham Faison
Womble, James Dawson
Wood, Edward Philip
Wood, George Collins
Wood, Word Harris
Woodall, Charles Lawrence
Woodall, Junius Chester
Woodard, David Warren
Woodard, Graham
Woodard, James Edwin
Woodard, Wayne Owen
Woodson, James Leake
Woody, Eugene Munday
Woollcott, Philip
Woollen, Charles Thomas, Jr.
Wooten, William Preston
Worsham, Buford Blackburn
Worth, Henry Venable
Wrenn, Creighton
Wrenn, Elmer Alexander
Wright, Auburn Leslie
Wright, Henry
Wright, Irby
Wright, Isaac Clark
Wright, Lenoir Chambers
Wright, Robert Herring
Wright, Robert Hazlehurst, Jr.
Wyrick, Charles Lloyd

Yates, William James
Yarborough, Charles Hill
Yeager, Olin Ray
Yeomans, Edgar Dawson
York, William Marvin
Younce, George Alexander
Young, Thomas Bayard
Young, William Leslie

Zaiser, Eugene Carl
Zealy, Robert Lyles
Zollicoffer, Allen Caulain

271

FOOTBALL LETTERMEN

1936

Adams, R.L., Avery, I.T. Jr., Bartos, Henry, Bershak, A.A., Buck, R.D., Burnett, T.D., Cooner, B.R., Dashiell, Dick, Dermid, J.D. Jr., Ditt, A.H., Dunham, W.G., Hutchins, J.A., Little, Crowell, Maronic, S.J., McIver, C.M., McCarn, L.W., Palmer, E.J., Smith, F.P., Stewart, R.M., Trimpey, J.S., Watson, G.D., Webb, Van Wyck H., Hart, W.A. (Mgr.), Lindley, P.C. (Mgr.)

1937

Avery, I.T., Adams, R.L., Bartos, Henry, Bershak, A.A., Bricklemyer, E.C., Burnette, T.D., Ditt, A.H., Kline, C.R., Kraynick, J.J., Little, C.C., Maronic, S.J., Palmer, E.J., Palmer, Horace, Radman, G.R., Slagle, C.A., Stirnweiss, G.H., Watson, G.D., Woodson, J.L., Wrenn, E.A., Craige, Archie Jr. (Mgr.), Ray, R.M. (Mgr.)

1938

Abernathy, L.F., Adams, R.L., Cernugel, A.N., Desich, D.D., Graham, A.H. Jr. (Mgr.), Kimball, C.G., Kline, C.R., Kraynick, J.J., Lalanne, J.F., Mallory, J.B., Maronic, S.J., Maynard, Albert (Mgr.), Palmer, Horace, Patrick, L.N. (Mgr.), Peiffer, Carl, Radman, G.R., Sadoff, S.H., Severin, P.V., Slagle, C.A., Smith, R.B., Stirnweiss, George, Watson, G.D., Winborne, J.W., Woodson, J.L.

1939

Abernathy, L.F., Baker, D.C., Bobbitt, M.E., Brantley, J.T., Connor, R.L., Doty, F. deB., Dunkle, H.N., Elliot, J.D., Faircloth, W.H., Kimball, C.G., Kline, C.R., Lalanne, J.F., Mallory, J.B., Nowell, A.G., Radman, George, Ralston, G.F., Richardson, S.S., Sadoff, S.H., Severin, P.V., Sieck, R.C., Slagle, C.A., Slotnick, Leo, Smith, R.B., Stirnweiss, G.H., Stoinoff, R.R., Suntheimer, C.J., White, R.A., Woodson, J.L., Hines, W.W. (Mgr.), Holmes, F.M. (Mgr.)

1940

Austin, J.J., Baker, D.C., Barksdale, D.A., Benton, H.P. Jr., Bobbitt, M.E., Connor, R.L., Cooke, M.J., Dunkle, H.N., Dalton, M.R. (Mgr.) [Freshman manager granted major award.], Elliot, J.D., Faircloth, W.H., Heymann, R.L., Hodges, H.L., Kimball, C.G., Lalanne, J.F., Marshall, Alfred, Michaels, Edward, Miller, J.D., Nowell, A.G., O'Hare, F.V., Pecora, J.L., Richardson, S.S., Sadoff, Sidney, Severin, P.V., Sieck, R.C., Sigler, W.M. Jr., Smith, R.B., Suntheimer, C.J., Whitten, R.E., Wolf, J.L., Gray, J.A. Jr. (Mgr.), Wright, T.H. Jr. (Mgr.)

1941

Austin, J.J., Baker, C.R., Barksdale, D.A., Benton, H.P., Byrum, T.C., Cheek, M.E., Connor, R.L., Cox, J.H., Crone, J.C., Croom, W.C.,

272

Dunkle, H.N., Elliot, J.D., Faircloth, W.H., Gugert, F.A., Heymann, R.L., Hodges, H.L., Jordan, R.A., Marshall, Alfred, Michaels, Edward, Nowell, A.G., O'Hare, F.V., Pecora, John, Richardson, S.S., Serlich, E.A. Jr., Sieck, R.C., Stallings, F.D., Suntheimer, C.J., Turner, R.C., White, R.A., Wolf, J.L., Hogue, Cy (Mgr.), Hinkle, North (Mgr.), Brown, Roland (Mgr.)

1942

Austin, J.J., Byrum, T.C. Jr., Cooke, M.J., Cox, J.H., Croom, W.C. Jr., Graham, S.P., Heymann, R.L., Highsmith, C.L., Hussey, J.W., Jones, J.M., Jordan, R.A., Karres, A.M., Marshall, Alfred, Myers, Fred C., Pecora, J.L., Pupa, W.E., Sigler, W.M. Jr., Sparger, G.W., Strayhorn, R.N. Jr., Tandy, J.H., Turner, R.C., Webb, H.T. Jr., Wolf, J.L., Wright, J.W. Jr., Carlton, Graham (Mgr.), Thomason, Dan (Mgr.)

1943

Aland, J.W., Arbes, Samuel, Arfman, H.T, Bryant, C.E., Clayton, E.D., Cornogg, U.G., Cox, Hugh, Croom, W.C., Elliott, R.W., Erickson, W.C., Fitch, J.S., Grimes, G.S., Hamilton, F.S., Harris, R.A., Henry, N.H., Hodges, G.D. Jr., Hoey, E.F., Hussey, J.W., Johnson, W.O., Jones, J.M. Jr., Kosinski, J.S., Lane, T.A., McCollum, R.W., McDaniel, R.C., Maskas, J.D.,

Miller, F.W., Myers, F.C., Owen, T.B., Palmer, Wayne, Poole, G.B., Poole, J.R., Poole, O.L., Richardson, J.E. Jr., Roberts, G.R., Rodgers, H.W., Rohling, B.H., Spurlin, M.L., Staples, J.S., Starr, Edward Jr., Strayhorn, R.N. Jr., Teague, E.L. Jr., Thomason, V.D., Turner, R.C., Weldon, Howard, Powell, C.W. (Mgr.), Lockhart, J.W. (Mgr.)

1944

N.R.O.T.C.

Brown, H.C., Dean, J.R., Kraus, Walter, Twehey, E.L., Walters, Ray, Ellis, W.B. III (Mgr.)

MARINE

Camp, J.V., Elger, A.J., Ellis, J.T., Godwin, J.L., Kerns, J.E., Lane, Tom, Lowe, A.C.

NAVY V-12

Abell, T.G., Buchheister, J.B., Collins, A.E., Foster, J.E., Gilliam, Wm., Golding, E.I., Kinsey, J.H., Koffenberger, E.L., Lacy, E.H., Leatherman, D.R., Voris, C.W., Walker, J.N., Warren, R.C., Weant, R.A.

CIVILIAN

Bauen, F.C., Bay, Sam, Smith, W.G., Crowley, A.J. Jr. (Mgr.)

273

1945

CIVILIANS

Bernot, A.R., Camp, J., Cooke, M.H., Curran, F.E., Flamish, W., Grow, B.K., Gurtis, J.W., Hartig, D.C., Kennedy, R.M., Marczyk, S.W., Mitten, R.M., Norcross, M.M., Pritchard, W.G. Jr., Rizzo, P.J., Rubish, M., Steigman, D., Szafaryn, L., Varney, H.E., Wardle, W.J., Warren, R.

NAVY V-12

Ellison, C.A., Voris, C.W.

N.R.O.T.C.

Colfer, T.R., Golding, E.I., Gorman, T.C., Twohey, E.L.

MARINES

Bevers, B.B., Cox, R.V., Hazelwood, T.E., Oliphant, R.C., Walker, W.W.

1946

Britt, William D., Camp, James, Cheek, Marvin E., Clements, John L., Cox, Robert V., Fitch, Jack S., Fowle, F. Haywood, Grow, B.K Jr., Hartig, Donald, Hazelwood, Theodore, Highsmith, Chandos, Jarrell, Baxter, Justice, Charles, Maceyko, William S., Mitten, Robert, Myers, F.C., Powell, Kenneth, Pupa, Walter E., Roberts, George R., Rodgers, Hosea, Romano, Joseph A., Rubish,

Michael, Sparger, George, Spellman, M.A., Spurlin, Max, Stiegman, D.B., Strayhorn, Ralph, Sutherland, William J., Szafaryn, Leonard, Tandy, John H., Varney, Harry, Weant, Robert, Williamson, E.W., Wright, J.W. Jr., Weiner, Arthur, Isaacs, Wade (Mgr.)

1947

Bernot, Albin, Camp, James, Cheek, Marvin E., Clements, John L., Cooke, Max H., Cox, Robert V., Fitch, Jack S., Flamisch, William A., Fowle, F. Haywood, Hayes, William A., Hartig, Donald C., Hazelwood, Ted E., Justice, Charles, Kennedy, Robert M., Klosterman, Lawrence, Knox, Edward, Logue, Daniel, Maceyko, William S., Mitten, Robert M., Powell, Kenneth, Pritchard, William G., Pupa, Walter E., Roberts, George, Rodgers, Hosea, Romano, Joseph A., Rubish, Michael, Sherman, Fred E., Smith, William G., Sparger, George W., Stiegman, Daniel, Szafaryn, Len, Tandy, John H., Varney, Harry, Wardle, William J., Weant, Robert A., Weiner, Arthur E., Wright, Joel, Hogan, George (Mgr.)

1948

Bunting, Richard F., Clements, John L., Cooke, Max H., Cospito, Joseph A., Cox, Robert V., Flamish, William A., Fowle, Haywood, Hartig, Donald C., Hayes, William A., Hazelwood, Theodore E., Highsmith, Chandos, Holdash,

Irvin J., Justice, Charles, Kennedy, Robert M., Klosterman, Lawrence, Knox, Edward M., Maceyko, William S., Marczyk, Stanley W., Mitten, Robert M., Neikirk, Joseph R., Powell, Kenneth, Purcell, Gus B., Reynolds, Robert K., Rizzo, Paul J., Rodgers, Hosea, Romano, Joseph A., Rubish, Michael, Sherman, Fred E., Stiegman, Daniel B., Szafaryn, Len A., Varney, Harry E., Wardle, William J., Washington, Edward K., Weant, Robert A., Weiner, Arthur, Lindley, Tom (Mgr.)

1949

Augustine, Joseph F., Bestwick, Richard L., Bilpuch, Edward G., Bunting, Richard F., Carson, Leon H., Clements, John L., Dudeck, Joe, Gantt, Robert B., Gurtis, Joseph W. Jr., Hansen, Roscoe H., Hayes, William A., Hendrick, James P. Jr., Hesmer, Theodore C. Jr., Holdash, Irvin J., Justice, Charles, King, Julian B., Knox, Edward M. Jr., Kosinski, Joseph S., Kuhn, William O., McDonald, Richard L., Neikirk, Joseph R., Nickerson, Glendon B., O'Brien, Joseph W., Powell, J. Kenneth, Rizzo, Paul J., Ruffin, Dalton D., Rywak, Peter, Sherman, Fred E., Stevens, Thomas B., Verchick, George, Wardle, William J., Washington, Edward K., Weiner, Arthur E., Wiess, Richard T., Wiley, David E., Williams, Egbert P., Moore, Henry F. Jr. (Mgr.)

1950

Bestwick, Richard L., Bilpuch, Edward G., Bunting, Richard F., Carr, Joseph B., Carson, Leon H. Jr., Dudeck, Joe, Gantt, Robert B., Gruver, Richard M., Hansen, Roscoe H., Hayes, William A., Hesmer, Theodore C. Jr., Higgins, Thomas, Holdash, Irvin J., Kimel, Don H., King, Julian B., Kuhn, William O., Liberati, Ernest A., McDonald, R.L., Miketa, Andrew, Nickerson, Glendon B., Norris, George, O'Brien, Joseph W., Page, Robert, Port, Chalmers, Rizzo, Paul, Rousseau, Julius, Ruffin, Dalton, Sherman, Fred E., Stevens, Thomas B., Venters, Robert T., Wallace, William C., Walser, Grover B., White, C.C., Wiess, Richard T., Wiley, David, Woodell, John, Craft, Bill (Mgr.)

1951

Adler, Thomas James, Baker, William Luin Jr., Behrens, Charles E. (Mgr.), Berger, Charles Douglas (Mgr.), Bestwick, Richard Lamont, Carson, Leon Halden Jr., Cooke, Jackson Millard, Darnell, Louis A., Dudeck, Joseph Jr., Ellenwood, Charles, Gantt, Robert Baxter, Gaylord, John Freeman, Gravitte, Connie Mack, Gruver, Richard Myers, Hesmer, Theodore C. Jr., Higgins, Thomas Joseph John, Hursh, David Paul, Kelso, William Dunlap, King, Julian Baxter, Kirkman, William H. Jr., Kuhn, William Orville, Lackey, Norris D. Jr., Maultsby, John Warren, Miketa,

Andrew John, Nickerson, Glendon Barry, Norris, George Van, O'Brien, Joseph William Jr., Parker, Larry Hunter, Port, Chalmers Marshall, Ruffin, Dalton Dillard, Stevens, Thomas Brock, Venters, Robert Troy, Wallace, William Carter, White, Robert William Jr., Wiess, Richard Thomas, Wile, David Edgel, Williams, Egbert Pridgen, Williams, William Owen, Wissman, Francis John, Walser, Grover B., Yarborough, Kenneth Harold, Thornton, William E.

1952

Adler, Thomas James, Alexander, Wilson, Beaver, Ralph Grady, Bruton, Oren Douglas, Bullock, Leonard Storey, Cooke, Jackson Millard, Davidson, Harold Howard, DeWeese, James Charles, Eure, Thaddeus A. Jr., Foti, George Leigh, Fredere, Francis Bolton, Frye, William Jennings, Gaylord, John Freeman Jr., Gravitte, Connie Mack, Gregory, Miles Cunningham, Higgins, Thomas J.J., Hursh, Paul David, Keller, Kenneth K., Kirkman, William Hugh, Jr., Kocornik, Richard Wilborn, Lackey, Norris D. Jr., Lambert, John Marcus, Liberati, Ernest Anthony, Long, Albert Anderson Jr., Mainer, Daniel Iverson, Marcinko, Stephen Charles, McCormick, Donald Felix, McCreedy, James E. Jr., Motta, Charles Peter, Mullens, David Bobo, Neville, James Steve, Newman, Marshall Joseph, Norris, George Van, Opitz, Stephen Louis Jr., Parker, Larry Hunter, Patterson,

Edward Leonard, Port, Chalmers Marshall, Ridenhour, Charles Franklin Jr., Seawell, Howard Carter Jr., Wallace, William Carter, Wallin, George Franklin, Walser, Grover Bentley, White, Robert William Jr., Williams, William Owen, Worrell, Florenz Demoris, Yarborough, Kenneth Harold, Lingerfeldt, Robert Dewey (Mgr.)

1953

Adler, Thomas James, Bullock, Leonard Storey, Eure, Thaddeus Jr., Foti, George Leigh, Fredere, Francis Bolton, Frye, William Jennings, Gravitte, Connie Mack, Gregory, Miles Cunningham, Keller, Kenneth K., Kirkman, William Hugh, Kocornik, Richard Wilborn, Koman, William, Lackey, Norris Dixon, Lambert, John Marcus, Lane, Norman Ronald, McCreedy, James Edward, Neville, James Steve, Newman, Marshall Joseph, Parker, Larry Hunter, Patterson, Edward Leonard, Perdue, Roland Powell, Seawell, Howard Carter Jr., Starner, Richard Allen, Williams, Billy O., Yarborough, Kenneth Harold, Connell, Avery (Mgr.), Hawks, William, Weatherspoon, Van Louis, Newton, Adrian Jefferson Jr.

1954

Alexander, Wilson, Bilich, John Matthew, Bullock, Leonard Storey Jr., Foti, George Leigh, Frye, William Jennings Jr., Gravitte, Connie Mack, Jones, John

Columbus, Keller, Kenneth K. Jr., Kirkman, William Hugh, Klochak, Donald, Koman, William, Lane, Norman Ronald, Lear, Donald Joseph, Livesay, Darden Rawls, Long, Albert Anderson Jr., Marcinko, Steven Charles, Maultsby, John Warren, McMullen, Larry Daniel, Muschamp, Robert Larry, Neville, Jimmy Steve, Newman, Marshall Joseph, Parker, Larry Hunter, Patterson, Edward Leonard, Perdue, Roland Powell, Ridenhour, Charles Franklin, Shoulars, Wilson Hudson, Stavnitski, George Joseph, Sutton, Edward Wike, Malone, Douglas Owen, Callihan, Herbert A. (Mgr.)

1955

Bilich, Matthew John, Frye, William Jennings, Gaca, Giles John, Jones, John Columbus, Jones, James Harold, Keller, Kenneth Kay, Koman, William, Lear, Donald Joseph, Lineberger, Jackie Ray, Maultsby, John Warren, McMullen, Larry Daniel, Muschamp, Herbert Larry, Payne, Roland William Jr., Perdue, Roland Powell, Reed, David Robert, Robinson, Charles Filmore, Sasser, George Freeman, Setzer, Willis Marshall, Shoulars, Wilson Hudson, Smith, Richard Wayne, Stavnitski, George Joseph, Sutton, Edward Wike, Temple, Joseph Edward, Vale, Wallace Handle, Williams, William Howard, Johnson, William Holmes (Mgr.)

1956

Bilich, Matthew John, Blazer, Phillip Paul, DeCantis, Emil Joseph, Dillard, Robert H. (Mgr.), Ellington, William Banks, Farmer, Carl Douglas, Gaca, Giles John, Goff, Rowland Daley, Hardison, Willie Louis Jr., Hathaway, Curtis Harcum, Haywood, John Robert, Johnson, William Holmes (Mgr.), Jones, James Harold, Jones, John Columbus, Kemper, Donald, Koes, Ronald Paul, Lear, Donald Joseph, Marquette, Roland James, McMullen, Larry Daniel, Muschamp, Larry Herbert, Parks, William (Mgr.), Payne, Roland William Jr., Pell, Stuart Lamar, Pulley, William Paul Jr., Redding, Donald Sanborn, Reed, David Robert, Robinson, Charles Fillmore, Russavage, Leo Joseph, Sasser, George Freeman, Setzer, Willis Marshall, Smith, Richard Wayne, Stavnitski, George Joseph, Sutton, Edward Wyke, Swearingen, Fred Jones Jr., Turlington, Clyde McRae, Vale, Wallace Handel, Varnum, James Wilson

1957

Blazer, Phillip Paul, Coker, Donald Ray, Cummings, John Ballentine, Davis, James Edwin, DeCantis, Emil Joseph, Furjanic, Edward Francis, Gaca, Giles John, Goff, Rowland Daley Jr., Hathaway, Curtis Harcum, Haywood, John Robert, Johnson, William Holmes (Mgr.), Jones, James Harold, Kemper, Donald, Koes, Ronald Paul, Lineberger, Jackie Ray, Lipski, Edward Adam, Lowe, David Nelson, Marquette, Ronald James, Payne,

Roland William Jr., Pell, Stewart Lamar, Pulley, William Paul Jr., Redding, Donald Sanborn, Russell, Paul Jr., Schuler, James Randall, Shupin, Robert Rodney, Setzer, Willis Marshall, Smith, Wade Marvin, Stallings, Alva Donald, Steele, Ralph Thomas, Swearingen, Fred Jones Jr., Turlington, Clyde McRae, Goldstein, Alan

1958

Blazer, Phillip Paul, Buckley, Don S. (Mgr.), Butler, Earl Ray, Clement, Henry L. Jr., Coker, Donald Ray, Cummings, John Ballentine, Davis, James Edwin, DeCantis, Emil Joseph, Folckomer, Senford Lavern, Goldstein, Alan, Greenday, Michael, Hawkins, Ross Cooper, Kemper, Donald, Klochak, Donald, Koes, Ronald Paul, Lipski, Edward Adam, Long, James M. (Mgr.), Lowe, David Nelson, Mueller, Fred Otto, Redding, Donald Sanborn, Rice, James Alexander, Riggs, Francis Graham, Russell, Paul, Schroeder, John Jenkins, Shupin, Robert Rodney, Smith, Moyer Gray, Smith, Wade Marvin, Stallings, Alva Donald, Steele, Ralph Thomas, Stunda, John Francis, Swearingen, Fred Jones Jr., Turlington, Clyde McRae, Wall, Roy Milam, Walton, Rabe C., Crist, Takey, Hardison, Willie Louis, Goff, Rowland Daley, Hathaway, Curtis Harcum, Droze, Haywood Daniel Jr.

1959

Amos, Jerry W., Butler, Earl Ray, Carson, Gilbert M., Clement, Henry L., Coleman, Wilkes (Mgr.), Cummings, John Ballentine, Daniels, Allen (Mgr.), Davies, Joseph E., Davis, James Edwin, Elliott, Robert W., Farris, Ray Simpson Jr., Folckomer, Senford Lavern, Frederick, Larry G., Gallagher, Benjamin Baker, Goldstein, Alan, Greenday, Michael, Hawkins, Ross Cooper, Hegarty, John Francis, Klochak, Donald, Kordalski, Robert Edward, LeCompte, James Leonard, Lipski, Edward Adam, Lotz, Daniel M., Mueller, Fred Otto, Nead, Richard F., Ray, Herman E., Rice, James Alexander, Riggs, Francis Graham, Russell, Paul, Schroeder, John Jenkins, Shupin, Robert Rodney, Sloop, Max Conrad, Smith, Clayton Bernard, Smith, Moyer Gray, Smith, Wade Marvin, Stallings, Alva Donald, Steele, Ralph Thomas, Stunda, John Francis, Truver, Gary G., Wall, Roy Milam, Walton, Rabe C.

1960

Addison, James Haywood, Beck, Leonard James, Brennan, Edward Michael, Cabe, William Thomas, Carson, Gilbert Martin, Clement, Henry Littlefield Jr., Craver, Joe Malcolm, Davies, Joseph Edwin, Eanes, Carl Marshall, Elliott, Robert Whitlow, Farris, Ray Simpson Jr., Flournoy, John Francis, Folckomer, Senford Lavern, Fowler, Wesley C. (Mgr.), Gallagher, Benjamin Barker, Greenday, Michael, Greene, Duff Surgent,

278

Hawkins, Ralph, Hawkins, Ross Cooper, Hegarty, John Francis, Hennessey, Anthony James, Hokanson, James Richard, Knox, George Cowan, LeCompte, James Leonard, McMillan, Benton Lee Jr., Marslender, William Ward, Mendelsohn, Joseph S. (Mgr.), Mueller, Frederick Otto, Renger, John F. (Mgr.), Rice, James Alexander, Riggs, Francis Graham, Runco, John Anthony, Schroeder, John Jenkins, Shumate, Jimmie Roger, Sloop, Max Conrad, Smith, Moyer Gray, Smith, Robert Bernard, Stunda, John Francis, Talley, William Adolphus, Tillery, Jack Gregory, Truver, Gary Gene, Wall, Roy Milam, Welch, William Edward

1961

Addison, James Haywood, Alderman, James Blane, III, Ballard, Marshall III (Mgr.), Beck, Leonard James, Cabe, James Jerry, Carson, Gilbert Martin, Craver, Joe Malcolm, Davenport, Joe Conrad, Davies, Joseph Edwin, Edge, Bias Melton Jr., Elliott, Robert Whitlow, Esposito, Victor Michael, Farris, Ray Simpson, Jr., Flournoy, John Francis, Greene, Duff Surgent, Hammett, John Allen, Hegarty, John Francis, Hennessey, Anthony James, Knox, George Cowan, Lacey, Robert Reavil, LeCompte, James Leonard, Loflin, Samuel Wayne, McMillan, Benton Lee, Marslender, William Ward, Regan, John G. Breckenridge III, Renger, John Frank (Mgr.), Runco, John Anthony, Saffelle, Milton Franklin

Jr., Serenko, Stephen Anthony, Shuford, Gene Miles, Shumate, Jimmy Roger, Sloop, Max Conrad, Smith, Roger William, Spainhour, Walter Judson Jr., Taylor, William Henry, Tillery, Jack Gregory, Truver, Gary Gene, Yates, Stephen Keith, Zaback, Robert Joseph, Hobson, William Patrick (Mgr.)

1962

Alderman, James Blane III, Ballard, Marshall III, (Mgr.), Barden, Heywood Lamb, Black, Gary Ray, Boutselis, George John, Braine, David Thomas, Cabe, James Jerry, Cozart, William Taft Jr., Craver, Joe Malcolm, Eason, James Lawrence, Edge, Bias Melton Jr., Esposito, Victor Michael, Eudy, John Clinton, Flournoy, John Francis, Gallagher, Francis Joseph, Greene, Bruce Briant, Greene, Duff Surgent, Hammett, John Allen, Hanburger, Christian Jr., Hennessey, Anthony James, Hill, John Alvin, Hobson, William P. (Mgr.), Ish, Curtis Laws, Jackson, John Ronald, Kesler, Ralph Edward, Kortner, Coleman Kirth, Lacey, Robert Reavil, McLamb, Joseph Timothy, Marslender, William Ward, Robinson, Carroll Bennett, Runco, John Anthony, Sigmon, Wendell Gene, Smith, Roger William, Tillery, Jack Gregory, Tuthill, Ronald Floyd, Ward, Tom Henry Jr., Wells, Loren Worth, Willard, Kenneth Henderson, Yates, Stephen Keith, Zaback, Robert Joseph, Zarro, Richard John

279

1963

Alderman, James Blane, Atherton, John Warner, Baggett, Lee McLeod, Ballard, Marshall (Mgr.), Barden, Heywood Lamb Jr., Black, Gary Ray, Bowman, Frank Llewellyn III, Braine, David Thomas, Brooks, Thomas Eugene, Cabe, James Jerry, Chapman, Max Carroll, Constantin, Donald C., Cowles, Robert L., Eason, James Lawrence, Edge, Bias Melton Jr., Edwards, William Masters, Ellison, George Robert Jr., Esposito, Victor Michael, Eudy, John Clinton Jr., Gallagher, Frank Joseph, Hammett, John Allen, Hanburger, Christian Jr., Hill, John Alvin, Hobson, William P. (Mgr.), Hodges, Henry Latham Jr., Ish, Curtis Laws, Jackson, John Ronald, Kesler, Ralph Edward, Kinney, George Sandifer, Kortner, Coleman Keith, Lacey, Robert Reavil, Malobicky, John Joseph, Nance, Joseph K. (Mgr.), Naughton, James Michael, Ogburn, Robert Glenn Jr., Paulos, Raymond John, Ray, James Pendleton, Robinson, Carroll Bennett, Sigmon, Wendell Gene, Smith, Roger William, Stringer, Edward Hand Jr., Tuthill, Ronald Floyd, Ward, Tom Henry Jr., Wellman, Dana Richard, Wells, Loren Worth, Westfall, Barry Franz, Willard, Kenneth Henderson, Zarro, Richard John

1964

Atherton, John Warner, Axselle, Ralph Lewis Jr., Barden, Heywood Lamb, Black, Gary Ray, Braine, David Thomas, Brooks, Thomas Eugene, Chapman, Max Carrol, Churchill, Joseph Lacy, Clay, Neal Hargett, Darnall, William Carlyle, Davis, Charles Thomas, Eason, James Lawrence, Edwards, William Masters II, Eudy, John Clinton Jr., Frantangelo, Joseph Anthony, Gallagher, Francis Joseph, Gallagher, James Joseph, Hanburger, Christian Jr., Harmon, John Matney, Harrington, James Stewart, Hill, John Alvin, Hume, Robert Leo, Jackson, John Ronald, Kaplan, Ronald Martin, Kesler, Ralph Edward Jr., Kinney, George Sandifer, Lister, Stephen Craig, Loveday, Donald Ray, McArthur, Alan Francis, Malobicky, John Jay, Nance, Joseph Kinchin (Mgr.), Ogburn, Robert Glenn Jr., Phillips, Harold Lee Jr., Sadler, George Henry, Stringer, Edward Hand Jr., Stubbs, Stanley Lyon (Mgr.), Szymaitis, James Adam, Talbott, Joseph Daniel, Tuthill, Ronald Floyd, Ward, Tom Henry Jr., Willard, Kenneth Henderson, Wood, Charles Henry, Zarro, Richard John

1965

Addison, James Haywood, Alexander, Charles Edward Jr., Atherton, John Warner, Battistello, Gregory Alesandro, Beaver, Jeffrey Windsor, Boggs, Charles Irving, Byrd, James Edward, Carr, Charles Lee, Chapman, Max Carrol, Churchill, Joseph Lacy, Clayton, Felix Bernard, Critcher, John Calvin Jr. (Mgr.), Darnall, William Carlyle, Davenport, John Francis, Davis, Charles

280

Thomas, Davis, LeRoy Albert, Edwards, William Masters II, Ephland, Charles Ray III, Erimias, David Richard, Esher, John Joseph, Fisher, Lloyd Gene, Fratangelo, Joseph Anthony, Harmon, John Matney, Harrington, James Stewart, High, William Worley, Horvat, Michael Anthony, Hume, Robert Leo, Ingle, Archibald Tomlinson, Johnson, Ryland Earl Jr., Kaplan, Ronald Martin, Lampman, Thomas Smith Jr., Link, Malcolm Eugene, Lister, Stephen Craig, Malobicky, John Joseph, Masino, James Paul, McArthur, Alan Francis, Milgrom, Brent Marriott, Phillips, Harold Lee, Powell, Robert Franklin, Pukal, Louis Anthony, Riggs, David Lee, Sadler, George Henry, Shea, Patrick Joseph, Sledge, Charles Harold, Spain, William Joseph, Stringer, Edward Hand Jr., Talbott, Joseph Daniel, Twamley, Joseph, Vincent, Wood, Charles Henry, Zadjeika, George White

1966

Alexander, Charles Edward, Barnes, Francis Marion, Battistello, Gregory Alesandro, Beaver, Jeffrey Windsor, Blank, Landy Maitland, Bomar, Darley Gayle, Bradley, Eckel Clifton, Buskey, Thomas William, Carr, Charles Lee, Cowan, Everett Campbell, Darnall, William Carlyle, Davenport, John Francis, Davis, Peter Nils, Dempsey, Thomas Richard, Dodson, William Edward, Duncan, Lynwood Hart, Erimias, David Richard, Federal, William Aubrey, Fisher, Lloyd Gene, For-

tune, James David, Horvat, Michael Anthony, Hume, Robert Leo, Ingle, Archibald Tomlinson, Karrs, Timothy Louis, Knott, Robert Allen, Lampman, Thomas Smith, Link, Malcolm Eugene, Lister, Stephen Craig, Martin, Tilden Silas (Mgr.), Masino, James Paul, Mazza, Mark Anthony, Milgrom, Brent Marriott, Phillips, Harold Lee, Powell, Robert Franklin, Pukal, Louis Anthony, Quick, John Craig (Mgr.), Renedo, Thomas Henry, Richey, James Michael, Riggs, David Lee, Ringwalt, David Lewis, Rogers, James Nielsen, Rowe, Terry Lee, Sadler, George Henry, Shea, Patrick Joseph, Smith, Michael Thomas, Spain, William Joseph, Sparks, Edward Francis, Talbott, Joseph Daniel, Wall, William Battle, Warren, William Edwin, Watts, Clifton John (Mgr.), Wesolowski, Richard Raymond, Wood, Charles Henry

1967

Beaver, Jeffrey Windsor, Blank, Landy Maitland, Bomar, Darley Gayle, Bradley, Eckel Clifton, Burdulis, Stefen Wayne, Cantrell, Thomas Franklin, Carr, Charles Lee, Chalupka, Edward Stephen Joseph, Connolly, Robert James, Cowan, Everett Campbell, Davenport, John Francis, David, Douglas Edward, Davis, Peter Nils, Dempsey, Thomas Richard, Duncan, Lynwood Hart, Hanna, Robert William, Hollifield, Michael Stephen, Horvat, Michael Anthony, Ingle, Archibald Tomlinson, Karrs,

Timothy Louis, Knott, Robert Allen, Lewis, Meriwether (Trainer), Lowry, Ronald Eric, Martin, Tilden Silas (Mgr.), Masino, James Paul, Mazza, Mark Anthony, Miggs, James Lewis, Price, Kenneth Wayne, Pukal, Louis Anthony, Quick, John Craig (Mgr.), Richey, James Michael, Riggs, David Lee, Rogers, James Nielsen, Sheehan, James Edward, Smith, Michael Thomas, Wall, William Battle, Wesolowski, Richard Raymond, Zadjeika, George White, Zemaitis, Saulis Michael

1968

Blanchard, Felix Anthony, Bomar, Darley Gayle, Borries, Kenneth Roy, Bounds, Walter Samuel, Bradley, Eckel Clifton Jr., Chalupka, Edward Stephen, Cowan, Everette Campbell, Davis, Peter Nils, Dempsey, Thomas Richard, Dodson, William Edward, Grzybowski, Ronald Anthony, Hanna, Robert William, Harris, John Lacy, Hartig, Donald Clarence Jr., Hicks, Keith Pegees, Hollifield, Michael Stephen, Hoolahan, Paul John, Jackson, David Whitney Jr., Karrs, Timothy Louis, Lanier, Ricardo Edwin, Lowry, Ronald Eric, Mazza, Mark Anthony, McCauley, Donald Frederick, Papai, James Joseph, Perry, Louis Wiley Jr., Pochucha, Larry Arthur, Price, Kenneth Wayne, Ray, Phillip Duckworth Jr., Renedo, Thomas Henry, Richardson, William Wayne, Richey, James Michael, Rogers, James Nielsen, Ross, Russell Thomas Jr., Schult,

Robert William, Smith, Garland Jan, Smith, Michael Thomas, Sparks, Edward Francis, Stone, Raymond Harvey Jr., Styers, Richard Stanley (Mgr.), Wall William Battle III, Wesolowski, Richard Raymond, Wynn, Curtis Brice, Zemaitis, Saulis Michael

1969

Alvis, Stephen Griffin, Anderson, John Bryan, Blanchard, Felix Anthony, Bobbitt, Michael Joseph, Bounds, Walter Samuel, Brafford, William Allen, Bunting, John Stephen, Cantrell, Thomas Franklin, Chalupka, Edward Stephen Jr., Cook, John Samuel, Cowell, John William III, Culbreth, Stanley Collins Jr., Eckman, John Charles III, Garrett, Richard Eugene, Grissom, Blois Carl, Grzybowski, Anthony Ronald, Hambacher, James Richard, Hamline, Geoffrey Scott, Hanna, Robert William, Hartig, Donald Clarence Jr., Hicks, Keith Pegees, Hodgin, Steven Francis, Hoolahan, Paul John, Hyman, Eric Cartwright, Jackson, David Whitney, Jolley, Lewis Elman, Lanier, Ricardo Edwin, Mattocks, Judge Stanley Jr., McCauley, Donald Frederick, Miller, Paul Felix II, Packard, Douglas Richards Jr., Perry, Louis Wiley, Price, Kenneth Wayne, Ray, Phillip Duckworth Jr., Richardson, William Wayne, Riddile, Mel James, Ross, Russell Thomas Jr., Schult, Robert William, Serbousek, Michael George, Sigler, William Montague, Simpson, George Herbert III,

Smith, Garland Jan, Stilley, Richard Graham, Swofford, John Douglas, Webster, James Murphy Jr., Working, Richard Michael, Zemaitis, Saulis Michael

1970

Alvis, Stephen Griffin, Anderson, John Bryan, Angelo, Louis Francis, Blanchard, Felix Anthony, Bobbitt, Michael Joseph, Brafford, William Allen, Bridges, William Tracey, Brown, Eugene Laurance, Bunting, John Stephen, Cantrell, Thomas Franklin, Chapman, William Sherard Jr., Cook, John Samuel, Cowell, John William III, Craven, Randall Ken, Culbreth, Stanley Collins, Garrett, Richard Eugene, Grissom, Blois Carl Jr., Grissom, Richard Charles, Grzybowski, Ronald Anthony, Hambacher, James Richard, Hamlin, Geoffrey Scott, Hicks, Keith Pegees, Hodgin, Steven Francis, Hoolahan, Paul John, Jolley, Lewis Elman, Kirkpatrick, Thomas Morgan, Lanier, Ricardo Edwin, Lemmons, Michael William, Lookabill, Reid Davis, McCauley, Donald Frederick, Mansfield, Michael Brian, Miller, Paul Felix II, Oglesby, Isaiah Vincent, Packard, Douglas Richard Jr., Papai, James Joseph, Perry, Louis Wiley Jr., Ray, Phillip Duckworth Jr., Richardson, William Wayne, Riddile, Mel James, Ross, Russell Thomas Jr., Rusnak, Ronald Lee, Sain, Jerry Steele, Schult, Robert William, Sigler, William Montague III, Smith, Garland Jan, Stilley, Richard Graham, Swofford, John

Douglas, Taylor, Barry Ray (Mgr.), Taylor, Kenneth Hall, Taylor, William Frederick, Thornton, Robert Edwards, Vandenbroek, Robert Glenn, Ward, Gregory Alan, Webster, James Murphy Jr., Whitehorne, Leslie Greg Jr.

1971

Anderson, John Bryan, Angelo, Louis Francis, Bethea, James Earle, Bradshaw, Joel Grey, Brafford, William Allen, Brown, Eugene Laurance, Bunting, John Stephen, Chapman, William Sherard Jr., Chesson, Earl Goodwin, Cowell, John William III, Craven, Randall Ken, Culbreth, Stanley Collins Jr., Early, William Steve, Grissom, Blois Carl, Hamlin, Geof Scott, Hite, William Thomas, Hodgin, Steven Francis, Hyman, Eric Cartwright, Jolley, Lewis E., Kirkpatrick, Thomas Morgan, Klise, John Weston, Lamm, James Philmon, Leverenz, Ted Louis, Lookabill, Reid Davis, Mansfield, Michael Brian, Miller, Paul Felix, Newton, John William, Oglesby, Isaiah Vincent, Packard, Douglas Richards Jr., Papai, James Joseph, Pratt, Robert Henry Jr., Riddile, Mel James, Rusnak, Ronald Lee, Sain, Jerry Steele, Sigler, William Montague III, Stilley, Richard Graham, Swofford, John Douglas, Talty, Peter James, Taylor, Barry Ray (Mgr.), Taylor, Kenneth Hall, Taylor, Terry O'Dell, Taylor, William Frederick, Thornton, Robert Edwards, Turco, Charlie Louis, Vandenbroek, Robert Glenn,

Vidnovic, Nicholas Charles, Walters, Robert Bruce, Ward, Gregory Alan, Webster, James Murphy Jr.

1972

Alexander, Ellis Turner, Andrews, Thomas Deacon, Angelo, Louis Francis, Arnall, Randolph Hamilton Jr., Barrett, David Alvis, Bethea, James Earle, Bradley, Thomas Winfield, Bradshaw, Joel Grey, Brown, Eugene Laurance, Chacos, Andrew Bedell, Chapman, William Sherard, Chesson, Earl Goodwin, Cowan, Gary Landis, Daly, Philip Niland Jr., DeRatt, James Harold Jr., DiCarlo, Mark Charles, Donahoe, Beaufort Harper, Early, William Steve, Elkins, Robert Theodore, Embrey, Thomas Carl, Frerotte, John Francis, Hite, William Thomas, Hollingsworth, William Harry, Huff, Kenneth Wayne, Hyman, Eric Cartwright, Jerome, James Daniel Jr., Johnson, Samuel Lee, Kirkpatrick, Thomas Morgan, Kupeck, Chris Charles, Lamens, Edward Patrick, Lamm, James Philmon, Lemmons, Michael William, Leverenz, Ted Louis, Lydecker, Dale P., Mansfield, Michael Brian, Newton, John William, Norton, Patrick Joseph Jr., Oglesby, Isaiah Vincent, Oliver, Richard Reginald, Pratt, Robert Henry Jr., Robinson, Ronald Edward, Rusnak, Ronald Lee, Sain, Jerry Steele, Shore, Donald Craig, Shuster, John Michael, Sigmon, Richard Lee Jr., Smith, Charles (Mgr.), Talty, Peter James III, Taylor, Kenneth Hall, Taylor, Terry

O'Dell, Thornton, Robert Edwards, Ulicny, Gary Ronald, Vandenbroek, Robert Glenn, Vidnovic, Nicholas Charles, Waddell, Charles Douglas, Ward, Gregory Alan, Wicks, William James

1973

Alexander, Ellis Turner, Andrews, Thomas Deacon, Arnall, Randolph Hamilton, Barrett, David Alvis, Bethea, James Earle, Betterson, James Thomas, Bradshaw, Joel Grey, Broadway, Roderick Craig, Cantrell, Terrell Pierce, Chacos, Andrew Bedell, Chesson, Earl Goodwin, Conley, Michael Maurice, Cowan, Gary Landis, DeRatt, James Harold, DiCarlo, Mark Charles, Duffy, Michael Thomas, Early, William Steve, Elkins, Robert Theodore, Embrey, Thomas Carl, Frerotte, John Francis, Grainger, John Victor (Mgr.), Hite, William Thomas, Huff, Kenneth Wayne, Jerome, James Daniel, Johnson, Samuel Lee, Jones, Thomas Irvine, Kupec, Christopher Charles, Lamens, Edward Patrick, Lamm, James Philmon, Leverenz, Ted Louis, Lydecker, Dale, Newton, John William, Norton, Patrick Joseph, Oliver, Richard Reginald, Paschall, William Herbert, Pratt, Robert Henry, Robinson, Ronald Edward, Talty, Peter James, Taylor, Terry O'Dell, Townsend, William Frank, Trott, Robert, Ulicny, Gary Ronald, Vidnovic, Nicholas Charles, Voight, Michael Ray, Waddell, Charles Douglas, Walters, Robert Bruce

284

1974

Alexander, Ellis Turner, Andrews, Thomas Deacon, Arnall, Randolph Hamilton, Austin, Charles Stanley, Barrett, David Alvis, Bauman, Roc Winston, Betterson, James Thomas, Broadway, Roderick Craig, Burkett, Thomas Paul, Cantrell, Mark Lee, Cantrell, Terrell Pierce, Chacos, Andrew Bedell, Collins, Melvin Eugene, Conley, Michael Maurice, Corbin, Michael Lawrence, Cowan, Gary Landis, DeRatt, James Harold, Dusch, William Coltrane (Mgr.), Elkins, Robert Theodore, Embrey, Thomas Carl, Frerotte, John Francis, Funk, Craig Eugene, Gaines, Mark Allen, Gay, Robert Rex, Griffin, Mark Ashworth, Hardison, William David, Harris, David Andrew, Huff, Kenneth Wayne, Hughes, Brian Neil, Jerome, James Daniel, Johnson, Ronald Stuart, Jones Jeffrey Burton, Kupec, Christopher Charles, Lamens, Edward Patrick, Lydecker, Dale Paul, Murphy, William Edward, Norton, Patrick Joseph, Oliver, Richard Reginald, Paschall, William Herbert, Perdue, John William, Reynolds, Richard Scott, Robinson, Ronald Edward, Smith, Brian Peter, Smith, Charles Alan (Mgr.), Stanford, Earnest Ray, Trott, Robert Franklin, Voight, Michael Ray, Waddell, Charles Douglas, Wells, Terry Turner, Wicks, William James, Williams, Charles Theodore, Wilson, Kirt Taylor

1975

(First Award)

Aycock, Claiborne Benson Jr. (Mgr.), Ayscue, David Broughton (Trainer), Biddle, Thomas Franklin, Bunce, Gregory Paul (Mgr.), Burchette, James Michael (Mgr.), Caldwell, Alan Lorenzo, Caldwell, Jeffery Stephen, Cale, Robert Edwin, Corbin, Michael Lawrence, Davison, Scott David, Daw, John Luther, Dowdy, Ronnie Dean, Duffy, Michael Thomas, Dunn, Billy Eugene, Elam, Aubrey John Jr., Finn, Michael Steven, Hukill, Robert Peverley, Junkmann, Steven Alan, Lancaster, Stanley Earl Jr., Lee, Joseph Walker, Loomis, Robert Edward, Mabry, William Lloyd Jr., McCallister, Franklin Ford, McNeil, Barry Steven (Trainer), Nantz, Charles Benjamin (Trainer), Rhames, Ulysses, Salzano, Michael John, Sheets, Kenneth Edward, Shonosky, Robert Michael, Stratton, John Harvey III, Thompson, Charles Duke, Williams, Kim Brooks

(Second Award)

Austin, Charles Stanley, Bauman, Roc Winston, Burkett, Thomas Paul, Cantrell, Mark Lee, Collins, Melvin Eugene, Funk, Craig Eugene, Gay, Robert Rex, Griffin, Mark Ashworth, Hardison, William David, Hughes, Brian Neil, Johnson, Ronald Stuart, Perdue, John

285

William, Schleter, James Christopher (Mgr.), Smith, Brian Peter, Stanford, Earnest Ray Jr., Williams, Charles Theodore

(Third Award)

Betterson, James Thomas, Broadway, Roderick Craig, Conley, Michael Maurice, Paschall, William Herbert, Trott, Robert Franklin, Voight, Michael Ray

(Fourth Award)

Andrews, Thomas Deacon